THE COLORS OF NATURE

THE COLORS OF NATURE

Culture, Identity, and the Natural World

Edited by
**Alison H. Deming and
Lauret E. Savoy**

milkweed
editions

"Birth Witness," by Ofelia Zepeda, reprinted with permission from
Where Clouds Are Formed. © 2009 by the University of Arizona Press.

"In History," © 1997 by Jamaica Kincaid,
reprinted with permission of the Wylie Agency, Inc.

"Burning the Shelter" by Louis Owens, reprinted with permission from *Mixedblood
Messages: Literature, Film, Family, Place.* © 1998 by the University of Oklahoma Press.

Published 2011 by Milkweed Editions
Printed in the United States of America
Cover design by Hopkins/Baumann
Interior design by Rachel Holscher
Leaf transformation Hopkins/Baumann
The text of this book is set in 11/15 Adobe Garamond Pro.
21 22 23   9 8 7
Revised Edition

Please turn to the back of this book for a list of the
sustaining funders of Milkweed Editions.

The Library of Congress has cataloged the previous edition as follows:

The colors of nature : culture, identity, and the natural world / edited by Alison H. Deming
and Lauret E. Savoy.
    p. cm.
ISBN 1-57131-267-6 (pbk. : alk. paper)
1. Nature.   I. Deming, Alison Hawthorne, 1946– II. Savoy, Lauret E.
QH81 .C663 2002
508—dc21
                                                                    2002002391

This book is printed on acid-free, recycled paper.

To the voices that remember and those as yet unheard

THE COLORS OF NATURE

4 PRAISE

THE COLORS OF NATURE

WIDENING THE FRAME

Lauret E. Savoy and Alison H. Deming

> . . . most nature writing is barricaded with omissions
> to make it just another gated community . . .
> —*Rebecca Solnit*

Despite countless claims to the contrary in recent newscasts and articles, the United States is not a "post-racial" society. In fact, each day offers new examples of injustice that reveal a society determined to avoid the troubled legacy of our nation's founding and growth.

Consider New Orleans. Years after Hurricane Katrina made landfall on August 29, 2005, the wake of levee failure still points to long-embedded practices of *de jure* and *de facto* apartheid. For those who lacked access to shelter or higher ground, and for those who received little forewarning or relief aid, their disproportionate suffering was only another surge in a centuries-old pattern. After the Civil War, African Americans were forced to live in the least-desirable, flood-prone areas of New Orleans. Lawful segregation of the city's public housing and transportation before the mid-1960s only further entrenched this geography of poverty and race. When Hurricane Katrina arrived, then, it should have hardly been a surprise that the burden fell primarily on

3

low-income people of color: Weeks after the levees broke the majority of homes that remained submerged were owned or rented by African Americans.

By some measures New Orleans has recovered significantly. The Brookings Institution reported in late 2010 that the city's population had exceeded three-quarters the pre-Katrina numbers, that large-scale rebuilding efforts had boosted the economy there, and that the local unemployment rate was lower than national statistics. But who has moved back and who is being counted?

Even though most of those living in the Crescent City in August of 2005 were renters and low-income residents, recovery programs have favored property owners. Thousands of displaced families still, years later, live in "temporary" housing (trailers and tents), or are homeless, many "squatting" in abandoned buildings. Thousands more, particularly low-income (former) renters and public housing residents, have not been able to return to the city as rents there climb out of reach and as mixed-income homes replace affordable housing. Those affordable public housing projects that survived Katrina—more than 5,000 units—were demolished by the housing authority (backed by HUD and the city council), leaving only a small percentage of homes set aside or subsidized for those with little means. And corporate spending on rebuilding hasn't helped the situation, giving priority to privatizing or reducing many social services rather than ending the displacement and homelessness of poor people of color. With investment goals focused on a smaller but more affluent city footprint, redevelopment is targeting areas where the economically poor did not, or could not, live.

Reconstruction is changing the city's racial and economic complexion, rather than restoring separated families, communities, or the spiritual rootedness that made the city so culturally rich. Yet, polled by Gallup and other organizations on whether Hurricane Katrina and its impacts pointed to persistent racial inequality, fewer than half of white Americans thought so, while more than three-quarters of African Americans in the country said "yes."

"Do you know what it means to miss New Orleans? / and miss it each night and day. . . ." These lyrics, first sung by Louis Armstrong and Billie Holiday in 1947, might very well be the anthem of a whole generation of New Orleanians unlucky enough to be from the wrong ward.

This is not only happening in New Orleans. Across the nation polluting industries follow paths of least power or resistance, as the federal government has persistently weakened or simply failed to implement enforcement structures and health-protection measures for communities less capable of defending themselves. The recent study, *Toxic Wastes and Race at Twenty: 1987–2007: Grassroots Struggles to Dismantle Environmental Racism in the United States,* reports that more than half of the nine million people living within two miles of hazardous waste sites across the country are people of color. The study goes on to document systemic racial and socioeconomic inequities in the siting of commercial waste facilities.[1]

Anyone who looks closely enough can see that the ways in which the United States organizes its political system and economy—from *de facto* segregation and toxic waste sites to food production and trade policies—are far from neutral and even farther from "post-racial." And yet, despite clearly worded, well-researched studies proving racist policies—like *Toxic Wastes and Race at Twenty*—and despite one of the most massive and ongoing segregated depopulations of a United States city in history—New Orleans— citizens with great power in this country continue not to see the systematic injustices daily visited on communities of color. Why not?

The seed of this anthology was a troubling question: "Why is there so little 'nature writing' by people of color?" To respond we had to decide what "nature writing" was, and is.

Although writings about the natural world have existed from ancient times to the present in countless cultural traditions and languages, "nature writing" as a distinct literary tradition in Europe and Euro-America originated in the Romantic Age of the late eighteenth century. Romanticism, as a reaction against neoclassicism, was an affirmation of imagination over intellect and emotion over reason, and it celebrated a belief in the innate goodness of nature and of human beings in their natural state; but romanticism was also defined by a sense of separation from the natural world, the belief that nature was external to human existence. That "nature writing" became a strand in the weave of American literature was hardly surprising considering the compelling heritage of natural beauty, grand scale, and rich biodiversity of the continent. Many of the early, Euro-American luminaries of the genre wrote about solitary explorations of wild places from a poetic, philosophical, or scientific perspective; seeing nature as a place apart, where wisdom and inspiration could be harvested for day-to-day life in the "real" world of cities.

In the last few decades, "nature writing" has ranged beyond such narratives of solitary encounters and celebrations of pristine wildness to consider degraded habitats, cascading species extinctions, and global climate change—all providing incontrovertible evidence that our uniquely "American" relationship with this world has become unsustainable. This more contemporary sensibility understands that nature has been wounded and degraded throughout human history, that such wounding diminishes all of us, and that the wound must somehow be healed. If this is what "nature writing" is, the question then remains, "Why is there so little recognized 'nature writing' by people of color?"

African American, Asian American, Arab American, Latino/a, Native American, and "multiracial" or "mixed-blood" voices have profoundly enlarged and enriched our national literary identity. Yet while the previous question suggests, somewhat surprisingly, that little of that writing has had anything to do with the natural world, there is a wealth of literature on nature from culturally and ethnically diverse voices. *Black Nature: Four Centuries of African American Nature Poetry* (edited by Camille T. Dungy) is one recent example offering a vision of what African American poets have contributed to our understanding of the natural world and to nature writing. And it raises questions in our minds as to why other perspectives are missing from our nature literature, as it has been historically defined.

What if one's primary experience of land and place is not a place apart but rather indigenous? What if it is urban or indentured or exiled or (im)migrant or toxic? To define "nature writing" as anything that excludes these experiences does not reveal a "lack" of writing, but reflects, instead, a societal structure of inclusion and exclusion based on *othered* difference—whether by "race," culture, class, or gender.

If what is called "nature writing" aims to understand how we comprehend and then live responsibly in the world, then it must recognize the legacies of the Americas' past in ways that are mindful of the complex historical and cultural dynamics that have shaped us all. Perhaps some would say this isn't a goal of writing about nature or natural history. But if such writing examines human perceptions and experiences of nature, if an intimacy with and response to the larger-than-human world define who or what we are, if we as people are part of nature, then the experiences of all people on this land are necessary stories, even if some voices have been silent, silenced, or simply not recognized as nature writing. What is defined by some as an edge of separation between nature and culture, people and place, is a zone of exchange where finding common ground is more than possible; it is necessary.

Why do so many not see injustice in a place like New Orleans when it is so clear? Why do so many not see nature literature by people of color when it is written so well? These questions are not unrelated—they stem from the same force.

Today, as so much of "nature writing" details, we face many crucial challenges including losses of biological diversity and ecosystem integrity; anthropogenic changes to the atmosphere's composition; deforestation; and desertification. The same human institutions and values that have fostered this marginalization of the natural world also marginalize the life of a black farmer in the South whose ancestors, enslaved or freedmen, worked and knew the land with an intense generational intimacy. Their stories have a place in our nature canon, but they have been deleted by racist farm policies and bigoted bankers and ignored by scholars and publishers. Their stories could give hope to the children born and raised in a ghetto, barrio, or on a reservation. But the compromising of nature and the compromising of human beings by "racial" separatism and inequities in the past-to-present destroy both landscapes *and* stories of hope for the future.

What then, is Earth to American people of color? Of course there is no single or simple answer. For some, the land has been origin and continuity for millennia; for others the land holds the memory of those who worked it under a system of bondage; and for many, this is a place migrated to in search of new beginnings or a place of refuge from intolerable oppression. Today motion, dislocation, migration, and loss have come to define nearly all of our lives as groups or communities in the United States. But for people of color who do not fit easily into the mainstream structure of Euro-America, such motion can involve cultural erasure over time. What is left for too many is artifact, and for others, not even that.

Our intent here is not to paint a simplistic scene of victims and aggressors, with single proximate factors of cause and effect, but to recognize that the complexities and ambiguities of this nation's multicultural past and present, and the ways in which American culture has used or impacted the Earth, cannot be separated from underlying values that promote racism and systemic inequality. This is a stark and a sad reality—but it suggests a hopeful possibility: If the ignorance of stories can lead to ruin, perhaps the seeking out and understanding of stories can lead to rebuilding, in New Orleans, and everywhere else.

"No nation," wrote James Baldwin, "has ever made so successful and glamorous a romance out of genocide and slavery." Perhaps because the American past is stained, many of its citizens continue to see their lives as stories of rugged individualism rather than of (multi)culture making. Yet, how we see our lives is not necessarily how they are: Just as every day of one's life is embedded in nature, every day of one's life is also embedded in this complicated cultural legacy.

This anthology offers some of the fruits of that complication. Environmental thought and activism in the United States have old and diverse roots with a rich legacy of contributions by many cultures to the development of an environmental ethos, richer than just the contributions of those generally heralded. For example, as African American abolitionists fought and wrote against slavery in the early and mid-nineteenth century, they also fought and wrote against the use of arsenic in tobacco fields. Zitkala-Sa (Lakota-Dakota) and Sarah Winnemucca (Paiute) noted more than a century ago the close links between Euro-American racism and environmental attitudes that led to the degradation of what once was indigenous land. W.E.B. Du Bois's essay on the African roots of the First World War, in the May 1915 issue of the *Atlantic Monthly,* is as much an environmental essay as any piece written in that era on the need for a national park system.

The meaning of the word "nature" is derived from the Latin *nascor,* to be born. Perhaps a birth of sorts may yet occur in our ability to re-imagine and re-focus how we think and write about nature and environment. Then, perhaps all of us might finally begin to resist any mono-identity or mono-culture of mind, self, or knowledge—to celebrate the biodiversity of self and of others.

Field and street activists for environmental justice like Majora Carter and Van Jones are putting this principle into practice. As founder and first director of Sustainable South Bronx (SSB), Majora Carter worked in partnership with neighborhood groups, local government, and businesses to stop New York City's plan for a solid-waste plant to process 40 percent of the city's garbage along the Bronx River. SSB and other community groups have since reclaimed much of the waterfront—and improved the quality of life for local residents—by developing an ecological restoration workforce, building a park on old industrial land, increasing public waterfront access, establishing a community market, and introducing green roof technology. Both Carter and Van Jones, the founder of the Ella Baker Center for Human Rights and Green for All, have pioneered successful urban green-collar job training and placement systems.

Anishinaabe author and cultural critic Gerald Vizenor's term "survivance" is important here. Meaning more than survival, more than endurance or mere response, stories of survivance are an active, evolving presence that resists rigid categories, racialist stereotypes, or "manifest manners" sustained in a literature of dominance. Perhaps through such stories we might more fully imagine and comprehend who and what we are with respect to each other, to the land, and to our shared responsibility.

The Process and Themes

The envisioning, editing, and shaping of this anthology have been a rewarding collaboration, the great joy of which is that our two voices have prodded, questioned, celebrated, and challenged one another—not always ending in agreement but committed to delving where individual visions intersect into something larger than what either alone could conceive. In soliciting work we queried approximately one hundred writers and thinkers. We sought breadth in cultural, geographic, and disciplinary representation. We asked for essays or memoirs, suggesting that writers might consider how lifeways, homeplace, and identity of an individual or a community are linked with the environment. Ultimately we sought writing with grit, heart, and edge that could open provocative areas for reflection and move readers to bear witness and act.

Certainly there are many distinguished works already in publication that bear eloquent testimony to the richness of cultural perspective in our understanding of the natural world. Leslie Marmon Silko's essay "Landscape,

History, and the Pueblo Imagination" has been well represented in anthologies, as has N. Scott Momaday's "An American Land Ethic," and essays by bell hooks and Alice Walker. Gary Paul Nabhan's work as a literary ethnobotanist has been exemplary in exploring linkages between culture and nature among tribal people of the American Southwest. But we sought new work, trusting that our query would spur fresh thinking and words from writers already accomplished within their disciplines though not necessarily associated with the nature-writing genre. We were thrilled with the enthusiastic response.

The events of one's life "take place." Here are the words of essayists, critics, poets, scientists, policymakers, teachers, and novelists who feel that place down in their bones. They are African American, Arab American, Asian American, Latino/Latina, Native American; and they are "multiracial" and "mixed-blood" writers for whom such classifications are both limited and limiting.

Taken as a whole the writings creatively present how identity and place, human history and "natural" history, power and silence, and social injustice and environmental degradation are fundamentally linked. Some pieces reflect on how displacements and migrations have fragmented not only history and memories, but also language and names, the thin frames within which we try to order our lives. The reasons for such displacements are varied and many over time and space: war or occupation; embedded inequities in political and economic power; oceans separating places of origin from America; losses of language and indigenous connections to homeland across generations; need to find dignified work to support one's family; or borders both tangible and intangible that make "difference" a source of conflict rather than cultural enrichment.

Other pieces turn our attention to the role language plays in our understanding of nature and place, considering words and tropes that have remained unexamined or largely taken for granted. These essays recognize the failures of imagination that have widened false gaps between science and "non-science," humans and nature, us and them, subject and object, civilized and savage, "Third World" and "First World," as if such concepts named independent, separate realities. We are reminded that the scientific and the indigenous are not mutually exclusive instruments for reading the land, but parts in a conversation that resonates with relationship and meaning.

The distinct voices here weave very different experiences of place to create a larger and more textured cloth than the largely monochromatic tradition of American nature writing or of the mainstream environmental movement. The authors have written not from abstraction, but rather from their fingertips, their memories, their emotional and sensory beings. Together the contributions help us recognize how critical it is to think and write across threads of identity that are around and within us—those defined from within and those imposed from without—to understand more fully our place on Earth and connections with each other. And they ask us to contemplate the ways in which one can take possession of dignity and history, not in ownership but in honest relation.

As Francisco X. Alarcón and Enrique Salmon among others reveal, culture can offer new ways to see the terra incognita of America's ever-shifting identity. We agree with Kimberly Blaeser who suggests, "What we need are experiments in return." This is return not only to an intimate sense of belonging to the whole, but to storying that sense of dwelling and to recollecting what was left behind. We also agree with Ofelia Zepeda that we need language not merely to verify our existence to the census bureau, but to serve the poetic tasks that give music and meaning to our lives, "a language useful for . . . pulling memory from the depths of the earth," "for speeches and incantations that pull sickness from the minds and bodies of believers." And as bell hooks articulates, "to tend the earth is always then to tend our destiny, our freedom, and our hope."

We now live in a world substantially different from the world each of us was born into. This current historical moment is one in which the challenges of global climate change, fresh-water shortages, food insecurity, persistent fossil-fuel dependence, and the inequities behind poverty's spread demand the best of the human imagination. There are many unknowns about the threat of climate change. For example, the forecast holds that displacement of people who reside in areas most likely to be forcefully impacted will be a challenging reality, and one that will aggravate cultural conflicts. The need to enrich our understanding, our ability to listen and empathize across differences, will grow as the need for adaptation to these challenges increases. The political temper in the United States, as this collection goes to press, is one of anger, fear, and hate-mongering: Islamophobia in New York and Tennessee, Latinophobia in the border states, ceaseless wars of dubious purpose, and the troubling gridlock in Washington, D.C., where problem-solving seems the last thing on many legislators' minds—these are the troubles of the day. Our modest hope is that these writings make a contribution to both understanding and compassion at a time when "the better angels of our nature" could use some encouragement. Come, explore.

1

RETURN

BIRTH WITNESS

Ofelia Zepeda

My mother gave birth to me
in an old wooden row house
in the cotton field.
She remembers it was windy.
Around one in the afternoon.
The tin roof rattled, a piece uplifted
from the wooden frame, quivered and flapped
as she gave birth.
She knew it was March.
A windy afternoon in the cotton fields of Arizona.

She also used to say I was baptized standing up.
"It doesn't count," the woman behind the glass window tells me,
"if you were not baptized the same year you were born,
the baptismal certificate cannot be used to verify your birth."

"You need affidavits," she said.
"Your older siblings, you have some don't you?
They have to be old enough to have a memory
of your birth.
Can they vouch for you?"
Who was there to witness my birth?
Who was there with my mother?
Was it my big sister?
Would my mother have let a teenager watch her giving birth?
Was it my father?
I can imagine my father assisting her with her babies.
My aunts?
Who was there when I breathed my first breath?
Took in those dry particles from the cotton fields.
Who knew then that I would need witnesses of my birth?
The stars were there in the sky.
The wind was there.
The sun was there.
The pollen of spring was floating and sensed me being born.
They are silent witnesses.
They do not know of affidavits, they simply know.
"You need records," she said.
"Are there doctor's receipts from when you were a baby?
Didn't your parents have a family Bible, you know,
where births are recorded?
Were there letters?
Announcements of your birth?"

I don't bother to explain my parents are illiterate in the English language.
What I really want to tell her is they speak a language much too civil for
writing.
It is a language useful for pulling memory from the depths of the earth.
It is useful for praying with the earth and sky.
It is useful for singing songs that pull down the clouds.
It is useful for calling rain.

It is useful for speeches and incantations
that pull sickness from the minds and bodies of believers.
It is a language too civil for writing.
It is too civil for writing minor things like my birth.
This is what I really want to tell her.
But I don't.
Instead I take the forms she hands me.
I begin to account for myself.

IN HISTORY

Jamaica Kincaid

What to call the thing that happened to me and all who look like me?

Should I call it history?

If so, what should history mean to someone like me?

Should it be an idea, should it be an open wound and each breath I take in and expel healing and opening the wound again and again, over and over, or is it a moment that began in 1492 and has come to no end yet? Is it a collection of facts, all true and precise details, and, if so, when I come across these true and precise details, what should I do, how should I feel, where should I place myself?

Why should I be obsessed with all these questions?

My history began like this: in 1492, Christopher Columbus discovered the New World. Since this is only a beginning and I am not yet in the picture, I have not yet made an appearance, the word "discover" does not set off an alarm, and I am not yet confused by this interpretation. I accept it. I am only taken by the personality of this quarrelsome, restless man. His origins are sometimes obscure; sometimes no one knows just where he really comes from, who he really was. His origins are sometimes quite vivid: his father was a tailor, he came from Genoa, he as a boy wandered up and down the Genoese wharf, fascinated by sailors and their tales of lands far away; these lands would be filled with treasures, as all things far away are treasures. I am far away, but I am not yet a treasure: I am not a part of this man's consciousness, he does not know of me, I do not yet have a name. And so the word "discover," as it is applied to this New World, remains uninteresting to me.

He, Christopher Columbus, discovers this New World. That it is new only to him, that it had a substantial existence, physical and spiritual, before he became aware of it, does not occur to him. To cast blame on him now for this childlike immaturity has all the moral substance of a certificate given to a schoolgirl for good behavior. To be a well-behaved schoolgirl is not hard. When he sees this New World, it is really new to him: he has never seen anything like it before, it was not what he had expected, he had images of China and Japan, and, though he thought he was in China and Japan, it was not the China or Japan that he had fixed in his mind. He couldn't find enough words to describe what he saw before him: the people were new, the flora and fauna were new, the way the water met the sky was new, this world itself was new, it was the New World.

"If one does not know the names, one's knowledge of things is useless." This is attributed to Isidorus, and I do not know if this is the Greek Isidorus or the other Isidorus, the bishop of Seville; but now put it another way: to have knowledge of things, one must first give them a name. This, in any case, seems to have been Christopher Columbus's principle, for he named and he named: he named places, he named people, he named things. This world he saw before him had a blankness to it, the blankness of the newly made, the newly born. It had no before—I could say that it had no history, but I would have to begin again, I would have to ask those questions again: what is history? This blankness, the one Columbus met, was more like the blankness of paradise; paradise emerges from chaos, and this chaos is not history; it is not a legitimate order of things. Paradise then is the arrangement of the ordinary and the extraordinary. But in such a way as to make it, paradise, seem as if it had fallen out of the clear air. Nothing about it suggests the messy life of the builder, the carpenter, the quarrels with the contractor, the people who are late with the delivery of materials, their defense which, when it is not accepted, is met with their backchat. This is an unpleasant arrangement; this is not paradise. Paradise is the thing just met when all the troublesome details have been vanquished, overcome.

Christopher Columbus met paradise. It would not have been paradise for the people living there; they would have had the ordinary dreariness of living anywhere day after day, the ordinary dreariness of just being alive. But someone else's ordinary dreariness is another person's epiphany.

The way in which he wanted to know these things was not in the way of satisfying curiosity, or in the way of correcting an ignorance; he wanted to know them, to possess them, and he wanted to possess them in a way that must have been a surprise to him. His ideas kept not so much changing, as they kept evolving: he wanted to prove the world was round, and even that, to know with certainty that the world was round, that it did not come to an abrupt end at a sharp cliff from which one could fall into nothing, to know that is to establish a claim also. And then after the world was round, this round world should belong to his patrons, the king and queen of Spain; and then finding himself at the other side of the circumference and far away from his patrons, human and other kind, he loses himself, for it becomes clear: the person who really can name the thing gives it a life, a reality, that it did not have before. His patrons are in Spain, looking at the balance sheet: if they invest so much, will his journey yield a return to make the investment worthwhile? But he, I am still speaking of Columbus, is in the presence of something else.

His task is easier than he thought it would be; his task is harder than he could have imagined. If he had only really reached Japan or China, places like that already had an established narrative. It was not a narrative that these places had established themselves; it was a narrative that someone like him had invented, Marco Polo, for instance; but this world, China or Japan, in the same area of the world to him (even as this familiarity with each other—between China and Japan—would surprise and even offend the inhabitants of these places), had an order and the order offered a comfort (the recognizable is always so comforting). But this new place, what was it? Sometimes it was just like Seville, Spain; sometimes it was like Seville but only more so; sometimes it was more beautiful than Seville. Mostly it was "marvelous," and this word "marvelous" is the word he uses again and again, and when he uses it, what the reader (and this is what I have been, a reader of this account of the journey, and the account is by Columbus himself) can feel, can hear, can see, is a great person whose small soul has been sundered by something unexpected. And yet the unexpected turned out to be the most ordinary things: people, the sky, the sun, the land, the water surrounding the land, the things growing on the land.

What were the things growing on the land? I pause for this. What were the things growing on that land and why do I pause for this?

I come from a place called Antigua. I shall speak of it as if no one has ever heard of it before; I shall speak of it as if it is just new. In the writings, in anything representing a record of the imagination of Christopher Columbus, I cannot find any expectation for a place like this. It is a small lump of insignificance, green, green, green, and green again. Let me describe this landscape again: it is green, and unmistakably so; another person, who would have a more specific interest, a painter, might say, it is a green that often verges on blue, a green that often is modified by reds and yellows and even other more intense or other shades of green. To me, it is green and green and green again. I have no interest other than this immediate and urgent one: the landscape is green. For it is on this green landscape that, suddenly, I and people who look like me made an appearance.

I, me. The person standing in front of you started to think of all this while really focused on something and someone else altogether. I was standing in my garden; my garden is in a place called Vermont; it is in a village situated in a place called Vermont. From the point of view of growing things, that is, the gardener's, Vermont is not in the same atmosphere as that other place I am from, Antigua. But while standing in that place, Vermont, I think about the place I am from, Antigua. Christopher Columbus never saw Vermont at all; it never entered his imagination. He saw Antigua, I believe on a weekday, but if not then it would have been a Sunday, for in this life there would have been only weekdays or Sundays, but he never set foot on it, he only came across it while passing by. My world then—the only world I might have known if circumstances had not changed, intervened, would have entered the human imagination, the human imagination that I am familiar with, the only one that dominates the world in which I live—came into being as a footnote to someone just passing by. By the time Christopher Columbus got to the place where I am from, the place which forms the foundation of the person you see before you, he was exhausted, he was sick of the whole thing, he longed for his old home, or he longed just to sit still and enjoy the first few things that he had come upon. The first few things that he came on were named after things that were prominent in his thinking, his sponsors especially; when he came to the place I am from, he had been reduced to memorializing a place of worship; the place I am from is named after a church. This church might have been an important church to Christopher Columbus, but churches are not important, originally, to people who look like me. And if people who look like me have an inheritance, among this inheritance will be this confusion of intent; nowhere in his intent when he set out from his point of embarkation (for him, too, there is not origin: he originates from Italy, he sails from Spain, and this is the beginning of another new traditional American narrative, point of origin and point of embarkation): "Here is something I have never seen before, I especially like it because it has no precedent, but it is frightening because it has no precedent, and so to make it less frightening I will frame it in the thing I know; I know a church, I know the name of the church, even if I do not like or know the people connected to this church, it is more familiar to me, this church, than the very ground I am standing on; the ground has changed, but the church, which is in my mind, remains the same."

I, the person standing before you, close the quotation marks. Up to this point I and they that look like me are not yet a part of this narrative. I can look at all these events: a man setting sail with three ships, and after many, many days on the ocean, finding new lands whose existence he had never even heard of before, and then finding in these new lands people and their things, and these people and their things, he had never heard of them before, and he empties the land of these people, and then he empties the people, he just empties the people. It is when this land is completely empty that I and the people who look like me begin to make an appearance, the food I eat begins to make an appearance, the trees I will see each day come from far away and begin to make an appearance, the sky is as it always was, the sun is as it always was, the water surrounding the land on which I am just making an appearance is as it always was; but these are the only things left from before that man, sailing with his three ships, reached the land on which I eventually make an appearance.

When did I begin to ask all this? When did I begin to think of all this and in just this way? What is history? Is it a theory? I no longer live in the place where I and those who look like me first made an appearance. I live in another place. It has another narrative. Its narrative, too, can start with that man sailing on his ships for days and days, for that man sailing on his ships for days and days is the source of many narratives, for he was like a deity in the simplicity of his beliefs, in the simplicity of his actions; just listen to the straightforward way many volumes featuring this man sailing on his ships began, "In 1492 . . ." "In 1492." But it was while standing in this other place that has a narrative mostly different from the place in which I make an appearance that I begin to think of this.

One day, while looking at the things that lay before me at my feet, I was having an argument with myself over the names I should use when referring to the things that lay before me at my feet. These things were plants. The plants, all of them—and they were hundreds—had two names: they had a common name, that is, the name assigned to them by people for whom these plants have value; and then they have a proper name, or a Latin name, and that is a name assigned to them by an agreed-on group of botanists. For a long time I resisted using the proper names of the things that lay before me. I believed that it was an affectation to say *"Eupatorium"* when you could say "joe-pye weed." I then would only say "joe-pye weed." The botanists are from the same part of the world as the man who sailed on the three ships, that same man who started the narrative from which I trace my beginning. And the botanists are like that man who sailed on the ships in a way, too: they emptied the world of things animal, mineral, and vegetable, of their names, and replaced these names with names pleasing to them; the recognized names are now reasonable, as reason is a pleasure to them.

Carl Linnaeus was born on the twenty-third of May, in 1707, somewhere in Sweden. (I know where, but I like the high-handedness of not saying so.) His father's name was Nils Ingemarsson; the Ingemarssons were farmers. Apparently, in Sweden then, surnames were uncommon among ordinary people, and so the farmer would add "son" to his name or he was called after the farm on which he lived. Nils Ingemarsson became a Lutheran minister, and on doing so he wanted to have a proper surname, not just a name with "son" attached to it. On his family's farm grew a linden tree. It had grown there for generations and had come to be regarded with reverence among neighboring farmers; people believed that misfortune would fall on you if you harmed this tree in any way. This linden tree was so well-regarded that people passing by used to pick up twigs that had dropped from it and carefully place them at the base of the tree. Nils Ingemarsson took his surname from this tree: Linnaeus is the latinized form of the Swedish word *lind*. Other branches of this family who also needed a surname drew inspiration from this tree; some took the name Tiliander—the Latin word for linden is *tilia*—and then some others again who also needed a surname took the name Lindelius from the Swedish word *lind*, which means linden.

Carl Linnaeus's father had a garden. I do not know what his mother had. His father loved growing things in this garden and would point them out to the young Carl, but, when the young Carl could not remember the names of the plants, his father gave him a scolding and told him he would not tell him the names of any more plants. (Is this story true? But how could it not be?) He grew up not far from a forest filled with beech, a forest with pine, a grove filled with oaks, meadows. His father had a collection of rare plants in his garden (but what would be rare to him and in that place, I do not know). At the time Linnaeus was born, Sweden, this small country that I now think of as filled with well-meaning and benign people interested mainly in the well-being of children, the well-being of the unfortunate no matter their age, was the ruler of an empire; but the remains of it are only visible in the architecture of the main square of the capitol of places like Estonia. And so what to make of all this, this small detail that is the linden tree, this large volume of the Swedish empire, and a small boy whose father was a Lutheran pastor? At the beginning of this narrative, the narrative that is Linnaeus, I have not made an appearance yet; the Swedes are not overly implicated in the Atlantic slave trade, not because they did not want to, only because they weren't allowed to do so; other people were better at it than they.

He was called "the little botanist" because he would neglect his studies and go out looking for flowers; if even then he had already shown an interest in, or the ability to name and classify plants, this fact is not in any account of his life that I have come across. He went to university at Uppsala; he studied there with Olaus Rudbeck. I can pause at this name, Rudbeck, and say *Rudbeckia,* and say, I do not like *Rudbeckia,* I never have it in my garden, but then I remember that a particularly stately, beautiful yellow flower in a corner of my field garden is *Rudbeckia nitida*. He met Olaf Celsius (the Celsius scale of temperature measurement), who was so taken with Linnaeus's familiarity and knowledge of botany that he gave Linnaeus free lodging in his house. He became one of the youngest lecturers at the university. He went to Lapland and collected plants and insects native to that region of the world; he wrote and published an account of it called *Flora Lapponica*. In Lapland, he acquired a set of clothing that people native to that region of the world wore on festive occasions; I have seen a picture of him dressed in these clothes, and the caption under the picture says that he is wearing his Lapland costume. Suddenly, I am made a little uneasy, for just when is it that other people's clothes become your costume? But I am not too uneasy, I haven't really entered this narrative yet, I shall soon, in any case I do not know the Laplanders, they live far away, I don't believe they look like me.

I only enter the picture when Linnaeus takes a boat to Holland. He becomes a doctor to an obviously neurotic man (obvious, only to me, I arbitrarily deem him so; no account of him I have ever come across has described him so) named George Clifford. George Clifford is often described as a rich merchant banker; just like that, a rich merchant banker, and this description often seems to say that to be a rich merchant banker is just a type of person one could be, an ordinary type of person, anyone could be that. And now how to go on, for on hearing that George Clifford was a rich merchant in the eighteenth century, I now am sure I have become a part of the binomial system of plant nomenclature narrative.

George Clifford has glass houses full of vegetable materials from all over the world. This is what Linnaeus writes of it: "I was greatly amazed when I entered the greenhouses, full as they were of so many plants that a son of the North must feel bewitched, and wonder to what strange quarter of the globe he had been transported. In the first house were cultivated an abundance of flowers from southern Europe, plants from Spain, the South of France, Italy, Sicily and the isles of Greece. In the second were treasures from Asia, such as Poincianas, coconut and other palms, etc.; in the third, Africa's strangely shaped, not to say misshapen plants, such as the numerous forms of Aloe and Mesembryanthemum families, carnivorous flowers, Euphorbias, Crassula and Proteas species, and so on. And finally in the fourth greenhouse were grown the charming inhabitants of America and the rest of the New World;

large masses of Cactus varieties, orchids, cruciferea, yams, magnolias, tulip-trees, calabash trees, arrow, cassias, acacias, tamarinds, pepper-plants, Anona, manicinilla, cucurbitaceous trees and many others, and surrounded by these, plantains, the most stately of all the world's plants, the most beauteous Hernandia, silver-gleaming species of Protea and camphor trees. When I then entered the positively royal residence and the extremely instructive museum, whose collections no less spoke in their owner's praise, I, a stranger, felt completely enraptured, as I had never before seen its like. My heart-felt wish was that I might lend a helping hand with its management."

In almost every account of an event that has taken place sometime in the last five hundred years, there is always a moment when I feel like placing an asterisk somewhere in its text, and at the end of this official story place my own addition. This chapter in the history of botany is such a moment. But where shall I begin? George Clifford is interesting—shall I look at him? He has long ago entered my narrative; I now feel I must enter his. What could it possibly mean to be a merchant banker in the eighteenth century? He is sometimes described as making his fortune in spices. Only once have I come across an account of him that says he was a director of the Dutch East India Company. The Dutch East India Company would not have been involved in the Atlantic trade in human cargo from Africa, but human cargo from Africa was a part of world trade. To read a brief account of the Dutch East India trading company in my very old encyclopedia is not unlike reading the label on an old can of paint. The entry mentions dates, the names of Dutch governors or people acting in Dutch interest; it mentions trade routes, places, commodities, incidents of war between the Dutch and other European people; it never mentions the people who lived in the area of the Dutch trading factories. Places like Ceylon, Java, the Cape of Good Hope are emptied of its people as the landscape itself was emptied of the things they were familiar with, the things that Linnaeus found in George Clifford's greenhouse.

"If one does not know the names, one's knowledge of things is useless." It was in George Clifford's greenhouse that Linnaeus gave some things names. The Adam-like quality of this effort was lost on him. "We revere the Creator's omnipotence," he says, meaning, I think, that he understood he had not made the things he was describing, he was only going to give them names. And even as a relationship exists between George Clifford's activity in the world, the world as it starts out on ships leaving the seaports of the Netherlands, traversing the earth's seas, touching on the world's peoples and places they are in, the things that have meant something to them being renamed and a whole new set of narratives imposed on them, narratives that place them at a disadvantage in relationship to George Clifford and his fellow Dutch, even as I can say all this in one breath or in one large volume, so too then does an invisible thread, a thread that no deep breath or large volume can contain, hang between Carolus Linnaeus, his father's desire to give himself a distinguished name, the name then coming from a tree, the linden tree, a tree whose existence was regarded as not ordinary, and his invention of a system of naming that even I am forced to use?

The invention of this system has been a good thing. Its narrative would begin this way: in the beginning, the vegetable kingdom was chaos; people everywhere called the same things by a name that made sense to them, not by a name that they arrived at by an objective standard. But who has an interest in an objective standard? Who would need one? It makes me ask again what to call the thing that happened to me and all who look like me? Should I call it history? And if so, what should history mean to someone who looks like me? Should it be an idea, should it be an open wound and each breath I take in and expel healing and opening the wound again, over and over, or is it a long moment that begins anew each day since 1492?

TALES FROM A BLACK GIRL ON FIRE, OR WHY I HATE TO WALK OUTSIDE AND SEE THINGS BURNING

Camille T. Dungy

I have always loved to be outdoors. From a young age I've enjoyed hiking with a goal, or just ambling, exploring. Even sitting still in one spot can be relaxing. I've hiked alone. I've hiked with strangers. Without a care in mind, I've wandered through fields, trying my hand at identifying the plants and animals whose paths mine crossed. It never occurred to me that I would desperately fear an entire landscape, until I tried to duplicate this pleasure in an old plantation state.

The first indication of trouble was a hike I attempted along the Cumberland Gap, where Tennessee borders Virginia. Earlier that summer, while an artist in residence at Colorado's Rocky Mountain National Park, I'd taken a three- to five-mile solo hike nearly daily. Still, not one mile into the Cumberland Gap trail, I was forced back by fear. The trees were so thick around me it seemed I could see nothing, and every snap and shuddering branch sounded like an assurance of approaching danger.

Perhaps I'd read too much pre–Civil War history. Why would I, with both feet in the twenty-first century, fear dogs or malicious white men? Of course, I also read the contemporary news and so had current reasons to fear dogs and malicious white men. Still, I was bemused and somewhat shamed when I jumped at yet another squirrel, turned my back on the dense rows of pines ahead of me, and headed toward the comforts of a couch and air-conditioning.

During the years I lived in Virginia, I occupied several historical planes at once. I lived my personal experience of a community that was legally desegregated and essentially welcoming; but I also lived my mother's and grandparents' pre–civil rights era experience. I knew I was free to pass wherever I chose, but I retained the legacies of the centuries before, when liberty was not a given. I heard and saw each creaking limb and trotting hound I encountered through one lens and just as easily another. Living in that old slave state, I regularly fought my fear. How dare the past keep me huddled up inside? To resist these imagined restrictions, I worked to ignore my trepidation each time I received an invitation to join a group outside.

And so one night, I drove deep into the country. Thick-branched trees grew densely on either side of the road, absorbing all peripheral moonlight. Wind shook limbs until they waved, although I didn't recognize these gnarled and night-blackened trees. Now and then something startling broke loose and knocked hard on my rear window, my moonroof, my windshield. An acorn, of course. Maybe a pinecone. A twig. Dead ropes of kudzu dangled here and there, and all my people's horror stories worried through my head. Didn't I know better? The path illuminated in front of me seemed to lead directly to a cemetery. I could see the crosses staked throughout the lawn, the cut flowers, some newly upturned dirt. A white angel guarded the entrance, but as I approached I discovered the road turned sharply. I passed the churchyard, the church, more woods. Then, behind the big house, I saw them. Though they'd seen me first. Seven or eight revelers, beer bottles in their hands, an old-time country tune still on their tongues, were pointing in my direction. Their bright skin glowed pinkly in the light of a ten-foot fire. They'd been expecting me. Now I'd arrived. In the broader light I could see bats the bonfire had disturbed. These were their hours to consume.

I came to associate open fires with historically informed terror. Many of my new Southern white friends enjoyed hosting bonfires, but I started to decline

their gracious invitations. Though their gatherings often began with a pleasant hike and a lovely dinner outside, I could never relax on these outings. I
knew the woods we walked through would reveal their malice because I was
so guarded, so conditioned to fear. I knew eventually the fire would be lit and
my friends' faces transformed. There had been plenty of lynching parties in
this part of the country. I couldn't help wondering, while wandering through
these southern woods, if one such event might have happened on the ground
where I stood. I knew the acts of history could not be denied, and I had no
interest in living them again, in memory or experience.

Fear limited the scope of my experience. Campfires and bonfires represented a conflation between the natural world and the human. The wood
in those piles was innocent and yet acted out a role. Because I was afraid of
what humans had done to other humans in those woods and on those tree-
provided fires, I'd come to fear the forests and the trees.

Whenever the opportunity arose, I left that neck of the woods. I found
myself spending the summer at an artist's colony in Maine. There the legacy
of racial violence didn't haunt me the same way. I could hike solo again. Deer
in the distance filled me with wonder, not fear. Ravens warned me off their
path and I felt no sense of personal foreboding. I could spend hours hunting for wildflowers, losing myself in the dense forest, and never be afraid of
whom or what might find me there. I was, again, at liberty in the wild.

After several days of such freedom outside, it began to storm. The rains
lasted six days and all the residents of the colony were trapped inside. On the
seventh day it cleared. After dinner, reluctant to return to the cabins we'd
worked in all week, we decided on a party so we could linger outside listening to the birds, the rustling leaves, and lapping waves.

The bonfire pit, expertly dug by a sculptor, was perfectly safe. Still, I
couldn't get comfortable. All the writers brought drafts to use as tinder. I
torched the one about the wild iris's melancholy glister under the moon. The
fire warmed all of us, even the dogs. The hound who ran the woods circled
me twice before laying its head at my heels.

A painter found a log that looked like the torso of a man. It had a knot
where the navel should be, a twig protruding from the juncture where the
solid trunk branched in two directions. There was some banter about the fac-
ile ease with which certain artists impress human experience upon the natural

world. This was a log, we understood. Nothing but a tree trunk. Still, "Man on fire." Some of them laughed. I diverted my eyes from the limbs that reached out of the greedy flames. The hand that extended toward me, whiter than ever silhouetted by the fire, passed me some wine. Everything around the fire was still wet from the rains, so we leaned against each other, watching sparks join the stars, flying heaven knew where.

Calm down, it's safe out here. I had to repeat this to myself many times.

You've been taught not to play with fire. You've been taught to show respect. Your whole life, you've known the rules. When you live in this country, you have to know the rules. Yucca, ice plant, chaparral pea, bigcone Douglas-fir: even the plants here make provisions for hard times. There are those that hoard water, and there are those gamblers that reproduce best in scorched terrain. Don't tell me you didn't know. It's inhospitable here, dry and danger-ous. A desert unless you own the water rights. Sudden Oak Death strikes and dead limbs litter the landscape. It's a tinderbox, this country. Now look what you've done. The whole family's in danger now. The whole neighborhood. Acres of wild country. All the beasts and all the birds. You had to look. You wouldn't look away. A child with a magnifying glass. That thin-waisted wasp caught beneath your lens's gaze and then those sparks and you too slow to quench the fire. And now, this terrifying blaze. You knew. You know. You've been taught not to play with fire.

I'd grown up in the semiarid hillsides of Southern California, where the spark from a campfire, a stray cigarette, or an insect burned under a magnify-ing glass could ignite a firestorm that burned a hundred homes, scorched innocent animals, and demolished thousands of acres of habitat. From a young age, I heard warnings about open fires. I was told to be cautious around anything that might ignite and people who find pleasure in starting a blaze. Just as I'd grown up aware of the historical dangers of being black and discovered outside, I knew to fear fire.

History is its own crucible, but that night in Maine, I realized African American history alone was not at the root of my fear of succumbing to flames. History and experience had linked my fear of violence against the body to those bonfires, the trees and the woods that permitted them, and the people who allowed them to blaze, but it was the sparks that erupted from the fires and the violence they could visit on a whole landscape that I most fundamentally feared. The danger fire posed to a human body and the danger fire posed to the natural landscape: I had conflated these so that when I encountered large fires, these separate fears became one and the same. Concerned about my own well-being and concerned about the land, I grew up learning reason upon reason I should fear walking outside and encountering flames.

CROSSING BOUNDARIES

Jeanne Wakatsuki Houston

We are speeding along U.S. Route 395, my daughter Cori behind in the backseat, ready with video camera to film the first sight of the Alabama Hills. After passing the white crusty expanse that was once Owens Lake, our excitement grows. Lone Pine, a small town facing the portal to Mount Whitney, lies not far ahead, signaling that the hills will soon be emerging on the left—low, purplish, and magenta. They still remain in my memory as potent markers of Manzanar's southern boundary. How often as a child had I gazed at them, terrified by tales of Indian ghosts roaming the slopes, rattlesnakes writhing in every jagged crevice.

From the age of seven to eleven, I spent the World War II years—along with ten thousand other Japanese Americans—in a mile-square encampment of barracks surrounded by barbed wire. Manzanar ("apple orchard" in Spanish) was, from 1942 to 1945, the most populous city between Reno and Los Angeles. Looming to the west, a two-mile-high wall, the Sierra Nevada, separated the camp from California's Central Valley; eastward, the Inyo Mountains and Death Valley formed another natural barrier.

More than fifty years have passed since I left. I returned once, in the early seventies, when my husband and I and three children made a pilgrimage. Cori, our eldest, was ten then. Today she is in her late thirties, eager to film with her new video camera what remains of Manzanar, a place she knows only as a traumatic event in her mother's history, remembering little from her short visit as a child.

I am working on a novel—a lifelong project, it seems—that has changed its focus numerous times in the past years. Recently, I learned some interesting facts that again have stimulated a change. A remarkable pattern of "displacement" has occurred on this particular stretch of land in the high California desert. For over a thousand years, Indians had flourished, living off the earth and the game and fowl teeming about streams and lakes fed by the Sierra Nevada runoff. When prospecting and mining on the eastern slopes began in the early 1850s, it heralded the end of the Indians' stewardship.

Until that time there were no preexisting white settlements, although Euro-American trappers and official mapping parties had traversed the region, with John C. Frémont passing through in 1845 to name the valley, river, and lake after Richard Owens, a guide on some of his trips through California.

In 1861 the first mining district east of the Sierra was formed. Cattlemen and farmers soon followed. Within the next year hostilities broke out between the Paiutes and white settlers, and in 1863 nearly one thousand Indians were imprisoned at Camp Independence and force-marched to Fort Tejon, a reservation 175 miles south. As years passed, some of the displaced Paiutes returned, but not to their independent life. They had become dependent on the firmly established Euro-American economy, and most found jobs as farm laborers—as expert irrigation managers—on this land inhabited for centuries by their ancestors, who had created intricate water systems and lush game reserves.

The township of Manzanar prospered until 1924 when Los Angeles bought the water rights to streams used for irrigation and siphoned the precious resource south to its ever-increasing population and urban spread. Farmers and ranchers were ruined, and, again, another group was "displaced," forced to abandon the valley once fertile with apple and pear orchards they had planted.

Then in March 1942 the first Japanese-American internees arrived. The town of Manzanar became an internment camp leased by the United States Army from the Los Angeles Water District for twenty-five thousand dollars a year. (The district first had demanded ninety thousand.) Relocated from areas of Los Angeles, the Central Valley, and Bainbridge Island in Washington, the new inhabitants were to add another layer of history to the site.

As a child I had been intrigued by stories of Indian spirits that supposedly roamed the surrounding desert terrain. I wanted, somehow, to incorporate an Indian presence into my novel. Thus, I had decided to make this trip with my daughter to revisit the ruins, now a national park, and meet with one of its guides, a Paiute Indian named Richard Stewart.

"Are those the hills?" asks Cori.

Looking like hillocks of smooth sand I had molded at beaches when I was a youngster, the Alabama Hills rise into view, purple and burnt mahogany cones. My throat constricts and beginnings of tears sting my eyes.

"Sure are," I say lightly, covering my emotion. I am irritated at myself. Hadn't years of therapeutic work and the catharsis of writing *Farewell to Manzanar* with my husband healed the trauma associated with World War II and the internment? I take a deep breath. Post-traumatic stress syndrome never goes away, they say.

I slow down so Cori can film our approach. In the rearview mirror, I see her run the camera nonstop, recording every rolling knoll, every dried scrub and tumbleweed overlaying the dry earth. She lifts the lens toward the mountains. I stop the car while she scans the granite grandeur of Mount Williamson, majestic with its cape of white snow.

We come to the camp's entrance, where the stone gatehouse once guarded by military police looks remarkably as I remembered it a half century ago. The low stone building with a sloping pagoda roof stands aloof, disdainful of the spiked tumbleweed, wheeling from a gust of wind, crashing against it. The flurry quickly dissipates. It is still again, the air growing hotter in the noon sun. Should we come back later in the day when it's cooler? We decide to continue and I turn west onto a rutted road leading into a jungle of overgrown Scotch broom, madrone brush, and the ever-present sage and tumbleweed. Scarred with deep channels cut by rushing runoff from the mountains, some resembling minicanyons over which the car pitches precariously, the road skirts the perimeter of the actual campsite. It's obvious the National Park Service has not been able to maintain this newest addition to the park roster.

After some minutes of intense navigating, we see a tall white obelisk rising in the distance. It marks the cemetery. We emerge from the darkness, almost blinded by light reflected from the monument. Standing tall and alone, the obelisk is a loyal sentinel guarding the sanctuary for the dead. Japanese characters on its face read "Soul Consoling Tower."

Surrounded by a barbed-wire fence installed to keep out cattle, the cemetery consists of several rock-outlined graves. Out of respect, Cori leaves her camera in the car and we wander inside the enclosure. It is quiet. I feel the antiquity, the calm energy that accumulates with years of undisturbed tranquility. Except for modern-day reminders left as offerings by visitors—a pair of mirrored sunglasses, plastic flowers, key chains, a rag doll, mounds of coins—I easily can imagine myself back in time to the 1940s.

We leave the cemetery, and Cori retrieves her camera before we penetrate dense brush hiding the camp's remains. At the eastern edge I recognize the hospital's concrete-slab foundation, wildly tilted and cracked, as if jolted by a quake. As we venture farther into murkiness, the air turns thicker and muggy, reminding me of extreme weather changes that could come on quickly. One moment clear sunshine, the next air darkened by a sandstorm or raging whirlwind.

Rusted pipes protrude from the dirt like periscopes. They are remains of water faucets attached to each barracks. Finally we come to an area I determine is Block 28, where I had lived. A line of gnarled, aged pear trees still neatly defines the edge of one barracks. I recognize them, and I am amazed. Barely alive, these old trees are still sprouting some sparse green leaves! They are survivors, just like some of the old Issei I remember—lean, weathered, and tough (ojichan and obachan), dried-up-looking as twigs. But underneath that leathery exterior, just as in the old trees, the juice of life still trickled, sustaining them through the harshest of times.

I think of my father nurturing those trees back to life. Previously abandoned before camp was built, they were barely kept alive by underground streams seeping from the mountains. When rescued by my father, the trees were emaciated and gray. But they soon revived after he built irrigation ditches around them and pruned their brittle branches. For our entire time in camp, they produced delicious pears, which we gathered and stored in the cellar dug under the barracks.

I tell Cori the story. Eyes wide with wonder, she gently touches the prickly limbs. I know she is seeing the grandfather she never knew handling those trees, perhaps the very branch she is now holding. She films the trees for several minutes and breaks off a twig, which she deposits in her satchel.

We leave Block 28, and Cori continues filming the rock-garden ruins of the orphanage and hospital. I look for signs of any firebreak, the open sandy spaces between blocks where we played baseball and searched for Indian arrowheads. Indian ghosts were said to roam in the firebreaks, especially on full-moon nights. I remember late one evening while crossing the break alone, I suddenly saw a group of Indians on horses galloping in a circle. The illusion lasted a few minutes and disappeared when a whirlwind rushed in. I told my family about it the next day, and they said I was suffering from sunstroke.

But the area is now grown over. No open spaces at all. We are tired, sweating in the airless dry forest. After trudging for what seems like miles, we finally emerge into glaring light, Mount Williamson rising before us in the distance, my spirit's life, as I remember how that peak inspired us during our imprisonment. Solid and steadfast, it remained immovable through all times. Around it the terrain and people changed, but the mountain stood constant, its stately aura sustaining our spirits, as its water sustained our bodies.

We leave Manzanar and check into a motel on the outskirts of Lone Pine. The clerk is a mustached man around forty who immediately asks if we are here to visit the ruins of the internment camp. Surprised at this unexpected question asked so quickly, I answer somewhat defensively. "Why do you assume that?"

He smiles, seemingly unoffended by my curt response. "Well, we get many tourists who come to visit Manzanar, especially Asians. It's been very good for business, and I want to welcome you." Times certainly have changed on this side of the Sierra. I remember when names of towns such as Lone Pine, Independence, and Bishop only brought up feelings of rejection and fear. They once hated our presence; now we are welcomed back.

Richard had suggested meeting for lunch in Independence. The cafe is small, with an oblong counter enclosing the grill, and, strictly out of the forties, three steel-legged Formica-topped tables and chairs crowding the remaining space. Cori and I are there only a few minutes before he arrives. He is an imposing figure, tall and lean, shoulder-length hair tied at the back. In a fringed tan suede jacket, Levis, and boots, he looks like many of the locals we've seen walking about town. But the resemblance stops there. He sits down across from us, and we see a dark copper-toned face, high-boned cheeks, and eagle-wing eyebrows jutting over eyes that twinkle as he smiles.

"Welcome to Independence," he says in a deep voice. "Or rather, welcome *back*." He directs the words to me. I notice his teeth are white and even. I guess his age to be around forty-seven.

"Thanks so much for seeing us," we both gush. Cori has never met a full-blooded Indian. I fully understand her rapt eyes, glistening with awe, as I, too, feel myself swept back to childhood fantasies. Not all were fantasies, though. One of my most vivid memories is the day Indians from the nearby reservation came to Manzanar and danced. Beating drums similar to the Japanese Taiko, they danced in full dress, singing in deep voices what sounded like mournful chants of Buddhist priests.

After polite small talk, he begins to speak more intimately. He tells of his love for the land, about the Northern Paiutes and their history. Confirming the pattern of "displacement" I had come upon, he relates the "dispersement" of Indians by white settlers, the "water wars" of Owens Valley between Los Angeles and local ranchers, the creation of another "reservation" for Japanese Americans during World War II. This history of exploitation and exile, he says, has left a residue of dark energy that pervades the site.

In my mind's eye I recapture the violent riot of December 1942, when two young men were shot to death by soldiers; the "stalag-17" whiskey brewing in barracks, soddening the Issei men's minds; tension and fistfights between internees over the loyalty oath. I see myself at my first funeral, witnessing, with a child's curiosity and awakening compassion, the sight of a relative named Charley, held up on his feet by his brothers as he unashamedly cursed and wailed the death of his wife. Yuri, young and beautiful, had died hemorrhaging from a miscarriage. Yes, Richard is right. Already saturated with sorrows of the past, the land had again been assaulted by violence and grief. I agree energy never leaves a place. Perhaps that is one reason why places of worship—throughout centuries—retain a special emanation, a feeling of sacredness and peace.

I ask how he came to be a docent for Manzanar, since he is not a park ranger. He reveals that he is also a poet, now focusing on haiku. Bashō, the great haiku master of seventeenth-century Japan, is his idol. After seeing similarities in the uprooting of his people and Japanese Americans—who he says are from the same ancient tribe—he began delving into the internment camp's history.

"I know every block barrack, latrine, mess hall, and laundry room. Every firebreak, road, and garden. I know them like the back of my hands," he says, displaying one, large and ruddy, ridged veins like streams and creeks traversing its broad fleshy terrain.

I envision him leading groups, kneeling on one knee to trace the outline of a pond or rock garden, a modern-day Indian guide tracking a path through a forgotten wilderness.

His latest poems are of Manzanar, he confides, and he hopes to write a series called *Thirty-Six Views of Manzanar*.

I tell him of my plan to incorporate the Indian presence in my novel. "Probably a love story," I add hesitatingly.

"Great! Even if it never happened, it could have."

Encouraged by his reply, I ask for his opinion of a scene I have written, in which a teenage girl interned at Manzanar has a vision of a granite obelisk transforming into an Indian warrior. "I mean, is that vision believable in the Indian sense?" I had made up the episode, spinning off the multitude of rock gardens created within camp.

He laughs and informs me there is a Paiute legend of a warrior who turns into stone. "The whole desert is filled with spirit-rocks. The Big One," he points toward the mountains, "is our grandfather."

I am stunned. Could my imagination have tapped into some unconscious field of myth? I look at the jagged spires reaching to the sky. Suddenly the range takes on another dimension. I realize that when I gazed at those mountains as a child, it was a grandfather's protective power I felt—protection and the unconditional acceptance of an unwavering grandparent.

After lunch he takes us to the Eastern California Museum, which contains a sizeable section of Manzanar memorabilia, including a poster of *Farewell to Manzanar*'s book cover. We meet the director and staff, with whom we spend the afternoon learning about the area's history and plans for

Manzanar as a national park. When it is time to leave, Richard gives Cori and me each a clay pottery mug, henna-colored with black petroglyph-like drawings adorning the sides. His name is inscribed on the bottom. Not only a poet, curator, historian, and educator, our new friend is also a potter. He wishes me luck on my novel, and I wish him the same for his haiku poetry.

The next morning we are up early and on the road before the sun rises above the Inyo range on the eastern side of Owens Valley. My mind is sharp, lucid as the crisp air. We have been here not more than thirty-six hours. Yet it seems like weeks, as if time backtracked while we rummaged in the ruins and stood still in the past. I now feel eager to get back to work.

We pass the stone guardhouse and I look again at the terrain. With the barbed wire gone, the land is continuous from mountain range to mountain range. Oddly, since yesterday, the landscape seems different. Or perhaps it is myself, my perception. During my childhood in camp, the barbed wire was an unforgiving wall, physically and emotionally. Trespassing its boundaries could end in death, as it did in another camp for a young boy collecting firewood outside the fence.

When I asked my mother why we were in prison, she answered in the simplest way she could without explaining the politics of war, "It's because we are Japanese." From that moment on, in my innocent mind, I perceived it was not only bad to be Japanese, it was criminal. I can see how growing up within a square mile surrounded by this unmistakable punishment for being the very person I was could account, in ways, for my reluctance to take risks, to test certain boundaries, to press limits—in myself and in my writing.

Today I feel a sense of liberation. My talk with Richard had affirmed one boundary crossing, giving me a new permission to trust my visions, to break through a barbed-wire confinement I had placed around my imagination. Despite the dark energy that still must pervade Manzanar's ruins, I feel only lightness as we drive past on the highway. Its clumped site of brush and trees is small, almost lost in the now clear and open space of ochre desert and gleaming rock. In the rearview mirror, I watch it disappear as we round the Alabama Hills.

WORKING IN A REGION OF LOST NAMES

Fred Arroyo

We stood in the middle of the pier, looking out on the blue freshwater sea. My father was very thin, his *guayabera* and freshly pressed black pants elegant in the August sun, and there was something peaceful in his bony, gnarled hands holding those rails as if he were vacationing. A few boats bobbed on the white-crested waves. The people on the beach were distant, yet I could easily make them out: sitting on colorful blankets and sheets, children building castles and running along the shore and splashing in the rising and falling waves.

My mother and sister had walked to the end of the pier. Now they were making their way back; the henna strands of my mother's hair were full of sun, and the yellow ribbons in my sister's hair gently twisted in the soft breeze. My father would have been about thirty-seven (close to my current age, though I was then only fourteen or fifteen), and though he had shaved closely that morning, his face smooth and clean and lean, he had missed those glittering gray and silver hairs just at the ends of his sideburns.

The wind picked up and a sheet of thick, white clouds moved in from the southwest, the July air turning hotter, the sky blanketed by a dulling haze of gold.

My father rested his chin on the palm of his hand, his elbow leaning on the guardrail. Lately, he had taken to having my mother drive us thirty miles from Niles to Saint Joe, so he could walk out on the pier and look at the freshwater sea of Lake Michigan.

The sea stirred with the breeze, the blue water pocked with discs of gold. My father seemed lost, as if he momentarily vanished and became the waves, crested and bobbed, disappeared, and then appeared out there in the blue, the more and more he stared into the horizon.

What was he searching for?

My father hardly ever talked to me, and from the time I was around nine years old, he never seemed to want to talk in English, and there arose between us a great distance like a turbulent sea I didn't know how to cross. That summer he had been even more silent, and we all began to live within our own lonelinesses. He had lost his job at a factory, I'm not sure if it was because of cutbacks or his drinking, and he had sobered for a time by moving to Chicago to live with his sister's family and to work at a different factory. In Michigan he had been arrested at one point for drunk driving. Given his previous offenses, he had to serve time in a program that allowed him to work and stay at home during the week, but on Friday nights he had to check into the county jail in Saint Joe for the weekend.

I looked out at the horizon, tried to find the spot my father searched for. There were special days I waited for, days that never arrived. A high, clear, blue summer sky. One stood along the lakeshore, or, better yet, one looked from the vantage point of a high bluff or a tall dune, and then the Chicago skyline—ninety miles away—would rise out of the freshwater sea, the buildings forming like black boxes on the horizon, the straight line and pointed top of the Sears Tower making it all the more alive. On that day I couldn't see Chicago—there were the waves, the warm wind on my arms, the white clouds, the horizon, but no distant-appearing buildings, no sudden realization of things arising out of nothing. But maybe my father knew of those days too, maybe, at times, he dreamed them, and so up on the far bluff, when he spent his Saturdays and Sundays in the county jail, maybe there was some small window he knew of, and on a clear day he had a way of looking I may one day discover.

My sister and mother walked toward us. My father waved for us to follow, and we all walked back toward the shore, and then to the car. My father sat in the passenger's seat while my mother drove, and we were all silent as the countryside unfolded in gold and green and blue that late afternoon, the darker shapes of the orchards coloring with apples, plums, and peaches. Without saying a word, almost as if by instinct, my mother pulled off the highway into Vollman's Market.[1]

There was the smell of cantaloupe and dust mixing in the warm air drifting in through the pole-barn doors that I still can't seem to lose. Tomatoes, zucchinis, mounds of green beans were piled on tables, and on three fifty-five gallon drums set side by side, their tops covered by a red and white checkered cloth, there were quart-size cardboard baskets filled with fat blueberries. The cantaloupes were in a small pyramid. Bushel baskets were filled with red and gold apples, and the baskets were on pallets. Fruit flies filled the air. There were clear packages of dried fruit and nuts on the table next to the cash register, along with canning jars of red, deep purple, and orange preserves. Against the wall there was a set of clear coolers filled with gallons of milk, sodas, eggs, and butter.

A woman straightened some ten-pound bags of potatoes on a pallet, the sound of the thick paper crunching as she pulled on a bag, lifted, and dropped it into the pattern she was making; the smell of wet, beginning-to-rot potatoes stinging my nose. I stood there for a moment. Then she turned to me. She was short and heavy, with black hair and glasses. I asked her about a job. Most of the work, she told me, was picking corn and some odd work around the market, helping to unload deliveries, sweeping and cleaning, maybe helping to pick and bag potatoes. She yelled over to an older man (the concrete floor was splotched with dark stains, and suddenly I felt a spasm of shame deep in my stomach, as I flicked away a green fly crawling down my arm). The man, who was her husband and the owner of the market, came over. She told him I was interested in work. He had a thick, bristly mustache that was turning gray, his hands and arms trembled with a slight tick as he stood there, and it was hard to see his eyes because of his green hat, the bill pulled down low. He simply said, "That'd be fine," after looking me over a bit, and he mentioned the picking of corn, and like his wife, the extra work of loading and unloading trucks, some cleaning, bagging potatoes. I turned and looked across the market at my mother, sister, and father standing behind a table of lettuce, and behind them, the open door and the cars passing by on their way north.

I asked, "And my father? Can he work too?"

Mr. Vollman tipped the bill of his hat back, and then he and his wife both looked past me across the market, their eyes not widening but their faces filling with some strange recognition. They looked at each other, as if they were used to talking without ever saying a word, and then she said, "Yes, your father can work too. We'll see you both here tomorrow at six in the morning."

Returning to that summer I have a difficult time pinpointing the exact year—conflicting memories of work, drink, and those long, unending, sickening days when getting sober meant sitting with my hate and loss, are what return to me. That summer must have been in 1982, when I was fourteen. I'm not sure why I asked about that job on that day. When I close my eyes I see the black and orange Help Wanted sign tacked to a thick cottonwood tree as we pulled into the dusty driveway, the sign's squared perfection and how it seemed to float there surrounded by the black and green of the tree. I don't remember my father mentioning the sign, and I don't remember him asking about the job. In my memory—as I recall that day becoming grayer with thick, wet clouds; my father trying to sober up after a three-month bout with drink; the quiet stillness of the market save for a small fan blowing by the cash register; and then the sound of rattling glass as my father tried to steady his hand and the bottle of ginger ale he had lifted from the cooler—the feeling for my remembrance tells me he hadn't said a word. I asked, suddenly, about the job because I had always worked in some way (various paper routes, detasseling corn, picking blueberries), and I felt the money earned would be helpful since school would start soon, since my father wasn't working.

In that one moment when I turned, gnats drifting back and forth in the gold, dusty light falling on the fruits and vegetables, I turned because I felt something rise in me, because I remembered my father, turned to find him, and then asked if he could work too.

There was an odd chill in the market; I looked outside, the sky predicting rain. We headed from the market, my father drinking his ginger ale, my sister and mother eating a peach. We passed the cottonwood tree, and when my father opened the passenger-side door, I pointed at the sign on the tree and I said, "They gave me a job." Everyone looked at my extended arm for a moment, almost as if my words had come from my hand, and then I asked my mother if she could drive me out here in the morning before she went to work.

"They're paying $4.35 an hour," I said, and thought how it was a good amount above minimum wage.

"I asked if Chago could work too."

My mother said, "Yes, I'll bring you out."

There was no more discussion, no questions asked as we got into the car, nor as we drove home. Once home, my mother and father put together some lunches for the next day. My father pulled from below the kitchen sink a scotch plaid thermos. He raised it next to his ear, shook it, listened for any broken glass. I never heard whatever he heard in his shaking; a gust of wind hit the side of the house, a branch striking the roof crazily, and out past my mother and father's darkened profiles the sky turned blue-black, then silver sparks of rain shattered against the windowpane. My mother turned from the counter and placed two bowls, each with a spoon inside them, on the table. She placed a coffee cup next to each bowl. In the morning we'd have oatmeal and coffee, and in that darkening kitchen of summer rain I knew the morning would arrive soon.

My decision to ask about the job was weighted by memory. Perhaps the summer before (or the summer before that) my mother's brother had returned to town and was looking for work. He, my father, and I had driven out into the hot August fields of Berrien County looking for work. Driving along those long roads flanked by fields and orchards, they would turn onto dusty one-lane roads that led into migrant camps comprised of small green or white shacks, children standing in the hard sun or running under dust-covered trees, and always the women hanging laundry—a bright confetti of colors— along precariously secured clotheslines. These camps where mostly inhabited by Mexican families, but back then, in the early eighties, we also drove through compounds of three or four shacks inhabited by Haitian families. My father seemed free and easy—speaking either Spanish or his fast, musical English—in the camps. Usually, at first, the women would look at us strangely, but then once my father began to talk they told us where we needed to ask about work, often a mile or so down the road on the edge of a field, where we would find a green or silver trailer. We never found work at any of those trailers; there were already too many workers, and I remember a kind of awe in my father's voice when he said we could've worked at one farm, but we needed to bring our family to work there and live in one of the shacks.

I wonder, as I return back to this colored geography of green trees and deep brown fields, the wind rushing through the car lifting my hair, if there was some larger memory behind our going out to the fields. My uncle, perhaps, asked my father to help him search for work because it was something my father was accustomed to doing all his life, and he did it well. When my mother and father moved us to Michigan from Hartford, Connecticut, in the mid-1970s, my father had, in fact, found—right away—work picking apples; and, of course, the only reason my parents met was because my father came to Michigan to work at the Green Giant cannery in Niles.

My father and I must have worked a day, maybe two at Vollman's Market, yet I don't recall any of those first days of work. What I remember is a morning—gold, everything—the grass, the trees, a long clothesline—speckled with dew—when my mother dropped us off at the market, and there in the driveway were three men. Two of them leaned against the hood of a long blue car, and the third man stood inside the open door of a cream-colored truck, his arms resting against the door. My mother stopped the car and looked at my father, but neither said a word. Once I stepped out of the car, I recognized the men as my father's friends.

At some point, my father must've told them that there was work (he must've easily understood that there was more work than he and I could do, that there was the possibility that his friends might ask for work too). I remember that when Mr. Vollman pulled up with the tractor and wagon to pick up my father and me, he didn't seem to look at all strangely on the scene. He shut down the tractor and jumped to the ground. He pushed the bill of his hat back, and then took off his gloves as he approached. We all stood in a semicircle, Mr. Vollman in the middle. My father stepped forward, and in a voice of ease and confidence said (his arms spread wide at his sides), "They work too, if you like."

Mr. Vollman looked around briefly, looking each man in the face. And then he looked at me.

I'll always remember his smile, the twitch of his graying, bushy moustache, and how he waved us all toward the wagon, and how we all jumped on

the back end, the sudden sound of talk and laughter, and how when the tractor hit the dirt lane and jerked, I was immediately aware of the cold morning
air and how the cornfields were endlessly beautiful in the golden dew.

My sense of our work back then has become dull over the years; I never
experience the deep-in-the-bones pain from that time, I never have those
afternoons and nights of undisturbed sleep because sleep is what the pain in
my arms and legs call for. The work only comes back to me in the strange
weather of July: the fields cold and wet in the morning, and then by noon—
my face red and cut by the sharp cornstalk leaves, my thighs raw and swollen
from my soaked jeans rubbing between my legs as I stoop up and down in
those tight lanes—the sun high and hot. The smell of the wet burlap sack at
my side mixing with the smell of my sweat and wet clothes, and then an odd
odor I can't seem to place but imagine as my skin rotting like the bruised,
overripe fruits found in the trash heap behind the market.

The work returns finally as a rhythm, a faint music: I follow it in the soft
beat of a lightly tapped conga drum, the quickly scratching tempo of shaking maracas, my hands pulling ears of corn from a stalk and sliding them
into my burlap sack, my feet lifting slowly and coming down in what felt
like light, giant steps that took me further down the row of corn toward
the bright light at the end, as a new, quieter music arose within my thighs
and spread up into my stomach, chest and arms, a tender, invisible yet flute-
like music that called me to work with it, to keep on moving, to not lose the
music, to know that soon we'd be done.

The wagon piled higher and higher with the bags of corn we dumped
there, and then eventually we jumped on the back and Mr. Vollman jerked the
tractor on the lane and headed back to the market. Once there, we headed
into a pole barn where there was a wagon filled with dark, dusty potatoes.

My father stepped on an overturned milk crate, a pitchfork in his hands,
and then placed his feet broadly and with assurance on the wagon as he began
to shovel the potatoes onto a running conveyor, the potatoes bouncing and
nudging against each other as they made their way down the line. One of my
father's friends stood on the side looking for stones, plants, weeds, and bad-
looking potatoes that he threw into a wooden box at his feet. At the end of
the conveyor the potatoes gathered into a pool that continued to rise the more
my father shoveled potatoes. Another of his friends scooped up with his hands

the potatoes from the pool into a scale, and once loaded with ten pounds, he dropped the potatoes into a new open white bag, and then placed the bag on a waist-high table where another of my father's friends twisted the tops of each bag closed with a copper band. He lifted and tossed the bag free into the air toward me—I caught each bag in my cupped elbows, one of my hands immediately grabbing the bottom and the other forming around the twisted, copper-banded top. Twisting at the waist I laid it down on a pallet, twisted up and caught another, twisted, laid it down, beginning to create a three-by-five pattern, twisting and laying down, twisting and laying down, the pattern growing into the layered rows of ten-pound bags of potatoes I stacked on the pallet, the rising pattern of bags clean and new and vivid, the paper and copper bands etching themselves within the grain of my palm, and the pain of the work sometimes forgotten as I focused on the image of the red mountains and a thin green stream running between those mountains on the bags.

Right away I became aware that I was not a man like my father or his friends. I could not keep up with them; I didn't have the body, experience, and memory of work most of them had since childhood, my father beginning to work in the fields of Puerto Rico when his own father made him quit school in the third grade.

My father and his friends asked Mr. Vollman if we could go out to the edge of the potato fields, out back behind the market, and use one of the white migrant shacks during our breaks between picking corn, bagging potatoes, and the afternoon potato picking. There were two out there, side by side, and although they seemed bright and clean and freshly painted, I think they were the remnants of a time long past, a time when the market was a much bigger farm, when families had traveled to live there and work all summer and deep into the fall. My father and his friends picked up some of the still-edible fruits and vegetables that had been thrown away at the market, a few bruised peaches or a cantaloupe soft with rot yet still good on one side, some wet celery, a blackening onion. We walked the quarter mile or so out to the shack. Someone dug some potatoes from the field. Someone started a small fire of sticks within a ring of broken bricks and stones. The potatoes were peeled and washed in the spigot in between the two shacks, and then boiled in an old pot on the fire. Someone had brought a small jar of mayonnaise, an off-white set of salt and pepper shakers, and what was salvaged from the celery and onion was chopped up, mixed with the cooked and cubed and salted and peppered potatoes and mayonnaise.

The warm potatoes melted the mayonnaise velvety smooth, the celery crunchy and briefly bitter, the onion burning the roof of my mouth and nose. I drank a coffee cup of cold water from the spigot.

Inside the shack the walls were bare and dark, the smell of cracked and crumbling dusty boards, and then the faint scent of wet soil and rain. An old mattress dusty and stained by water or sweat or what—I did not know—lay on the floor. It felt so cool and good to step out of the sun. I sat down on the mattress entranced for a time by that summer doorway, the square of gold and blue vividly present and real because of the darkness of the shack, and the talk and laughter of my father and the men outside. It became an original moment I couldn't—I still can't—frame; and now, just as then, I let it exist, as it needed to exist after a morning of wet work. I lay back on the mattress, the gold and blue coloring the insides of my eyelids, as I fall into a deep colored sleep that, no matter how brief, is only broken when I hear the men call from outside that it's time to go back to work.

Somewhere in the region of my mind are the names of those men, my father's friends. When I close my eyes they all seem to blur together, lying back against a pile of corn we've just picked, walking behind a wagon of potatoes, their figures like brown shadows in the drifting dust, their faces indistinct because of the sun and sweat in my eyes. Their names are nowhere to be discovered.

I recall an old man with a droopy long gray mustache, his eyes a sharp silver blue. His chin and his cheeks are speckled with silver and gray, and it seems he might have shaved every three or four days. I only heard him speak Spanish, yet his hair—a light sandy brown—is the longest I have ever seen a Puerto Rican man keep, striking the collar of his shirt. He always wears a very clean and neat white or light blue dress shirt. His dark blue pants attract dust. It's almost as if when taken together these features don't create a definitive portrait, and so I can only see them in the simplest of terms: the features of a man getting old and in need of money, who worked in a field alongside other men who lived with similar circumstances, men he had worked with—in countless regions and fields—for at least five decades.

There is also a very dark man working with us, and his face stands out because his eyes are coal black, his cheeks deeply defined as if chiseled into their smooth slenderness, and he has the wickedest smile, and each time he smiles I see a worn knife drawn across his lips, and then hear heavy laughter inhabited by cigarettes and something deep within him that he likes to share, but will never give away. I have to remember his face the only way I can: *Asian*. An ancient face I've seen in museums on masks and figurines, and a face I've passed countless times on the streets of New York, San Francisco, Madrid. And I seem to remember his face because his hair is the black of a raven's wing. His name—like all their names—remains a mystery. But he always wore, no matter how hot, a green plastic helmet. With some certainty I assume it was a leftover from his past; he probably worked at the Green Giant cannery in the sixties or seventies, and the helmet he wore, back then at the cannery, would've been fitted with a little light for working in the dark bunkers where mushrooms were grown. *Raphael.* Raphael returns to me without certainty, but as I repeat this name a few times I discover a timbre—shaped by a lonely piano and a sorrow-filled cello—that does justice to his face.

The man I remember the most I'll name Juan. (I hear this name no matter how empty the region of lost names.) Ever since I suddenly discovered that things can be beautiful in themselves because of the care I take to see them, Juan's handsomeness has supported my search for elegance and perfection. Juan's skin is a rich copper color, and in the right circle of sunlight his skin glows and tints his hair with red and gold, his hair always swept back with pomade and combed smooth and glossy and perfect. In his middle years he must've begun to develop a beer belly. No sooner, though, since his T-shirt revealed a chest and biceps defined by muscles, as well as a particular youthfulness that would continue on until he died (and in my memory that youthfulness lived beyond his sad death).

He was quiet, like me. Perhaps he was shy like me. He looked at things a long time, all the while making valuable discriminations (something I'm still learning). When he worked he wore a yellow baseball cap, the bill turned down and curved, the perfect shape a pitcher needed when standing on the mound on a bright sunny day. I'll always remember watching him as he leaned against the doorway of a migrant shack, the sun brilliant against his arms folded across his chest. I have brief memories of baseball when I was eleven, a few practices, a game, a yellow baseball hat, and a man standing inside the open door of his cream-colored truck watching me as I worked on throwing low strikes. Juan gave me a hand when I often fell behind picking corn or bagging potatoes. Later, when I forgot Juan without intending to, I heard he committed suicide by shooting himself in the stomach with a rifle. Something about his quietness stays with me.

Now, as I look out on the bare trees of late November—Thanksgiving has passed, the leaves have fallen, the sun becomes weaker and weaker as the fall ends and winter begins—I see that something seemed continually etched on Juan's brow, appeared at work in his memory. What was Juan doing, given the life he seemed to have created in town, out there in those fields? Why did he want or need to work out there? Something must have been at stake for him—*but what?* And when did he reach the point where he felt he had nothing else to wager?

There were years when I drove past the old Green Giant cannery almost every day, or at the least once a week. Sometimes I would pull over, get out of my truck, and look at the crumbling buildings, the broken, sagging roofs, the cement walls seeming soft to the touch, grass and weeds growing up through the sides of cracked walls, many of the fences surrounding the property rusty and weak, some fallen on their sides. I have no choice but to acknowledge the fact that my mother and father only met because my father traveled from the East Coast in response to a call for workers needed at the cannery. This call is more than likely the only reason a dozen Puerto Rican men ever lived in Niles, Michigan. But I won't accept the possibility that the closing of the cannery and the loss of a job pushed Juan toward death. I have to imagine another possibility: when the presence of the Green Giant cannery no longer exists, when it seems wiped away from Niles's memory, I'll still return to a region of lost names, a region where I can work to remember how those men lived with dignity. I need the chance to stop on the side of the road in southwestern lower Michigan, look out on the orchards and fields, and demand from the sky and the sun and the soil something like memory and hope and justice . . . even if I can never fully redeem Juan's life.

I'll need to move backward and forward, I'll need to invent the past within the present, the present within the past, if I'm ever to come to terms with

Juan's death. Juan's taking of his life placed him, I recognize now, within a larger pattern crisscrossed by departures, migrations, and arrivals. A larger pattern crisscrossed by sons and daughters within the silence and solitude their fathers leave behind when they depart. A pattern sometimes shaped by violence and death. In my extended family, I have relatives who have never known their fathers. I often forget that my cousin is part Puerto Rican because her father, a contemporary of my father's, has been lost from memory—deliberately forgotten, it seems. Her mother, my mother's sister, was briefly married to this man, who migrated to Michigan in order to work at Green Giant like my father. They had a daughter, my cousin, born three months before I, and then they split up. I often heard him evoked in what seemed like a mysterious whispered tone, or in a voice that seemed filled with rage. I have the image of a man with longer black hair, brown skin, and a long Pancho Villa mustache—but the image is vague, and it fades away.

I'm not sure I ever actually encountered him as a child, and as far as I know my cousin did not either. I do distinctly remember my father—his eyes wide, his hands shaking—saying he had learned that my cousin's father was killed in a bar in Puerto Rico. My father's right hand was clenched into a fist, and then his arm extended, his thumb rising, and he said my cousin's father had died from a knife wound as he jammed his hand violently into some imaginary space, just about waist high.

This man, who I continue to evoke without a name, I place alongside Juan, adding him permanently to the pattern. Yet what he adds is too sharp; it cuts away whatever meaning I try to create with words. As if the words too must depart when they are exhausted, when they become lost fathers *tired of putting up with certain conditions.*

I see now that when I wrote earlier of memory and hope and justice, I meant that there must be hope for the bloodline—of fathers, language, memory, generations, and history—to continue, that I have to work to continue the bloodline, even though I will always face the hard reality that I may fail to provide what's needed to help someone carry the bloodline into the future.[2] We each make our own wagers in this life, and I have to see that my wager—through a life of writing—can be placed alongside those men I worked with. I can continue work in a way that honors the struggle and dignity of their lives, no matter how much of their lives I'll never know. I have to try to bring them—the words, too—*back home.*

My work alongside those men didn't last very long. We may have worked four weeks together. Perhaps only three. We made some good money together, but that money helped my father to begin drinking again. School was starting; I wanted to be on the football team, and practice commenced a few weeks before the first day of school. Our time together fell apart. When I left the fields for the beginning of the football season and school, my father started riding to work with his friends. There wasn't that much work left at Vollman's Market. There was no more late sweet corn to pick; whatever was left in those unpicked fields was plowed back into the soil or left to dry and wilt in the sun. There were no more potatoes to bag; a semi trailer had left the market full of neatly stacked pallets of ten-pound bags, and the pole barn, too, still housed some of the pattern I tried to design, I tried to hold together, even if for only the briefest of times. My father started to drink with great fever (as he liked to say in Spanish of the most exciting things) and went into his last time—a year—of being drunk, before he began the long sober dream and plan of his departure for Puerto Rico.

Those days of dew, sun, corn, and potatoes will always be a part of me. They are a part of the bloodline I'll work to continue until I die, and then maybe they'll fall apart like crumbled dirt and turn to dust and become a part of the sun and the sky and the earth. Although I don't remember the work that much anymore, I nevertheless continue to return to those white shacks, how clean and strong they appeared amid those rich brown fields, those thick tall swaying green trees, and the miles of potato fields that went on and on and on.

My father and his friends shared stories and memories I'm grateful to have been a part of. Their loud laughter and their broad smiles are so important, as is their happiness in each other's company. They helped me to know whenever I ate my lunch or whenever they called for me in my colored sleep inside that shack, that there could be much more difficult things in life than working together on a hot summer day.

When I look back I'm haunted by seasons—those seasons of fruits and vegetables, cold and heat, birth and death. My looking back has never been to simply emphasize a season of change, nor about my living beyond change. My looking back is more of a deep recognition of how a season leaves and we then suddenly return to who we are, a temporary vessel of ragged skins and brittle bones filled with the loss of what has just departed. Yesterday the sun was topaz and warm in the leaves, and the sun stayed with twilight for some time as I started to count the emerging stars tinged with gold. Today the clouds hang heavy and wet in a bunched-together sky, the leaves falling heavily to the ground when the northwest wind shakes the trees. Yesterday a man in a yellow baseball cap walked at my side down a farm lane, one of his arms tucked under my arm in support, the other helping me to hold up a wet burlap sack brimming with ears of corn. Today I can't find him no matter how long I linger in a region of lost names.

NOTES ON THE NEW WORLD

Faith Adiele

Trying to Leave Horse Heaven

For years nature and I didn't speak. I grew up ignoring the world outside our house, determined to resist this smalltownamericaplace that was not-Africa, not-Europe: not like us. A dry indentation of earth cupped in a ring of sage-brush hills so matte and purple they could have been a painted backdrop for one of the countless westerns my mother grew up on—a different double feature every weekend—red-felt cowboy hat dangling from a string around her neck. Hills holding back the big blue bowl of sky wherever we looked: the Rattlesnake Hills to the north, the Horse Heaven Hills to the south. The sour smell of the feedlot at the entrance to town enveloping the car and worming its way through vents and window cracks. Endless days of punishing sun with not enough trees, broken sidewalks refracting the light with blinding intensity. Escape that.

Two Houses

When I think about childhood, those perfect years between the ages of six and twelve, I picture my grandparents' farmhouse, pale yellow, nestled among the densest cluster of trees on Route 2: the lemon, tangerine, and mint-colored kitchen; the pink music room; the rose-and sea foam master bedroom; the black-walnut tree with the rope swing that smelled of musk; the raspberry patch buzzing with fat bees; the cool, green fields of spearmint; Mummi bent over dusty zinnias and sugar-pea vines in the garden. Never the flimsy mobile home behind the house. Where—except for that first summer—Mom and I actually lived.

I never consider the trailer's shameful boxiness. Its hollow walls, panels of dark veneer stapled together and camouflaged with battered posters from Mom's college days: van Gogh's *Starry Night,* Picasso's *Mother and Child.* Its seventies gold-and-green-brown color scheme. The kitchen's muddy-avocado appliances. The drabness of the olive bathtub against mustard wallpaper. At each window the same rough, open-weave curtains with machine embroidery.

Was there a moment I didn't hate the trailer? Perhaps an initial thrill when poring over the dog-eared factory catalog with Mom and choosing the fifty-foot single wide? The weeks of waiting for our ready-made home—the first in the neighborhood, its tinny, simulated-panel siding gleaming white. The call-and-response of the workmen as they wheeled our home into the backyard and cranked it down onto the waiting foundation.

In the beginning, surely we must have loved the trailer. Old Pappa set concrete stepping-stones into the lawn between the two houses. Their shapes echoed the raised pattern of linoleum that ran through the trailer—coolly smooth like so many dark, mossy stones in the trout streams we fished each summer. He built a porch outside the front door and steps from the back door down to Mom's flower beds. As soon as he constructed a lattice to hide the foundation, the barn cats moved in. At night we could hear yowling through the floor as boundaries were crossed and territories invaded.

Then came puberty and with it, shame. Now mobile homes were no longer unique. Now they fell into rusted disuse, symbols of the dark-skinned migrant workers who perched on the edge of the county line near the fields they worked: apples, asparagus, cherries, peaches, pears, hops. Now a subtle shift in relationships began: my friends no longer kids on the bus, but those who lived in town on the Hill, slept in pastel rooms with canopy beds, and walked to school.

The New World Shifts and Steams

I'm nearly sixteen before I learn the true story of my birth. It's spring 1979, fifteen months before snowcapped Mount Saint Helens will wake up a couple hundred miles away and forever change the weather and landscape we thought we knew, seventeen years after my teenage mother lay down on the floor of her father's house and contemplated suicide. I can picture her in 1962, with her apple cheeks and light brown ponytail, prone against the gray carpet, looking too brunette to be Nordic and much younger than her nineteen years. She might have been wearing a sleeveless blue cotton smock, the patch pockets stuffed with half-used tissues, and a mannish pair of black glasses. Those droopy blue eyes of hers, so deceptively sleepy, would have been open. Seventeen years later, except for the short bowl haircut swirled with cowlicks, she looks exactly the same.

Time has stopped in the living room of our tiny house. It's as if, with my mother's silence, a spell descends over us like the ash will when Mount Saint Helens erupts, turning cars and flower beds silver. We'll have to wear surgical masks outside, as will the thousands of spectators and beauty queens waving to each other from behind white paper cones at the annual Portland Rose Festival to the south. But for now, my mother contemplates the ceiling, and the cats on the roof fall asleep, whiskered chins upturned in the shade of the honeysuckle vine.

No one on Gregory Avenue moves. Next door, Mr. Graham turns to stone in the midst of his prized hybrid teas. Across the street, Tommy the Plumber stalls, tattoos motionless in the hairy forests of his arms and legs and chest. At the end of the street, the boys on the high school wrestling team—state champions for three years straight—slump drooling onto gym mats, while next door at my mother's junior high, three kids smoking joints topple over on the football field.

The entire town of Sunnyside, Washington—where, according to the chamber of commerce then, the sun shone 360 days a year—holds its breath. At the feedlot near the sign welcoming visitors to Sunnyside—Home of Astronaut Bonnie Dunbar, the milk-faced Herefords and polled Angus stand vacant-eyed and slack-jawed, just like they will when the volcano blows. In the tiny business district, the Rotarians and Kiwanis and Elks and Eagles stop singing midsong; the neon warrior on the awning of the Safari Restaurant watches his spear and shield blink and fizzle out; and the Golden Pheasant Chinese restaurant actually closes.

The blond kids up on the Hill continue drifting in their blue swimming pools, while Mexican workers doze on ladders in the sooty fruit orchards, their burlap bags slipping to the ground. Nothing much was happening to begin with at the big Catholic and Mormon and Episcopalian and Methodist and Baptist and Presbyterian churches, but in the tiny new churches that are continually forming and separating at any time of day—so many that Sunnyside, according to Old Pappa, is in the *Guinness Book of World Records*—the congregations begin to snore right in their folding chairs.

This hush while I wait for my mother to call the true tale of my origins up from hibernation carries out of town, past Old Doc Querin's big-animal practice, past the huge Dutch dairies with their tin-roofed barns, past fields strung high and beaded with hops. It wafts along the restricted road to the Hanford Nuclear Reservation, which did the plutonium finishing for the bombs dropped on Hiroshima and Nagasaki, and where people say that strange new insects breed in the chalky limestone. It floats by the Moore farm with its collapsing barn and twelve kids, the Kludas farm with its narrow lambing shed and single giant son, and my grandparents' farm wedged in between. For once the woodpecker attacking their trees is quiet, enjoying the bright pink blossoms on the thorny hawthorn, the heart-shaped leaves of the catalpa, the drooping weeping willow. The silence wends along the irrigation ditch to the asparagus fields at the tiny airport, the same fields where my mother walked barefoot in 1962, the soil damp between her toes, and began to consider killing herself and her unborn child.

Places We Don't Remember

In 1962 everyone understood that as soon as a girl got out of the Home, she would spend the rest of her life trying to forget it. It was a nonplace, one of a network of places that weren't talked about and therefore didn't exist. As her due date approached, my mother too began to disremember things. She waddled through the shabby, cheerless rooms, omitting each detail from her memory. She would forget that couch in front of the television, sagging with dazed, pregnant teens. The card table with the bent leg near the piano. Now, seventeen years later, she can barely remember how long she was exiled there, or anyone's name. Silence has managed to erase almost all of it.

A New Country

The spring of 1979, the year before Mount Saint Helens decides to awake from her 123-year slumber, the self my mother has kept dormant these seventeen years creeps out of the past. The last time the mountain blew was 1857, the year the U.S. Supreme Court decided blacks were not citizens. And like the pressure building now beneath our feet, the *Dred Scott* case weakened the fault line between Northern abolitionists and Southern slaveholders, four years later exploding into civil war.

Mount Saint Helens' very first outburst was the stuff of legends, an origin tale that also pitted brother against brother. According to the Klickitat, who call her Tah-one-lat-cha (Fire Mountain); the Puyallup, who call her Loowitlatka or Loowit (Lady of Fire); and the Yakima, our local tribe, the mountain was a lovely, white-clad maiden with whom both sons of the Creator fell in love. They battled each other for her, causing the sun to darken and the earth to tremble. As they hurled molten rock back and forth, entire forests and villages disappeared in flames. Angered, the Creator turned one son into Mount Adams, the other into Mount Hood, and Loowit into the symmetrical, beautiful Mount Saint Helens, perennially encased in ice and snow.

For three months in 1980, prior to the eruption, the ground beneath her will tremble—ten thousand quakes in seven weeks. A crater will yawn in her mouth, growing at a rate of six feet per day. Though geologists and biologists recognize the signs, they will ignore them. When at last Loowit succumbs to the pressure, the avalanche preceding the blast will splash water 850 feet high, temperatures will reach one thousand degrees, and five hundred million cubic yards of rock will be released in one of the largest volcanic explosions in North American history. The entire mountaintop will slide into the Toutle River valley.

Two hundred miles away in Sunnyside, we will sit open-mouthed before the television, watching thick, white smoke curdle like brain matter against a blackened crater. We will hear the stunned cries of journalists and rescue workers. "It doesn't even look like the same country!" someone shouts into a radio. "I can't find any landmarks. It doesn't look like anyplace I've ever been before!"

The Lady of Fire will forge an entirely new country. Before the explosion, Sunnyside is so dry that when it rains, school closes. My mother tells me tales of the west, just over the Cascade Mountains, where there are cities and water, people who read. When Loowit blows, the largest landslide in recorded history will level 230 square miles of forest in three minutes, wiping out entire populations of elk, deer, bear, and coyote. Glistening Spirit Lake, where my cousin Heidi and I spend summers cresting through snow thaw, will become a bowl of mud, as will the Columbia River, plummeting from a depth of forty feet to thirteen and stranding four dozen freighters in the process. The silvery ash will drift in a fifteen-mile-high column all the way here to southeast Washington. By noon, ash will be falling in Idaho. In two weeks, it will circle the globe. After that, rain in my hometown becomes normal and school is never canceled. The very earth outside the door changes but still, I want out.

In Horse Heaven

The spring before our geography irrevocably changes, my mother breaks the spell that binds us to the living room sofa, the cats to the roof. "Well," she says, recalling my father's return to Nigeria, her expulsion from the farm by the very grandparents I trail each day, the hazy arrival to the unremembered Home—all new information: "this is the story."

The spring, seventeen years before, when the Rattlesnake and Horse Heaven hills were buttery with yellow wildflowers and the irrigation ditches clogged with velvet-silver pussy willows, I entered the world, joining my mother in exile at the Home and then somehow, in less than a year, leading us back.

Demographics

For years I was an only child, the only child. The only black baby born to a white girl in the Home. The only New World African in Sunnyside with a doting Nordic immigrant family. The only child raised on a farm in a valley of pale landowners and Mexican field hands, nestled at the edge of painted Native American lands. The only one on the playground with no father and no good excuse like "He died." The only one whose mother had to swear not to overthrow the United States government, me balanced on her hip, so that the National Security people would give her the money to finish college and spend the next six years teaching in dry school districts where no one had a father and yet I was still, *still* the only black one.

Invaders

As a child I studied my African folktales and Norse legends and waited for Anansi the Spider and Loki the Half-Giant, both tricksters who amused themselves at others' expense, to come scuttling over the purple mountains that ringed the town, cupping us in the curve of dry earth. The invaders would be half-Nigerian, half-Nordic and look like me. They would say "Welcome, sister!" in a special language that only we understood. But no one ever came, other than the occasional earth-colored rattlesnake, and in the end, I got on a plane and left in hopes of increasing my odds.

In college territory is marked by color. I learn to read the subway's deceptively cheerful hues: Red Line linking Harvard Square's monied tourists and college students with Dorchester's Irish bars and dog-shit-speckled sidewalks. Green Line running from green suburbs and designer shopping to brick, white-steepled colonial buildings and cement, monstrous Government Center. Blue Line focusing on the always-under-renovation airport and Wonderland, the intriguingly named racetrack. The odd Orange Line, spanning both Charlestown, infamous for school busing violence, and black stronghold Roxbury. Miles, seemingly, between cobblestone streets and high-rise projects. Rocks. Baseball bats. Black body splayed across the electrified third rail, white hot. T stops like landmines. When traversing the landscape, I learn to choose wisely.

Increasing My Odds

Boston is destined to become my disremembered place, the place I will spend the rest of my life trying to forget. In the end, I get on a plane and leave in hopes of increasing my odds.

Suddenly—Nigeria. I arrive, hungry for my people, and yet, every day I stare open-mouthed at the place: My father's village in Igboland, nestled in the shadow of a giant *achee,* the largest tree I've ever seen. Huge, gnarled roots arcing out of the ground higher than a man, a series of natural seats that stretch nearly a block along the forest floor. Evenings the villagers gathering and laying the day to rest. The sun dropping into a cluster of branches and the moon disentangling itself to provide some light amongst all that shade.

My raised-in-Nigeria sister tells me that the tree saved the village during the civil war. "When the Federal troops finally made it this far south," she begins in that lilting voice of hers, as if speaking from far away, "they marched into the village and began looting houses and setting farms on fire. Our house was one of the first to go."

"When they saw the prize *achee,* they rushed to chop it down." My sister smiles, her fingers seeking mine, our feet clogged with red earth. "They say that wherever Federal axes struck the tree, blood ran like sap. The soldiers fled the village in terror."

What am I fleeing? Mummi's village in Finland, Old Pappa's in Sweden—long empty roads, strands of thin, white-barked trees, vacant farmhouses—pale landscapes you abandon for the New World. My mother's village of America with its hills that held us in, not danger out. With its volcanoes and cities that attacked not our enemies, but us.

Morning in *Alaigbo* arrives with a variety of sounds and smells: First the mournful, pre-dawn dirge of hymns learned from missionaries. Then the rustle of family members returning to the morning's tasks, the splash of water rising from the well, the sizzle as palm oil heats up, releasing its nut-musk scent, the plop of thick slices of *ji* dropping into a water-swollen pot. True yam—not the sweet, orange-yellow, New World pretender. This white-fleshed tuber balances on the head, thick and dark as firewood.

I dream the glottal murmur of Igbo, thick and restful to my untrained ears. Someone picking fruit from his or her natal tree, the crack of stick against trunk, the rustle of leaves resisting the harvest, accompanied by the blooming floral bouquet of pawpaw and citrus and mango. The bleat of the goats that follow me everywhere from a careful distance. That wait around the corners of the house for me like a gang of bearded thugs, smelling my difference.

When the air thickens, burning mist off the tangled greenery, my body shifts in sleep, positions itself to process Igboland swirling through the open window. Bugs purr steadily like the generator out back. I open my eyes to a dim room, a Welcome! banner strung across the wall: Samson House, a dollhouse-size pastel bungalow my father built on the ashes of the burned homestead and named for my grandfather. I see Old Pappa, my other grandfather, in the pink and blue rooms. In the courtyard ringed with trees.

I wonder if my modern, educated stepmother buried my siblings' umbilical cords and afterbirths beneath the taproots of their natal trees. It must be comforting to know under which tree one's origin rests. When my born-in-Nigeria siblings stand on ancestral land, they can feel themselves growing beneath. When they eat the fruit from their natal trees, they taste themselves.

No wonder the Igbo always return to the village to build a house in which to grow old. How far, across how many oceans, can we stray before Ala, goddess of the earth, calls us home? We return, fleeing notplaces and New World shames, to sit in the spot where our father's father's father sat and watch the sun go down. Remember. Or, we return, drawn to trees that taste of our blood and are prepared to shed theirs for us. Death surely comes as no great shock, burial merely a return to the familiar network of roots that have held us close since birth.

I open my eyes to a sister who could be my twin, stranger-brothers who sit and stand and laugh like me. Finally, nature—calling me to plant myself, blood and all.

INVOKING THE ANCESTORS

Aileen Suzara

My mother tells me that if the scent of white church candles or jasmine appears without a source, it is a sign of a visiting spirit, perhaps that of a relative or an old friend. The smell lingers for a moment and then departs, dissipates into thin air. As a child I was fearful and secretly excited for these rare times. I searched for blown-out candles in the kitchen, or looked outside for a climbing spray of tiny blossoms, whenever a sweet, sourceless scent permeated the room.

It seemed impossible that ancestral spirits would find our family in America—how could they navigate across the Pacific Ocean? Over forty years ago, my parents arrived in this country from their Philippines. The only remnants of home were the clothes on their backs, dried tears, and suitcases stuffed with photos, visas, and clothes too thin for winter. In America, their address changed every few years. Like nomads or permanent tourists, my mother and father rooted and uprooted themselves across the land, moving steadily west. Our tiny family found itself in industrial New Jersey, a windy huddle of houses in eastern Washington, a dry town in the Mojave Desert, and the rainy uplands of Hawai'i. Even living relatives lost touch with us, the rootless ones.

Even if they could find us, I didn't understand why the ancestors would be interested in visiting us. My sister and I would not be able to speak with them in their language. We hardly knew their names and had never seen their faces. We did not wake in the morning to witness what I imagined they knew intimately: street vendors bringing the town to life, rice paddies stepping into the sky, children running in the rain. Even if they did come to America, it seemed too confusing to find our exact living rooms, to navigate through the intermingling of so many living descendants from so many ancestors.

But now I am more hopeful. I scribble invocations to the past in my journal. I do not wait for a perfume or a trail of smoke to remind me that we are visited constantly by our ancestors. We are they: you can smell it in the rain.

Ancestors—in Tagalog, *ninuno*. In Ilocano, *nag-anak*. In Bicolano, *ginikanan*. Ancestors—they are called by the names of Soledad, Pepe, Jose, Jan. There are many more names, many more dialects birthed across the geography of an archipelago, across oceans; birthed from that endless thread of bloodlines, of lovers and mothers and betrayals that came before us. They emerge from within us, taking the shape of dreams and the movement of the clouds, even when the names die from our tongues, even when the bones are forgotten and the books closed.

I write as the descendant of ancestors. I write to my Filipino ancestors, to those whose languages I cannot speak and whose names I do not know. I write this as a prayer, in the hopes that you will recognize me, one of the generations born into North America, born young and with a memory so tiny it fits in one mouthful. I have no ancestral tongue to guide me through the dark. My father's Bicolano is a stranger to me, as is my mother's Pangasinan. The syllables flow like water through my fingers. And yet, I am drawn to their relentless energy.

I write this because I have no apology to offer for the distance between land and body, only excuses: because I was born Stateside, because I am second-generation Filipina American, because I must learn what we can create by digging for what has been destroyed. I speak, write, and dream in English, without subtitles and with no trace of an accent. I write this as a prayer against erasure, praying to be claimed.

I write in resistance to the Spanish conquistadores who disrupted a sovereign people, to the colonizers who burned a trail of greed through the Philippine archipelago for four hundred years. This was the same trail that led through Native America and the lands now known as Puerto Rico and Hawai'i. I write to recapture Magellan, whose accidental arrival on Philippine shores opened the floodgates of history into each other.

Yo escribo para los antecesores, I write to the Spanish ancestors in me who did not make their appearance in my face, who did not give me the skin of a mestiza, but who linger in a name passed down through generations. *Los antecesores,* to the mestizo men and women buried in the family graveyard in my father's town of Daet. To my great-grandfather, Fructuoso Suzara, a Spanish businessman. When I first greeted him in our family graveyard in Daet over a decade ago, I was surprised to find him looking back as a painting on a pale headstone. To my mother's maiden name, Muyargas, which translates to *muy argas*—very bitter, to the bitter medicine of our history. We have a past, the names will not disappear with us.

I write in recognition of Filipino as a mestizo culture and myself as part of it, the entanglement of histories, of borders interweaving, and name-making and name-taking. I write to syncretic Catholic faith that mixed piety with animism, to the mixed blood of language. I write to understand this psychological splitting of selves, to what has fractured and sustained our people as a culture.

I write to recognize how I inherited this language, the syllables I love and at times feel betrayed by. Over one hundred years ago, the Philippines was taken over as an American colony. As a part of the imperial regime, pro-expansionists, including President McKinley, argued for the reeducation of and teaching of English to Filipinos. In the 1902 *Philippine Affairs,* Jacob Gould Schurman wrote, "The hope for the future of the Philippines is in education. The majority of the Philippine people are uneducated and very ignorant. But they have a high appreciation of education and a strong desire to have their children instructed. . . . English should be taught in the schools of the archipelago to the utmost extent feasible."

Like with other dispossessed peoples across the globe, deculturation through language was justified as one of the necessary measures to civilize and uplift the "savage." My grandfather, Jose Muyargas, was rapped on his hand when speaking his native tongue in school. With the loss of a language, entire ways of knowing, of naming, disappear.

I wonder if I, like others of our generation who have never learned the history of our bones and of the lands that have nourished us, will become weightless, a ghost without history. Questions beg to be asked: Is this a slow and painless death? Should we grieve? How do we forgive? Where does reclaiming begin? Can we survive our own forgetting?

I write this as a prayer to the ancestors.

There are no clear maps. I was never taught directions. It is difficult to stay awake these days when mass extinctions of species, languages, cultures, natural environments, and entire ways of life tell me to close my eyes. I write this to remember, to remember not from nostalgia but from hope. Hope to create. Hope to become. Hope to return to abundance, to that which strengthens us and keeps us sane. I search for the ancestors everywhere: in passersby on the street, on the Internet, in textbooks and poetry, in snatches of song. The truth is, they could be anywhere. They are everywhere. Ancestors rise on the backs of stories when we are children, until we are told to forget this way of knowing them and of trusting ourselves.

In the mirror, I search the landscape of long fingers, dark hair, a scattering of beauty marks. Read what has been written onto flesh: the deep brown of eyes, the narrow hips of my mother, the thick lips of an ocean people. Balance on my legs as though they are the deep roots of trees. It is a good gravity, to be filled with the weight of stories.

I search for stories to unearth and reclaim. Like wild animals, stories do not go by a single name or respond to the same voice. They defy repetition, cannot be caught and domesticated in the way that written history would have it. In defying capture, spoken stories take meaning in the voices and the bodies, the minds and the memories of those who carry them. It is a good gravity, to be filled with the weight of stories.

Nameless ancestors. I don't want to wait until I meet them on the other side of life; I pray to find them in the here and now, to receive their breath, their affinity to song, into the daily patterns of living, of movement in the world.

My father, Emilio Linan Suzara, was born of Soledad Lang Suzara in the small town of Daet. He grew up in the eastern province of Bicol, a region open to the ocean and often devastated by typhoons and the monsoon. When the town flooded, the boys left class, made small boats from the green trunks of banana trees, and floated through their streets. In the river waters they might see the swimming bodies of snakes or the bloated corpses of dogs. My mother, Eleanor Muyargas, was born of Pacita Muyargas in Quezon City, in a time before Manila had fully sprawled outward in a tangle of shanty towns and shopping malls, but not before the once-legendary Pasig River was already polluted. During part of her childhood she lived with her aunt in the rural province of Pangasinan. When they cut the heads off chickens, she watched the feathered bodies fly up into the air. She tied threads onto the thin legs of beetles and flew them like tiny, winged kites. I was born in Kennewick, a small desert town in eastern Washington. The area is currently famed for the "Kennewick Man," but was mostly known in the past for its large nuclear power plant, the largest in the Western Hemisphere. I have no memory of that place.

My father gives me the bones of his stories, barely enough to imagine by; he is not generous with these stories. I must always be vigilant, ready for the next tale to emerge from the silences. It is in these bones of story that I glimpse a place I can only dream of, to meet my father as a child who once crouched in the dirt with ants, knowing with certainty the shared breath between himself and the smallest world under his fingertips.

In the country of my imagination, fifty years ago, it was late afternoon in Daet, that time when thick yellow beams angled through the banana leaves, illuminating the veined sheaves into living green panes. A lone rooster crowed its afternoon cry, restless. Under the *balete* tree, a mother dog lay sprawled on her side in the dust. Tongue lolling, she offered milk to three nearly blind, speckled pups. A fly lighted down on her warm, rough fur; her pale skin trembled under the winged irritation. Only a kilometer away, a still-new jeepney nearly collided with a tricycle. The smaller vehicle, loaded with three screaming, excited boys, skidded over the dirt road, as the jeepney driver honked, swerved left, then sped off, honking away a huddle of uniformed schoolgirls linked at the elbows. Dust and diesel fumes from the machinery rose like smoke, and the schoolgirls coughed delicately, bringing worn handkerchiefs to their noses.

Stopping at a *sari-sari* store at the corner, one girl hunted out a few hoarded *centavos* from her pockets, and passed them to the store owner, the one who perpetually fanned her broad, warm face with a woven palm. Like magic, the coins became a *supot,* a clear bag, full of sweet, brown *sarsaparilla* which the three girls sucked thirstily from a neon green straw as they walked slowly home.

The boy crouched in the golden dust was not concerned with any of this. He was unaware of these everyday occurrences in the same absent-minded way you forget the rest of the world that is not sitting on the top of your mind. Kneeling close to the skin of the earth, he smelled the scent of heated grass mingled with moist dirt. Distant metal shrieking filtered through his cupped ear. He shifted slightly; powdery dust clung to his knee.

Even as these living images swirled around him, he was gone, absent, because his eyes were, at that moment, a microscope, and the visions at the tips of his fingertips swallowed him completely. There it was, the wonder: a tiny black ant crept along his fingertip. If he sat still enough, holding his breath, he felt the miniscule tickling of its hairlike feet picking among the swirling crevices of his skin, the quivering antennae brushing epithelial cells, navigating the unfamiliar fleshy terrain. Under that delicate, nearly invisible touch, he imagined the size of his cells, the intricate network of tiny nerves weaving through his skin, the indentation and rebounding of skin as the nearly weightless creature padded threadlike feet over the surface of his body. A thought flashed suddenly, surfacing and submerging in less than a moment: My hand is its world. The boy quickly dipped his fingertip into the sweating jar of water by his feet, and the surprised insect fell into the lukewarm water.

The ant was so light that it did not sink immediately. Instead, legs flailing and antennae soaked, the creature was borne up on a watery skin, its own body forming a lifeboat. The boy hunched closer, wide eyes even with the rim of the glass, the deep pupils retracting in the brightness. He held his breath. Slowly, slowly, the ant slipped through the dividing membrane, first one leg, then the other, then the next. Thorax, eye, whipping antennae became submerged, saturated, and for a few more breaths the ant appeared to be swimming upon a clear, glass-rimmed sea. A few more breaths. Water crept over its lustrous brown body. As the floating ant grew still, the boy gently unmoored more ants from the dust, dropped them to drift like leaves in the river. His foot had fallen asleep, and he stood up to stomp the numbness out. The immobile ant and his struggling cousins looked like specks of black pepper.

Not yet, not yet. The boy held his excitement in check. The ants had stopped struggling; their bodies swirled over the surface, and still he waited a few moments more. Ants were the best for these games. Other insects— *ipis,* spiders, pillbugs—never worked. Besides, he liked ants better. Ants were almost like humans, only smaller and stronger. They built entire kingdoms. They spoke a silent language of scent and gesturing antennae, carried entire, still-living earthworms home for ant food, built ant hills, waged ant wars, marched secret paths in a trail of living beads.

Once, during a game of tag, the boy had accidentally stepped on an ant colony concealed within the tall grass. *Tabi po!* He apologized respectfully, remembering the warnings about spirits that lived in mounds of earth and in the branches of the balete tree. Yet despite the caution, curiosity tugged. Looking closer, he discovered that the mound did not contain *dwende,* the little people, but glistened with innumerable, tiny forms, living granules that followed an intricate geometry. He knelt. Tiny ants angrily escaped the crushed dirt, trailed in long lines, stopped to tangle and untangle antennae with other ants before running away. Tiny ants angrily crawled into the crevices between his toes, nipped with sharp, defensive bites.

It was time. Without a watch, there was no way to time himself, but he knew the moment was ripe. Two of the ants had sunk to the bottom of the jar, and a few still clung, waterlogged and flattened, to the side of the jar, but most of them had drifted to the center, floating and motionless. Using his hand as sieve, he poured the water and ants onto the dirt, caught the frail bodies. How still they were. The boy brought his palms to his lips and breathed. He blew warm air upon them, evaporating the water. The waterlogged antennae lifted in the warm wind of his mouth, quivered in his brown palm. The black specks shifted, grew suddenly, visibly alive. They straightened wet legs into the appropriate angles, uplifted drowned heads, stood up shaky as babies; they awoke as ants. Gently, the boy placed his hand to the cooling earth. The tiny ants stepped off and sped away quickly to unknown destinations.

He was still bent nearly nose down in the dirt when a rough tap was laid on his shoulder. *Tag, you're it!* his friend yelled triumphantly, as he darted away into the tall grass. The boy pushed off the hot earth, chased the disappearing flash of bare brown heels into the green. From behind the broad-leaved trees came the insistent call for dinner, *Kain na!*, Come eat! and the boy followed, belly suddenly hungry for the burnt end of the rice and sweet mouthfuls of *tocino*.

There are moments in the past of my father that are alive to me, a past I can always return to because it is imagined, because it is both fiction and real life. My father tells me stories of Daet. He tells me of the monsoons that drowned the town, of how he and other boys skipped school to float into the streets on the hollow trunks of banana trees, navigating the warm water with branches as water snakes and dogs passed by in the current. He tells me of a town that is closer to dreaming than reality, memories of another lifetime that survived the passage of time and immigration.

When my father returned to Daet for the first time after more than twenty-four years away in the States, he searched the unfamiliar streets for the world he had known.

Where, he asked townspeople, was the movie theater his family had owned? Where was their family home? He wanted to walk through the rain forest where they would have picnics on Sunday. He remembered a river they used to swim in, how they would dive into the green water and, afterward, burn the hungry leeches off their legs with the smoldering ends of cigarettes. The names of people and places suddenly returned to him—the priest, the neighbors, the children he went to school with who had become old men and women like him.

The forest had disappeared, we found out. The rivers were poisoned, and no longer ran pure enough for swimming. Many of the townspeople had died or moved away.

A stranger told us that his family home was gone, and their movie theater—no longer in the central part of the town—had also disappeared. Demolished. My father wanted to visit the site. Our family and the driver took us down a quieter street that seemed, to him, familiar. He stepped out onto the concrete, walked past a broken chain-link fence, stepped around rubble and trash. Surveyed the land. There was nothing left but disintegrated walls and cleared earth, but still he searched. Finally, my father called out, "I remember this tree!" He walked further, excited, and I followed. Out of the rubble, an arched and broken trunk shot out a few stunted green leaves like feathers, stubbornly clinging to life. "This is the *sampaloc* tree," he said quietly. "I remember it here, in the corner."

Later, he would whisper, "It's like a dream world and nothing I knew exists, except in my memory. . . ."

Daet is a place I must recreate and rebuild in my own mind from the rare words of a childhood too bitter and too sweet for my American ears. It is a past that he has almost lost with forgetting, a reality that I net and capture like the running of the fish, sieved out from every gesture and word.

On Mount Banahaw, some Filipinos say, the spirits live still. I read of the mountain by chance, and was drawn to the descriptions of a high peak thick with legends. It seemed to be a temple set in the landscape, a doorway to an animist Philippines, and my curiosity drove me to ask relatives and acquaintances about this mysterious place. The responses varied. To my devoutly Catholic grandmother, who had never seen the mountain, Banahaw was a traditional site for Christian pilgrimages. To Joe Boy, Banahaw was the scenery he had passed by on many long journeys, a destination for the spirits. To my sister, who had walked the mountain, Banahaw was a piece of earth possessing a sacred beauty that could not be conveyed in story; it was a place that needed to speak for itself. Although varied, these stories only affirmed the hints I had read. The region acquired a personality that encompassed not only the physical landmass itself, but the faceless masses of pilgrims I envisioned scaling the peaks and dipping brown palms in the rivers; a personality with an ancient past. In the years between my questions and my own eventual, unexpected visit, I waited with a formless craving—an anticipation—of walking in that holy, unknown space.

How does a single mountain—or any geographic expanse, for that matter, whether a pond or an entire archipelago—acquire meanings that may vary from person to person, culture to culture? There is no single, discernible answer, if there is any answer at all. Instead, there is a range of patterns that can be sifted through, tracked, observed, and commented upon.

One may consider individuals and their perceptions as the products of their ancestors and environments. I see myself as less of a product, and more of *transmittance*, a current vehicle in a genealogy and a history that stretches and speaks from a distant past into the future. As both a receiver and a transmitter of the past, the message I am carrying—the dialogue between self and history, self and environment, self and ancestor—is fluid, prone to interpretation, to obliteration and alteration. As a Filipina, I am a young woman whose heritage includes Mount Banahaw and the ancient rice terraces of Banaue, living "artifacts" of a time when my ancestors and the land lived in conjunction. As a Filipina, I am a receiver of colonization, of the historical events that are not of my own life experience, but form a past that I am both ignorant of and inheritor of.

As a Filipina, the genes in my cells are a synthesis of biology and history, resulting from the reproduction of the bodies of distant ancestors who nourished and formed their bodies from animal meat, from rice they tilled, from the roots they dug from the earth. I know that although the furthest reaches of my history are an unknown and perhaps unattainable knowledge, that although a history of colonization has been added to my own genetic mixture, that although I cannot locate ties to an indigenous past, I *must* accept the current incarnations of Filipino culture in what is now termed the "Third World," and not search for a static image of what it is to be authentically "Filipino." To do otherwise would be to deny the evolving nature of culture and history. It would deny the slums of Manila as realities in the Philippines, and only acknowledge the last "pristine" areas. It would deny the presence of nature surrounding and *within* the Philippines, whether seen as a developing country, a regenerating country, or a dying country. It would ignore the *un*dying tie between the people and the land. I have seen this evidence in my grandfather's garden in Quezon City, a garden that is surrounded by crumbling walls and rubbish but is thick with weedy guavas and watered by yearly monsoons. I have tasted this connection in the food, for the distinctive flavors and textures (or the closest substitutes) which expatriates and overseas Foreign Workers in Italy, Iraq, or Canada search for as a means to reconnect at least a part of their bodies to a distant land and culture. As a Filipina, I am not an artifact, but a part of an evolving and current past in which both the land—*lupa*—and her people have undergone constant transition. I am a piece in a continually regenerating culture, one whose survival has been and remains dependent on the earth. I cannot separate history and the environment, because the environment has been inscribed into my genes, and history has been written onto the land.

As an American, my consciousness and perception of the land have been shaped by my role as a citizen, my education, and the perceptions of those around me. Along with my classmates, some white, many of them Asian, black, and Latino, and most with American citizenship, I have repeatedly sung "This Land Is Our Land," mouthed the phrase "land where our fathers died" (although many of our forefathers never died in this land, but at the hands of her colonizers or on other, distant shores), and dogmatically saluted the American flag. With my classmates, I was taught the virtues of "our fore-fathers" who "founded" this nation that we, American citizens, now live in. I, along with my other classmates, have sat through history classes that instilled both a groundless pride in the formation of the American Constitution, and shapeless guilt for "our" role in the historical and continued dispossession of Native Americans.

As an American, I have questioned whether "American" is a citizenship based on geographical location, or if it is an identity that homogenizes and overrides individual culture. I have been educated to see nature in discrete parts, to break down and divide the world and her people into clearly demar-cated components. I have been taught to sieve and choose, to assign validity and authority to quantitative over qualitative, man-made over natural, citizen over immigrant, masculine over feminine, human over nonhuman, scientist over layperson, young over old, English over mother tongue, reality over leg-end. I have been taught to see trees and rivers as "natural resources." I have purchased and consumed both mass-produced and imported food whose en-tire life cycle—from planting, to tending, to harvesting—has been handled by machines, or by people used as machines. I have heard that finding the sacred in every aspect in nature is called "animism" and "paganism." I have been taught that, as Americans, we cannot trust what cannot be quantified, and that what cannot be quantified has no (monetary) value.

I am a Filipina born in America, caught between many modes of being. I have been born with the privilege to choose the message which I must carry and transmit. There is no clear-cut distinction where one begins and the other has ended: I cannot sift through this entanglement without finding ar-tifacts of Western and Filipino perceptions embedded in each. As a Filipina American, I have searched for a place that feels like home. My Filipino relatives have been integrated into the American economy and lifestyle as nurses and as farm laborers, and their children have grown up surrounded by pine trees or high rises instead of tropical rain forests. Many of us do not know where we came from, and for some it as if there has never been anything else. Living on the Big Island of Hawai'i, I became integrated and also felt alienated from an island culture which is a fusion of many seemingly disparate cultures that have come together as one. I have learned that the marker for Mauna Loa represents a region that I have walked through, a forest that is dense with koa and ohi'a trees that shiver in the breeze. I learned that Filipinos came to Hawai'i's shores to work in sugarcane fields, sharing plantation lullabies and sorrows with Japanese, Hawai'ian, Chinese, and Puerto Rican workers. Yet despite this connection, I still search for a deeper tie to my own history and environment, the same earth that my ancestors tread upon generations ago.

When I finally visited Mount Banahaw, my eyes were filled with deep green forests and a peak cloaked with continually dissipating and coalescing cloud. In the forest were large boulders painted with the seeing eye of God, the boy-child, the Santo Nino statue balanced on a mound of earth, surrounded by offerings of flowers. Candles left by pilgrims burned at the gnarled roots of trees. Walking through the forest, the local guide scolded me gently when I took a picture of an ancient tree without asking its permission. By the rivers, old women washed their hands and filled bottles with the clear waters. The shivering, metallic sound of bells filled the air at noon, rising upward with the woody smoke. At the caves, a trail of pilgrims set up camp on the earthen floor. As I peeked into the cool darkness of the caves, a light suddenly flared up in the shadows. Within, a woman lofting a burning torch paced the black interior, singing. It may have been a Christian song or another, older song, but in that still moment, with the dark and the light and the woman's rich voice resonating within the stones, I could not be sure.

The landscape is a narrative, not a narrator, because it has no human voice. It speaks through and is brought into being through the human-nature dialogue, in our voices and our perceptions, an internal geography which is, in turn, shaped by the exterior environment. We are simultaneously the *creation* of our environments and ancestors, and the *creators* of our environments and our descendants. It is necessary to suspend any expectations for a definitive "truth" and to approach with an open mind the varied frameworks and approaches that have been taken to interpret our environment. We can simultaneously inhabit multiple truths. Through this realization, it may be possible to forge a middle path, one that sees the immense power and frailty in human renderings of our environments.

HOPE AND FEATHERS

A crisis in birder identification

J. Drew Lanham

"The use of traveling is to regulate imagination by reality,
and instead of thinking how things may be, to see them as they are."
—*Samuel Johnson*

Africa is a place we all have in common. It is the widely acknowledged cradle of humankind, as most anthropologists agree that our hominid ancestors likely evolved there. So an Evolutionary Eve, mother to all of us regardless of race, ethnicity, or nationality, likely padded across the African plains.

Given this multimillion-year perspective, I or anyone else should've been awestruck at the prospect of treading the same ground as some australo-pithecine grandparent. But that was not necessarily the case. Twenty-one of us, including a dozen or so students and a handful of older lifelong learn-ers, were "sacrificing" spring break to study the wildlife ecology of the North Cape. I was along as the coleader, the trip ornithologist, the designated birder. Professionally, I was well equipped to do the job. Cleverly disguis-ing myself as a wildlife ecology professor, I've gamed the system, teaching field ornithology and researching bird habitat relationships, at times going to "work" to do things most folks only find time to do on vacation. For the wildlife work I do, the trip promised to be a dream experience. For the black man that I am, the promises were less certain.

Most black Americans would probably agree that there is something visceral about visiting the African supercontinent. It is a chance to get a little closer to the place from whence many of our ancestors were likely kidnapped and spirited away to places on the other side of the world that they were forced to call home. I know, from other black people who've been to sub-Saharan Africa, that the first trip "back" is often billed as nothing short of a life-changing pilgrimage to a place that provides the linkage between who we are and were.

Now it's true that South Africa played little if any role in the trans-Atlantic slave trade, and my ancestors probably came from somewhere in West Africa—maybe Nigeria or Ghana—far north of our southerly destination. But as an African-American who'd be stepping onto the same continent, I'd be one ocean closer to the connection—standing on the same tectonic plates as people whom I might rightly call relatives. There was another unavoidable piece of history as well: South Africa's entrenched system of apartheid that had come to dominate the world's conscience during my 1980s college years was only a few years removed. And yet, instead of pondering any of this in the weeks and months leading up to the trip, I'd selfishly spent most of my time thinking about expanding my life list with exotic things like lilac-breasted rollers and cartwheeling bateleur eagles.

Cruising at thirty-six thousand feet with almost twenty hours to go, I opened Sinclair's *Birds of Southern Africa* and began the final cram session. Perhaps I could somehow pack the dizzying array of what I might see, the thousands of field marks—bill shapes, tail lengths, wing bars, crests, and rump patches—into permanent memory and instant recall.

Somewhere in the middle of the night, the oceanic abyss that had offered no light or landmarks was interrupted by the flight attendant's announcement that we were landing for a crew change and refueling on Cape Verde. According to the little animated plane slowly creeping across the screen on the headrest in front of me, we were almost halfway to our destination. Looking out the postage-stamp windowpanes, there wasn't much to see. Where the verdant nomen came from was not obvious as the runway lights illuminated brown soil and scattered scrubby clumps of something not really green.

This complex of islands in the Atlantic was a crossroads for the African slave trade—a strategically centered set of dusty dots linking the middle passage to the other legs of the transatlantic triangle. As an African-American holding on to the mother continent by a hyphen, being there was, in that moment, eerie. All of that history and connection flew in and roosted somewhere in my head.

As we grew closer to our destination, the roosting musings became more restless. What would the reception in South Africa be like? Would I just be another black face among the many? Would the black Africans embrace me? Would the white Africans accept me as a professional ornithologist and not just another black face?

On the ground in South Africa, I'd never seen so many black people. They were everywhere seemingly doing everything—being human to the fullest extent of the right. This was Mandela's work, Tutu's dream. It was a black world and I felt like I'd gone down the racial rabbit hole. I was no longer a minority—at least not racially anyway. It was beautiful. I was overwhelmed by the beauty of so many black folks in charge of things. I felt oddly comfortable in a place I'd never been.

The birding would have to get better, though. Beyond the blacksmith plover loitering on the tarmac, I'd ticked a house sparrow and a European starling—both species proving that the noxious invasion of exotics is indeed global.

I'm frequently guilty of overanalyzing, thinking way too much about simple things. Ironically, in a country where more people looked like me than not, I began to feel like the odd man out as we made our way through the airport—me, the sole person of color among a horde of obvious white tourists. Why the stares? Did people think I was their porter or something? Carrying the negroid banner as I was, I had the self-appointed responsibility for our blackness. No one else was qualified.

On the way to pick up our group's rental vans the next day, the two other group leaders and I shared a cab ride with a white guy from Cape Town who spoke in what seemed like objective terms, talking about the good and bad of the new South Africa. The throngs of people walking everywhere were mostly the unemployed going nowhere. The rising jobless rate, ubiquitous poverty, lingering racism, and political malfeasance of the new leadership were all compressed into a fifteen-minute drive. As we described the mission of our trip, he asked with an air of assumption about our plans to visit the Apartheid Museum. Matter-of-factly, we said that our schedule wouldn't allow it. He seemed surprised. I was embarrassed. I suddenly felt as if I had neglected history, humanity, and, most of all, my own identity in order to put tags on the names of things whose freedom and dignity had never been curtailed like the people of color who lived in this place. I didn't share my feelings with anyone. After all, we were here for the ecology, and besides, maybe the colors of bee-eaters and rollers would be dramatic enough to overcome the silly black/white thing.

On the trip out of Johannesburg, our three Mercedes vans tucked head to tail like a family of white pachyderms, we saw legions of black folks on foot, heading somewhere and everywhere, or maybe nowhere. Street vendors dodged the morning's thickening traffic, and we drove by them as if they were nothing more than ebony traffic cones. If you stayed alert you might spot something new for the life list, but you might also miss what is as much a part of South Africa as the incessant droning of Cape turtle doves—the masses of people trying somehow to make freedom work. For all the people we passed and all the poverty we ignored, I was pretty sure that if Nelson Mandela himself had been selling papers on the streets, we probably wouldn't have recognized him as anything more than just another pedestrian.

As the skyline of the city shrank in our rear view, we began to pick up more of the unmistakable field marks of poverty, expanses of shabbily constructed wood, tin, and cardboard huts—not really houses, but huts—most maybe ten-by-ten-feet square. These were the shantytowns I'd heard about. In some places stretching for a couple of miles along the highway and back to some horizon defined by the abject absence of anything looking hopeful, these were textbook shanties—the habitats of the dispossessed. In between the townships, there were brick-and-mortar dwellings that might well fit the American description of middle class—but whatever color people they housed, these habitations were almost always fortified by a fence. Not pretty white picket fences inviting admiration, or even chainlink fences to keep the kids and pets safe. No, these were fortress walls built of concrete blocks with barbed or razor wire menacingly poised to keep something, or someone, out. Even along the rural portions of the route, we encountered skeins of hitchhikers with thumbs raised. In two weeks there and over a couple thousand kilometers traveled, I'm not sure I ever saw a hitcher picked up.

We pushed southwest and the kilometers clicked by hypnotically. Time seemed to stall, even as the landscape morphed from urban to agricultural to expanses of thirsty-looking thorn scrub and grassland. The road birding was unbelievable and changed with the scenery. Long-tailed widowbirds struggled with their encumbering retrices in reedy ditches; tuxedo-feathered fiscal shrikes sat with perfect pied posture on telephone lines, while pale chanting goshawks waited to become some rodent's nightmare. Ostriches, initially captivating, became common as cattle. Legions of smaller passerines, waterfowl silhouetted on shallow pans, and too many kestrel-like raptors had to go unidentified.

Sometimes the birds are a balm, an avian anesthesia that numbs pain or blocks unpleasant things. It is the Zen of putting field marks together—plumage, shape, behavior—into something that becomes a bird. This coming together, the gestalt, is what allows one to say what is seen, even when the views are fleeting and the song is incomplete. In that peaceful pursuit, the quarry is collected on a life list without having to give its life in return. It has been this way for most of my life: Me escaping to the birds. The birds providing something people couldn't—comfort in my own skin, peace in stressful times, and acceptance without question of who I am or what I do.

I struggled initially with putting names to the birds of South Africa. Each new bird helped connect me to places I will never forget: a night drive with broad-winged coursers flitting like moths in our headlights; a warbler-like pririt batis on the edge of a field of petroglyphs; ant-eating shrikes posed like lookouts on termite mounds.

Above us, the South African sky was never ending—even bigger and bluer than Montana's. Carved out of the cerulean, cumulous clouds climbed to impossible heights. This was the classic African savanna I'd dreamed of, a seemingly endless carpet of tawny brown Bushman's grass the color of a lion's coat with chalky, green acacia trees scattered sporadically across it.

Even the brilliant, brick-red soil underneath it all was striking. One day a sudden thunderstorm left a rainbow stretched across the canvas of blue, red, brown, and green, clearing away stale, humid air to usher in the cool, mind-clearing aroma of ozone and rain-settled dust. That evening, we climbed a kopje, a boulder-strewn, shrub-studded rock island in the savanna sea, to watch the sun settle behind the bush. It was a perfectly memorable day that brought some sense of peace, as did the fact that two of the birders escorting us through the bush were black people.

The next week in the Kalahari was absurdly spectacular. Kori bustards, big as tom turkeys, strutted within yards of us. Gangs of aggressive fork-tailed drongos harassed everything in sight. Sociable swallow-tailed bee-eaters posed cooperatively in iridescent splendor for the camera. A cornucopia of avifauna hung like feathered fruit from every tree. I even had encounters with several black park rangers who seemed to take mutual comfort in the appearance of a face of color among the typically white throngs of ecotourists.

When the washboard roads of the Kalahari pushed one of our vehicles past its mechanical limits, I got to talk with a black Botswanan man from the car rental agency who met us at park headquarters to deliver a new wheel. We engaged mostly in small talk, with me trying to get him to understand where in the world Clemson, South Carolina, was. But as my white partner excused himself to wrap up the business, the conversation's tone changed suddenly. Looking through my color to some deeper connection I think we both felt, he asked, "So, is it true you Americans think more of the animals here than the people?" It seemed as though he'd been waiting to ask the question of someone for a very long time. Perhaps because I had taken on the black baggage, I felt like I owed him the answer. "Yeah, that's probably true," I responded haltingly through the shock of the exposure. And then, as if to apologize, I tacked on, "But we're trying to do better." I'm not sure what his nod and half smile meant, but I felt relieved to have been found out. The conversation broke abruptly back to small talk when my white friend returned. Before departing the Botswanan wished me well with the three-grip handshake that I had come to expect from my African brothers.

So often on this trip, black South Africans seemed less willing to talk openly about the tough issues in the presence of white people. But I felt a connection with them that seemed genuine, and took some comfort in the handshakes, which seemed to linger a little longer with me than with my white counterparts. This time, the connection had opened up a wound in my consciousness that I was not quite ready for. Here I was, an "African-American" behaving more like the arrogant American tourist hell-bent on seeing everything but the real. At a traffic stop, I saw a little girl searching for something on top of a trash heap. For the few seconds that I saw her, I imagined that she might have to share what she found with the vultures and jackals. I'm not sure anyone else noticed. Maybe they were dumbstruck at the sadness of it, shocked that the human condition could sink to such levels. Maybe they were caught up in the birds like I'd been.

For most of my life, I've been one of the few or the only one. Aside from my family and a few close friends, or perhaps a rare foray to a black church, I often find myself among more white people than black. Throughout my school years I was placed in "advanced" academic tracks where whites were the overwhelming majority. I played bassoon in the symphonic band, went to band camp in the summer, became student council president. And though I had many black friends, played football, ran track, dated black girls, I was—am—still an outsider of sorts. I'm the black deer hunter, the black wildlife professor, the black birdwatcher.

I go to professional meetings and am the melanistic anomaly in the flock of white. I go hunting and people look suspiciously at the black guy wearing the camouflage "reserved" for the good ol' boys. I go birding and am stared at like some rarity blown in from a distant place. I can almost count the black birders I know on one hand. Pitifully, there are even fewer African-American wildlife ecologists. Even in South Africa, I did not meet a single black person working as a wildlife ecologist for SANParks, the nation's agency responsible for safeguarding the welfare of its incredibly diverse wildlife resources.

Henry was a savior of sorts. A skilled South African birder, he not only helped me pin down spike-heeled and Botha's larks, he also showed me that there were people who looked like me with a passion for feathered things. Congenial and competent in his role as a tour guide for DeBeers, he talked frankly of his aspirations one moment and the next was pointing out gabar goshawks and bokmakieries without missing a beat. Riding shotgun with Henry in his truck provided a valuable moment of honest exchange between two black men. He gave me more than he will probably ever know. I hope the feeling was mutual. After I returned home, I sent him a better pair of binoculars and a spotting scope with which to perfect his craft.

Another sort of redemption came on our final day in South Africa, as Julius Koehn, a soft-spoken wildlife ecologist, graciously shared his passion for falconry with us. The young peregrine sitting on his gloved hand was a beautiful bird, reflecting more wild in its eyes than willingness to be commanded. When the bird flew, oaring its angular wings against the evening sky, two preteen boys took a keen interest in the show. As all of us watched the sleek raptor's incredibly agile flight, my attention was drawn to the earthbound beauty of the two boys kneeling side by side, their heads swiveling in tandem as the bird swept by like a fighter jet on a low-level pass. The duo's simultaneous smiles reflected the wonder of the moment; the only mark separating them was the color of their skin. It was obvious that they were close—sharing a respect for one another and this wild place. The sight of them against a backdrop of thornveld that framed them in the golden light of the fading day moved me, and provided some reassurance that future generations might see beyond a difference in skin color to see one another as equals.

The pieces of South Africa I witnessed were at one moment the idyllic Eden, full of wildlife and the wonder of all Creation; at other times, purgatory, where people seemed stuck in some condition between despair and utter poverty. In many respects South Africa surpassed my most grandiose visions of what Africa is. I felt a visceral connection to a place I'd never been. The dramatic landscapes awed me at times to tears. I absorbed a modest 126 life birds, watching each new entry to understand it not as just a tick mark but as an organism within the context of the place. But my eyes were also opened to the poverty, the nasty racism still writhing beneath the new democracy, the long trek ahead for the new nation. And although I saw only a fraction of what the nation has to offer, it was enough to help me better understand my connection to nature and humanity, and to realize that the two are not as separate as I once thought.

The internal roller-coastering of my conscious will continue as I keep searching for my own identity, which unfortunately is not laid out clearly in any field guide. During the more challenging moments, I will recall that scene of the two boys watching the falcon and hope that that's the way things will be—that we can all understand our unique identities from the skin inward and be comfortable in that. Appropriately enough, it was the birds that reminded me to not neglect my fellow humans, and that helped me through my own crisis of identification to a clearer picture of who I am—and who I might become.

2

WITNESS

CONFRONTING
ENVIRONMENTAL RACISM
IN THE TWENTY-FIRST CENTURY

Robert D. Bullard

In the real world, all communities are not created equal. Some are more equal than others. If a community happens to be inhabited by poor, powerless people of color, it receives less protection than powerful, affluent white communities. Economics, politics, and race all play an important part in sorting out residential amenities and locally unwanted land uses (LULUs). Historically, exclusionary and expulsive zoning have been subtle forms of using government authority and power to foster and perpetuate discriminatory practices. Too often, zoning ordinances, deed restrictions, and other land-use mechanisms have been widely used as a not-in-my-backyard (NIMBY) tool against people of color.

Hardly a day passes without the media discovering a community of color fighting a landfill, incinerator, chemical plant, or some other polluting mechanism. Most of these conflicts can be grouped under the environmental racism umbrella. Environmental racism refers to any policy, practice, or directive that differentially affects or disadvantages (whether intentionally or not) individuals, groups, or communities based on race or color. Environmental racism combines with public policies and industry practices to provide benefits for whites while shifting costs to people of color.

Environmental racism raises its ugly heads through unequal enforcement of environmental, public health, transportation, and civil rights laws. It should not be forgotten that Dr. Martin Luther King Jr. went to Memphis in 1968 on an environmental and economic justice mission for black garbage workers on strike. They were demanding equal pay and better work conditions. Of course, Dr. King was assassinated before he could complete his mission.

Another landmark garbage dispute took place a decade later in Houston, when African American homeowners began a bitter fight to keep a garbage dump out of their middle-income neighborhood. Residents formed the Northeast Community Action Group. The group and its attorney, Linda McKeever Bullard, filed a class action lawsuit to block the landfill from being built. The 1979 lawsuit, *Bean v. Southwestern Waste Management, Inc.,* was the first legal challenge to the siting of a waste facility using civil rights law. Since *Bean,* dozens of civil rights lawsuits have challenged environmental racism.

A New Worldview

The environmental justice framework attempts to uncover the underlying assumptions that may contribute to and produce unequal protection. It brings to the surface the ethical and political questions of "who gets what, why, and how much." The environmental justice movement has changed the way scientists, researchers, educators, lawyers, and policy makers go about their daily work. It is led by a loose alliance of grassroots groups, networks, and leaders who question the foundation of the dominant environmental protection paradigm.

In 1983 the environmental justice movement was catapulted into the national limelight in rural and mostly African American Warren County, North Carolina, over the placement of a hazardous waste landfill. The landfill ignited protests and over five hundred arrests, and prompted a United

States General Accountability Office study, *Siting of Hazardous Waste Landfills and Their Correlation with Racial and Economic Status of Surrounding Communities.* The Warren County protests also led the Commission for Racial Justice to produce its landmark 1987 *Toxic Wastes and Race* report, the first national study to correlate waste facility sites and demographic characteristics. (The updated study *Toxic Wastes and Race at Twenty, 1987–2007* reports that more than half of the nine million people living within two miles of hazardous waste sites across the country are people of color.)

In 1990 my book *Dumping in Dixie* chronicled the convergence of the civil rights, social justice, and environmental movements. The book also highlighted African American environmental activism in the South, the same region that gave birth to the modern civil rights movement. A year later, the first National People of Color Environmental Leadership Summit was held in Washington, D.C. Summit delegates adopted seventeen "Principles of Environmental Justice." By June 1992 Spanish and Portuguese translations of the principles were being used and circulated by NGOs and environmental justice groups at the Earth Summit in Rio de Janeiro. In 2002 the Second National People of Color Environmental Leadership Summit took place in Washington, D.C.

In response to growing public concern and mounting scientific evidence, President Clinton, on February 11, 1994 (the second day of the national health symposium), issued Executive Order 12898, "Federal Actions to Address Environmental Justice in Minority Populations and Low-Income Populations." The order reinforced the three-decade-old Civil Rights Act of 1964, Title VI, which prohibits discriminatory practices in programs receiving federal funds. It also focused the spotlight back on the 1969 National Environmental Policy Act (NEPA), a law that set policy goals for the protection, maintenance, and enhancement of the environment.

Having the Facts Is Not Enough

There is clear evidence that racism influences the likelihood of exposure to environmental and health risks. Examples abound among migrant farm workers poisoned by pesticides and African American and Latino children injured by lead. Ironically, the people most likely to be exposed to harmful chemicals are also the least likely to have medical insurance. People of color are disproportionately represented among the forty-four million uninsured Americans. For example, one-third (33.4 percent) of Hispanics, one-fifth of African Americans (21.2 percent), and 20.8 percent of Asian and Pacific Islanders—compared to a little over one-tenth of whites (11 percent)—are without health insurance.

Scientists have known for decades that where you live can be hazardous to your health. Urban air quality is a major concern to people of color since they are disproportionately concentrated in the nation's polluted environments. According to National Argonne Laboratory researchers, 57 percent of whites, 65 percent of African Americans, and 80 percent of Hispanics live in 437 counties with substandard air quality.

Bad air hurts. It is also costly. The federal Centers for Disease Control and Prevention estimates that air pollution costs the nation $14 billion a year. Asthma alone accounts for 10 million missed school days, 1.2 million emergency-room visits, 15 million outpatient visits, and 500,000 hospitalizations each year. The hospitalization rate for African Americans and Latinos is three to four times the rate for whites. It is not surprising that grassroots groups across the United States—from Los Angeles to Atlanta to New York—are challenging transit racism that has allowed "dirty diesel" buses to proliferate in communities of color. These groups view clean air and affordable transit as a basic right.

Dumping in Dixie

Exploitation of land and exploitation of people are intricately linked. This is especially true in America's Deep South or "Dixie"—a region that has become a dump for the rest of the nation's toxic waste. The Deep South is stuck with the unique legacy of slavery, Jim Crow, and white resistance to equal justice for all. The region is characterized by look-the-other-way environmental policies and giveaway tax breaks that have left the area's air, water, and land the most industry-befouled in the United States.

Louisiana typifies this "sacrifice zone" pattern, with its African-American citizens bearing the heaviest toxic burden. Louisiana in the 1990s, like Mississippi in the 1960s, became a battleground against environmental racism. The state's chemical corridor has over 125 petrochemical companies.

Local activists dubbed the region "Cancer Alley." Louisiana is a leader in dol-ing out corporate welfare to polluters for a few jobs. A 1998 *Time* magazine article reported that in the 1990s Louisiana wiped $3.1 billion in property taxes off the books for polluting companies. The state's top five worst pollut-ers received $111 million dollars during this same period.

Despite uphill battles, groups are winning. After nine years on the battle-field, Citizens Against Nuclear Trash (CANT) won a historic decision in 1997 before the Nuclear Regulatory Commission (NRC). The NRC denied Louisiana Energy Services (LES) a permit to build a uranium enrichment plant in the middle of all-black Forest Grove and Center Springs. Racism rendered these two communities "invisible" since they did not appear any-where in the NRC's environmental impact statement. The communities date back to the 1860s.

After eighteen months of intense organizing and legal maneuvering, residents of the town of Convent, Louisiana, and their allies forced the Japanese-owned Shintech company to scrap its plan to build a polyvinyl chloride (PVC) plant in the black community. The plastics plant would have added over 600,000 pounds of air pollution annually to an already over-burdened community. Shintech's decision came in September 1998 as EPA administrator Carol Browner prepared to make a ruling on the permit public.

Racism in the Alabama "Black Belt"

The Alabama Black Belt is another favorite hot spot for environmental rac-ism. Sumter County is home to the nation's largest hazardous waste dump, the "Cadillac of Dumps." The county is 71.8 percent black. The facility re-ceives hazardous wastes collected from Superfund sites from forty-eight states and from foreign countries.

Alabama is a major "dumping ground" and garbage importer. The state's 25 dumps take in over 31,500 tons of waste daily. Alabamans generate only about one-third of the landfills' capacity. The other two-thirds come from out-of-state garbage. In the summer of 2000 a coalition of grassroots organi-zations, university officials, black elected officials, and national leaders joined forces and blocked the construction of a seven-to-eight-hundred-acre landfill slated to be located near historic Tuskegee University.

Lowndes County—also in the Alabama Black Belt—is located just sixty miles west of Tuskegee on U.S. Highway 80. Lowndes County is 75.7 percent black. The fifty-four-mile stretch of U.S. Highway 80 was made famous in 1965 by the historic "Selma to Montgomery March." Lives were lost and blood was shed along that highway. The civil rights marches and ensuing state-sanctioned brutality moved President Lyndon Johnson to sign the Voting Rights Act of 1965.

In 1996 the stretch of highway was designated the "Selma to Montgomery Historic Trail." The trail is also designated an "All-American Road" under the Federal Highway Administration's National Scenic Byways Program, created under the Intermodal Surface Transportation Efficiency Act of 1991 (ISTEA). Despite these federal government designations and strong sentiment held by black people, the Alabama Department of Environmental Management (ADEM) in 1998 approved a two-hundred-acre landfill permit on the trail, which many consider sacred ground. This action makes real the extent to which environmental racism is allowed to operate. It is highly unlikely that a garbage dump would be proposed next to the Washington Monument or the Lincoln Memorial.

Global Dumping Grounds

Native and indigenous peoples around the world are threatened by environmental racism. Dozens of sovereign Native American nations have been targeted for landfills, incinerators, and other waste-disposal facilities. The vast majority of these waste proposals were defeated by grassroots Indian groups on the reservations. However, "radioactive colonialism" is alive and well. In 1999 eastern Navajo reservation residents filed suit against the Nuclear Regulatory Commission to block uranium mining in the communities of Church Rock and Crown Point. In February 2001 a coalition of Native Americans and environmentalists defeated plans to build a nuclear dump near the Mojave Indian reservation in Ward Valley, California.

African Americans in Norco, Louisiana, have a lot in common with their African brothers and sisters in Ogoni, Nigeria. Shell oil refineries negatively impact both communities. This scenario is repeated for Hispanics in Wilmington, California, who live in the shadow of the Texaco oil refinery, and for indigenous tribes (Quichua, Cofan, Shuar, Siona, Secoya, Achuar, and Huaorani) who have also challenged Texaco in the Oriente region of Ecuador.

The conditions surrounding the more than two thousand maquiladoras, assembly plants operated by American, Japanese, and other foreign countries, located along the two-thousand-mile United States–Mexico border, endanger the environment and public safety and have placed border residents' health at risk. All along the Lower Rio Grande River Valley, maquiladoras dump their toxic wastes into the river, from which 95 percent of the region's residents get their drinking water.

People of color are at the forefront of the climate justice campaign. Several hundred delegates attended the 2000 Climate Justice Summit in The Hague, Netherlands. A 2001 report from the influential Intergovernmental Panel of Climate Change (IPCC) reveals that climate change will likely hit the poor nations of the southern hemisphere the hardest and thereby widen the economic gap between the "have" and "have not" nations.

Grassroots groups are fighting back and winning. They are forming alliances, coalitions, networks, and collaborations that stretch across the globe. Environmental justice is crossing borders and breaking down barriers. It is providing a vision for a truly global environmental and economic justice movement.

70117

A. J. Verdelle

Old New Orleans was a city well-matched to the muddy Mississippi, colored rich roux-brown by music, architecture, art, history, wit, writing, commerce, jazz. Old New Orleans had more personality than a choir of well-played horns. The old city had its traditions, flaunted its culture, and was always inviting. Hundreds of thousands of people each year accepted the old girl's invitation. Like a bride, old New Orleans was beautiful to approach; but the real truth and majesty of the old city smiled behind her veil. Intimacy with old New Orleans paid primarily cultural dividends; what a lively, secretive, deep old place. Old New Orleans was by no measure perfect—but when you found a failing, there were trade-offs: you could lean into history, follow a brass band, dance.

New Orleans had a syncopated heartbeat. On its up- and downbeats, the city produced and developed some of the greatest artistic and musical minds and talents this country has called its own. Now this lithe, nimble, near-ancient place has been mishandled; now the mistakes that have been made are growing shoots and taking root. The character of old New Orleans quite possibly left to die in heaps and piles. It's so historically American not to sort through a thunder of rubble, not to face disaster, to cart off and landfill a trash heap; not to salvage, not to save. There are whole industries of hand-recycling and preserving in other nations: whole cultures survive from the work of resuscitating what has been laid to waste. It's so historically American: to turn away from history, to think anything worth having can be recast in a new landscape, reborn without the lifeblood of its roots. Yet, nature always has an answer: there is life at every layer of a heap or a swamp, and sun always reaches in.

911

You could dial 911 from New Orleans today: there is still a bona fide emergency. Bumper stickers—*Make Levees, not war*—may be seen too infrequently or taken far too casually, but the cement that crumbled to cause levee walls to give way is not being replaced by materials more solid or more protective. Scientists who were asked to investigate, and who then told the truth, were argued with and de-tenured and then ultimately let go. Cast to the rubble of a wrecked career, a washed out neighborhood off Honesty Street, left stranded and unemployed on a roof between the Bywater and Treme. The landscape is still bereft, and people still need help getting home. When you call, will you reach a city service that can respond effectively? Maybe. Maybe not.

Calls for help at the height of the emergency called Katrina were botched by government and thwarted by high water. It's hard to imagine in service-rich America, but when Katrina happened, you could not use the phone. Lights went out, power ran out, water kept rising, and the people left there climbed, hacked openings in attics and roofs, tried to push old grandmothers through impossibly ragged holes. Old people perished in the heat. More than 30,000 struggled for days in two huge, impersonal, unequipped facilities. The president watched but did not touch down. Apparently, no one thought the levees wouldn't hold. Apparently, no one thought about busing the people who had no cars, no money, no evacuation options. Apparently, no one thought of tens of thousands stranded, in advance. Apparently, there were no rescue plans, but there was evening news. Helicopters. Fly-overs. Levees threatened, breached. Long nights of screaming, water lapping at stop signs, crossing streets.

For alluvial New Orleans, there was a care gap, a concern gap, a response gap, a prediction gap, a preparedness gap. Here in America, we have built and cultivated this operating system that tends to shut down for black and brown. The darker the crisis, the more the emergency is minimized. (Turn them loose. Lock them up. Get them off the good land.) Our long-held xenophobia and aversion to poverty got washed into visibility in New Orleans. Due to weather, due to wind, due to failing levees, due to storms we can anticipate so well that, while we wait, we give them names.

We applaud ourselves here in America: we call ourselves color-blind. Everybody and their mama knows that color blind is exactly the opposite of who or what we are. We are as color-conscious as day is light.

In the moment, now a number of years ago, phone lines went the way of wind and rain. The only way you could speak to someone you loved in New Orleans was to holler. Many of us did. We wailed. The news we got came by way of helicopter video feed—straight from the crisis zone to your television. And still we could not bring the necessary help.

How long will it be before I can forget? The mayor of New Orleans, sweating, with a towel round his neck, reporting conditions in the Convention Center and the Superdome—no food, no water, no sanitation. Tens of thousands of people. Babies, senior citizens, working people, parents. Hungry, hot, thirsty, shocked, enraged, bereft. Left waterless in a killing sea. Left waterless in a sweeping sea. *Water water everywhere and not a drop to drink.* What country do we live in? What landscape have we arranged?

Then-mayor Ray Nagin's radio-wave broadcast, his desperate SOS, his call for federal intervention, was a modern-day shout heard round the world. Replayed on the airwaves, translated into sympathetic languages. Technology, empathy, domestic disbelief, and international outrage brought pressure on the vacationing national leadership to attend: *Get yourself out of La-La land. Out of New York. Out of the Ferragamo store. Out of Air Force One. Tend to the black, the stranded, the hot, the hungry, the aged, the poor, the crowded, the drowning. Get thee to New Orleans, already. You're late!* This young mayor had to step outside protocol and tell the truth without memoranda; he stood sweating and toweled in a place so besieged that paper and pen, e-mail, and telephone had ceased to be available media. Ray Nagin was not the only "authority" in this crisis who doused us with honest emotion, who stood wet under the fallout from broken dams. There too stood the sobbing president of Jefferson Parish, Aaron Broussard, who helped galvanize the nation as he wept on *Meet the Press*. The emergency management director of Broussard's Parish lost his mother to high water even though he'd asked that St. Rita's nursing home be evacuated. The emergency management director was unable to save his own mother, an aged woman who could not evacuate herself. She, like the black children and the poor of New Orleans, had no rescue coming, without the support and emergency management training of our national guard, without the resources of our federal government. Sunday, hurricane; Monday, floods. His mother, trapped in a nursing home, drowned in risen water. How many other mothers, women, girls and boys, fathers, brothers, men found the same fate—wet, hot, thirsty, aged, tired, crazed—unable to survive delay? The answer to this question is, according to historical record: more than 1,830 people lost their lives.

HEADLINE:
More than eighteen hundred dead from heat, floods, dehydration and neglect. Catastrophic levee failure causes post-storm flooding over 90 percent of New Orleans. More than 80,000 people suffer through and survive. New Orleans, Louisiana, United States of America. In the heat of August, 2005.

311

Another storm has happened, providing opportunists the shield of bad weather, of hurricane season. Mike Brown "testifies" before cronies in Congress, responding to barely concealed instructions to take an offensive posture. His job is to make it seem as if some responsibility for this debacle has been placed. But this tragedy—of New Orleans, of Katrina and her aftermath—should occasion at least a pause: for us to look at how we see, read, and use neglect as a tool of power. We have the information we need to honestly collect and assess.

Here's more information. Hurricane Katrina didn't set these people swimming. Hurricane Katrina set the water moving. But the weakness in the levees caused the levees to give way, and then, the water broke. We have professionals in this country and in the world who deal with structures and stability; who predict safety and weight bearing; who manage restoring and reshoring; who calculate height and thickness and cost. We call them engineers. In the case of the New Orleans levees, we are talking about the Army Corps of Engineers. Over time, we have also engineered ourselves out of viable wetlands in coastal Louisiana: we have rerouted the wild river, we have flood-controlled and canalled ourselves out of natural hurricane protections. We have come to rely on man-made walls we call levees, that engineers built without the structural depth to withstand the weather and water we know will come.

There are many other cities in many other countries that thrive on top of water, and by watersides. Systems of locks and dams and even well maintained levees are built and managed and inspected and maintained.

Here in America, we want to make new or do nothing. We think, erroneously, that anything we lose, we can just build again.

411

New Orleans has Neglect to recover from—an n-word with a bold capital letter. Politicians who manage taxpayer money have for decades ignored the need to shore up levees, have failed for centuries to prevent poverty, and for days preceding Katrina turned a tin ear to the brewing crisis of a mandated evacuation for people who could afford to go nowhere. City officials did not plan for how to handle those who'd be left behind to bear the storm. Corporate media filmed people desperate on rooftops, chaos at the Superdome, and cacophony at the Convention Center. Every single sighting was a backdrop to the more important script the reporters had to read. The touching emotion of Anderson Cooper, the empathetic sadness of Jean Meserve, the spunky aggression of Soledad on scene, Oprah's high-fame angel network. Survivors finally finally finally get lifted out by military helicopters that looked a lot like the media choppers that flew over them for days—lenses extended from Saturday to Wednesday, but neither a rope nor a basket until the week started to wane. *Where is FEMA?* The media keeps asking, considering itself an advocate, and maybe rightly so. Mike Brown answered to Congress from his horse-high vantage point, engaged in a charade with his Republican colleagues, pretending to feel fire on Capitol Hill. They described him as beleaguered. No, these are the beleaguered: those who survived, those who succumbed, those who hacked their way out of attics, those who lost everything—from shoes, to phones, to homes, to parents. These are the beleaguered.

Word was, in the immediate aftermath of the debacle, there were meetings happening where the future of a changed New Orleans was being decided. Bigger, better, brighter, the president said. These meetings must have happened in the backest of back rooms, because no-bid contracts were arranged and initiated. Now we know the waste, the skimming, the vast amount of money that has not gone to rebuilding the city. Will New Orleans come back? Will New Orleans be even a sibling or stepchild of the cultural mecca it was, in the very recent past? I suspect that the men in those meetings will build in their own image.

What a Site

This disaster has behaved like a hot poker laid down on pulsating distrust and suspicion. Like a brand on thin skin. We[1] have been psychically burned by centuries of legalized callous treatment, by tens of scores of years of orchestrated abuse and neglect. I have felt supreme distrust since I learned to put good words to bad feelings. Any child who grows into learning like we do will ultimately ask: Why slavery? Why us? Why poverty? Why today, in the twenty-first century are we standing on rooftops, wondering still why, waving half-painted signs to an unhearing sky?

Data on how the hurricane and its survivors were mishandled is transparent. History will judge us, and harshly. Thinking citizens who come after us will ask all the obvious and pained questions. Why weren't we more proactive? Why can't we be reparative? Why do we not invest in restoring and rebuilding on our own soil? Why do we prioritize foreign wars? The American historical record does *not* make this travesty seem odd: theft and slavery, denial of the right to read, or to move freely or to be self-defined or to celebrate my culture or to earn and understand money or to call my children my own or to make the whole country, the whole world, available to my children—these are real and psychic wounds that got reopened with this inattention, with this dawning restatement of neglect. New Orleans was part of my positive history before, and has imploded to become part of my negative history now.

Think about it: every person stranded there thought they were going to die. Many did. Every person stranded there lived through two nights with water reaching to their knees, their ears, sweeping heavy refrigerators off their footprints. Every person who survived climbed to a roof or swam, or watched their neighbors or their houses wash away. This is terror. More precisely, this is terror witnessed by helicopter. Jean Meserve got in a rowboat, with a cameraman, and recorded for all of us the people trapped in their houses, wailing, screaming, boiling, fainting; trying to hold their mouths and noses up to air.

The exact number of how many media flew in and flew out is hard to find. Perhaps it wasn't counted. The helicopter video feeds, the daring rowboats, the alarmed morning news—well, this is how we got what truth we got.

A flood survivor I talked to who was sheltered in D.C. first used the word "dawning." I'm not sure I'll forget the unchecked sadness in his eyes when he talked about how it started to "dawn" on them, the stranded, that their being left out there was racial. He reported that that's when people started to shoot up at distant helicopters, asking with a gun report: Don't you see us standing here? He reported that people shouted in neighborhoods, from rooftop to rooftop, "They leaving us here 'cause we black!" This rumor or this fear or this fact spread like a shout, like a shot, like urban legend, oral tradition. The fear of collective abandonment could not be quelled. Think of it: standing hungry and thirsty, sleepless and half-crazed, trying to face down eight feet or six feet or twelve feet of water, unchecked. Trying to face down the low odds that your grandmother might stay alive. Trying to face down the screaming truth that you were black and hot and without support or supplies. A statistic of the flooded lower ninth. Had to be harrowing and had to seem like sure death. *This is terror.* I asked this man if he'd had to swim. Yes, he answered, I had to swim; that's when I lost my cell phone and my wallet and one of my shoes.

When you lose a phone and a wallet and one shoe in the high water after Katrina, you stand at the very beginning of an identityless, moneyless, shoeless road. There remains the ultimate question of your house. In the beginning, you are glad to stand, barefoot and safe from rising water, or be airlifted, finally, along with one thousand others. But, time soon reveals that the road home may no longer exist—gone the way of the ninth ward, of 70117, of Gentilly, of 70122, 70126, 70119.

HEADLINE:
Thirst will disorient you, hunger will make you primal,
heat will make you crazy. All three together: New Orleans, 2005.

Michael Moore, tongue-in-cheek, suggested that if this was not about race, then would Bush have left white people standing on their roofs for five days? Robin Williams asked if this calamity had happened in Kennebunkport, whether government response would have been any faster. New Orleans has been, in the past, a site where we could shore up, and find music, art, and heart so vibrant, so brassy, so restorative. This early twenty-first-century "horricane," as my daughter says, and its troubling, negligent aftermath, has reduced New Orleans, a former cultural mecca, into a site for sore hearts. The city has two-thirds the people who lived there before the levees failed. The second lines and social clubs may yet survive, but the African American population has declined by about a third, too.

I try not to succumb to predetermined pessimism. This is a long-term effort on my part. And I try not to cry that the city's future seems up for grabs. Distrust rises in me like mercury, like floodwater, based on an inherited and well-demonstrated national callousness toward my culture and kind. This sad and likely protective distrust comes as naturally to me as my hair. The calamity in New Orleans, the images of African Americans stranded and pleading, foodless and waterless, simply makes my suspicions seem warranted. My temperature has risen to the level of swamp heat in August—sweltering, stultifying. This pen lets off some steam.

77230

In this America of money and marketing and relentless pursuit of purchase power, zip codes speak mightily. Your zip code is packed so full of information it is downright predictive. When the New Orleans Superdome became untenable, its tens of thousands of locked-down inhabitants needed plumbing, lights, clean water, food, doors (at the very least) between adults and children, windows, the natural experience of outside air. The scene at the Superdome was different than the Convention Center, since many at the Convention Center refused to go in. (This turned out to be a good decision, because once in, the police and security cadres refused to let you out.) The Superdome is a football stadium, all eyes, all views, are trained to center, to the field. There wasn't a chance inside that hellish facility to see anything but this horrendous calamity. Children wailing. People half-dressed. Everybody sweating. Power out. Everybody worried. No water running. Everybody dazed.

By then, they'd promised buses, but the buses did not come. Flooding outside. Chaos in.

HEADLINE:
Being trapped can make you violent, or suicidal—same thing.

There were people who managed to remain outdoors. At the time, this didn't seem like the blessing that it was. But, to be confined indoors, locked in with the hysterics of a tragedy of this magnitude, with this temperature—outdoors, at least, you could breathe.

Some of those outdoors tried to walk to safety: to services, to telephones, to help. Some of those outdoors walked across the bridge to Gretna—a suburb, an unflooded site nearby. Eventually, evacuees were met on the "safe side" by gun barrels. Those flooded-out people who managed to get to Gretna, who had not heard national news reporting rumors of allegedly violent flood survivors, were met after their tragic experience and sodden trek by gun barrels. Picture this meeting at the foot of the bridge: survivors bedraggled, and struggling, yet hopeful. Our tired, our hungry, our citizens. Met by guns and witness to new violence. What price. What paucity. What color blindness? The bridge to Gretna: scene of new hope and new crime.

The trauma compounds. There was transfer to Texas, where the Astrodome had running water, a shower schedule, fresh cots, and a zip code all its own—77230. The Texas governor's photo opportunities were legion; his welcome seemed calm and dry and packaged. Talcum powder on a crisis of great national significance, of historic proportion. Fires burn on oil slicks in drowning

New Orleans while we turn our attention and follow the path of evacuees to distant brand-new locations all over our open-hearted landscape.

Lots of New Orleanians left in advance. Mostly the poor were trapped. We don't understand poverty here in this country. Or more likely, we don't want to. Even though we've created, and we cultivate, a lot of the poverty we have, the truth is we know how to make poverty but we show no willingness to break poverty. When you tell poor people to evacuate, you have to think that through. Evacuate to where? With what resources? Using what transportation? What resources will they use once they get where we'd have poor people go?

Poor people are poor. They do not have resources. They cannot get into cars and hit the road. They cannot go to solvent family members, or check into hotels. Poor people are poor. Where they live is what they have. They spend their money on what they eat. They do not have resources. Especially at the end of the month.

Culture U

I know an education when I see one. This is a teachable moment. I have two advanced degrees, and I hope to earn one more before this life dims its lights. I have called a few American cities my teachers and my homes, including Chicago and Albuquerque and New York. New Haven and Princeton are college towns that have nurtured me. I grew up under the influence of Banneker's prodigious intellect in Washington, D.C. I have traipsed through California's striking, shifting slants of sunlight—San Diego, Chula Vista, San Francisco, Oakland, Los Angeles. That's how I know that Dr. Spock was buried by way of a jazz funeral. I was in La Jolla when his widow raised her umbrella to the brass that serenaded Dr. Spock to his last parting; I was reading at the Museum of Contemporary Art. I have spent time in Lagos, Abidjan, Dakar, Mexico City, Amsterdam, Paris. I intend to know this world.

New Orleans is the one American city I have loved, and held close, and willingly adopted. The city of New Orleans teaches broadly and historically, especially if you can get beneath the glitz of Mardi Gras, the gloss of River Walk. In New Orleans, Africa and its American syncretisms have merged and been celebrated, slave culture and its survival strategies are known and

discussed, black Indians and their chanting practice remain alive and are retained. It's like Bahia. That jazz developed in New Orleans is no accident.
That Indians continue to practice old chants, lifting their voices in groups
to ancestors unseen, is miraculous. That altars to Saint Joseph are annually
decorated and celebrated and African-inspired is a marvel and a hope, a testament to living cultures that the city embraces and does not squash or malign.
New Orleans is a city with a dark, percussive heartbeat, and no ubiquitous
white superiority, no reckless quest for color blindness. The blunt instrument
of American racism cannot be cured by color blindness. And the knee-jerk
pursuit of color blindness creates culture blindness, which is also dangerous. Both these forms of blindness helped us fail a great city; have helped to
disable a venerable American port and cultural treasure. Whether or not we
admit it, this country devalues or despises what, or who, we call black.

My City Was Closed for Business

My city was closed for business. The whole city. Positively un-American, according to the America I learned. I have struggled to think of New Orleans
in the past tense, and have found myself unable to, unwilling to—although
the facts, the broken landscape, the black wards still sit morose for all to see.
The losses in New Orleans are a sobering, staggering, drastic, horrible truth.
Useless, needless waste. Go to the lower ninth ward. You will still see destruction. Listen for a horn. You will hear no swing, no brass. Ask after
Irvin Mayfield's father; you will find that after weeks of being unfound, un-
accounted for, he too emerged among the drowned. Lost to this man-made
municipally fueled government-aided post-hurricane disaster.

Whatever you think of poverty, whatever you think of colored people,
think of the waste, the gaping hole, the shame. The hurricane was a natural disaster, but the flood, its outcasts, its victims, its costs resulted from
pure neglect. What do you do with a Superdome with this history? How
do you revive a Convention Center so marked? Think of this scenario: your
town or city is closed for business. Your neighborhood is decimated, calami-
tously. Your neighbors are scattered hither and yon, without possessions,
childhood photos, or school clothes. None of you—doctors, lawyers, Indian

chiefs, waitstaff, chefs, or poor people—have jobs, or the practices you've worked so hard to build. Where is my daughter's pediatrician, the sweet and knowing Dr. Hales? Where is the local voodoo priestess—the legendary Ava Kay Jones? The cities you are now moved to are places you have not seen before. Baton Rouge absorbed you and your family. Houston absorbed your cousins. Then Houston closed. Said the mayor, Bill White: "Houston is full." The FEMA trailers finally came, and then, later, they left. The houses they fronted are gap-toothed, and doorless, rotting and sliding—many of them—back into the earth from which they came. The money dedicated to your city's rebuilding is still money; the rebuilding, you haven't seen. Your home city has flooded a second time since you've left. Your nearby sea has been flooded with oil. The federal government, to whom you pay hefty or precious tax dollars, had a horse man at the helm of the agency that responds to emergencies. Even as a horse man, his qualifications were inflated, his résumé a catalog of lies. Even with this masquerade as disaster executive, even with this charade of "hearings," can you care—homeless, jobless, city-less—about this blame game? Don't you just want your port active, your city revived, your house rebuilt, your homeland restored? Don't you just want to live on, where and how you lived? Don't you just want your city open for business, with you living there?

Tragedy causes trauma. There is plenty of post-tragedy trauma— homeless, roofless, rootless—walking our "color-blind" streets.

Do the Math

Eighty thousand stranded. *Water water everywhere.* Thirty thousand gathered in the Superdome, with thirty-six hours worth of food. Eight thousand trapped in the Convention Center. Sixty-five hundred gone missing. Four hundred unidentified dead. Forty thousand in hotel rooms. Trash five feet high in the Superdome. Bush's thirty-five-minute tour of the region from Air Force One. Three hundred fifty-five thousand occupied places to live, destroyed. Number of operating public schools reduced from one hundred sixteen, to *one.*

The exact number dead: for a long time, inexact.

Since Slavery

I am not the only person reminded of slavery by this tragic situation. The word *slavery* has been in the airwaves since "evacuees" could reconnect. This migration, this disorganized and barely recorded dispersion, reminds those of us who ever think of slavery, of slavery. This nation has not seen a migration of this magnitude since Emancipation. African Americans have not been involuntarily dispersed like this since our last names belonged to masters, and we were listed as possessions. Our kinships were disregarded in exactly this way when we were sold, inherited, given away as gifts. Now, the headlines are all about needing housing for three hundred thousand. These are three hundred thousand people who were not displaced by Katrina, but were stranded or displaced by levee breaks that scientists told our government were imminent. Now, if we'll listen, social science can tell us that trauma and heartbreak do not heal quickly. That wounds reopened do bleed and reinfect. That spin and cover-up do not change devastation brought on by a flood of hard facts, by neglect widely witnessed, by n-words.

Levee is a Creole/French word that references raising up. New Orleans has a Creole, French, African, American, Spanish, Cajun, Acadian history. Gumbo. Roux. Mea culpa is Latin for "Yep, I'm to blame." The president pronounced this Latin sentiment when he finally spoke to the nation two full weeks after the hurricane. He returned from a vacation to promise recovery and attention, and now he's out of office, with the recovery undone. Even though there's little room for dead language in New Orleans, there remains, to this day, plenty of room for recovery. Let's rebuild the city. Let's make up for our mistakes. Let's restore.

New Orleans needs sound levees—for infrastructure and for culture. There needs to be infrastructure that can handle high water: see Denmark, see Holland. Let go of American myopia. This is the only rational course of action, the only strategy that makes sense.

Gulf Opportunity Zone

When I first heard the words "Gulf Opportunity Zone," I reviewed what I knew about the Heritage Foundation, which was the organization touting this term. A sense of wry recognition rose in me, like mercury, or like seeping flood-water. I simultaneously began to worry about that single-minded president and his cadre of radical religionists, who seized every chance to remake America in their own image. Reasoning by religion, ribald creationists, they often see themselves as faultless, deified, right—as in unarguably correct. They rushed to repeal and to circumvent as if they knew their hold was tenuous, tempo-rary, or short-lived. Maybe this is wishful thinking. But the reach of their gerrymandering and finagling and cronyism and budget-busting and profit-skimming and deal-making far exceeded even the mandate they'd invented for themselves. Some argue that Bush did not win even once. New Mexico, courageous state, continued arguing to have their votes recounted. This alleg-edly unelected president's mother and wife blithely suggested that poor people flooded out not by weather but by neglect could feel better once removed. *The hospitality, in Texas, made them feel welcome; they were, you see, "underprivileged anyway."* We do not understand poverty in this country: being underprivi-leged does not take away attachment to where you live, does not make you respond to trauma, to dispersal, by feeling happy on a Houston football field.

There is a Gulf Coast opportunity zone here, all right—yet another time and place in American history where we can choose to bridge the gulf in op-portunity. A gulf that we choose to keep widening. A chance to refuse to give the lion's share to whomever successfully seizes, but to make civilized offer-ings to citizens directly damaged, most seriously maligned. Let the color of survivors not blind or prevent.

Of course New Orleanians should be invited to come back. People who lived in New Orleans should have a right of first return. In the future, which is now, the city should belong to the people the city belonged to. New Orleanians should be able to afford housing when it's rebuilt. The culture nearly washed away should be at the forefront of reconstruction. Rebuilding should involve those people who have really seen New Orleans. I admit this: I worry in this queer silence. The city is being stolen while debris rots in sunlight.

This Technological Time

It is unspeakable in this technological age that we could not track who went where, that we had people desperately searching for brothers, husbands, mothers, wives. That more than five thousand children endured the great crisis of being separated from their parents for weeks on end. That the corporate media made a backdrop of American citizens—stranded, dehydrated, moneyless, homeless—and by virtue of mute force also made survivors voiceless is also an act worth lambasting. That the president and the federal government tried to quiet this aftermath, sent unqualified Mike Brown on an offensive charade, is also tragic. That outcry about violence became elevated in the headlines is a huge twist of truth. In my culture we have this expression: *The pot is calling the kettle black.*

- Are the posses that stood at the gateway to Gretna violent?
- Is it criminal to take four or five days to "get to" people who are shown live on film, stranded and struggling?
- Is it violent to perpetuate poverty?
- When we say lawless, what exactly are we talking about? Shoes, bread, jeans, government? Letting people die because you don't know what you're doing, and you said, at interview time, that you knew what you needed to know?
- Is it lawless to fleece Indian casinos, to work like Tom De Lay?

The old-boy network lawlessness is more entrenched than the ability to respond to national emergencies. In my book, like other lawlessness, this is crime.

Beyond Poverty

Perspective is what makes us different from each other, here in this melting pot. Not color, not ethnicity, not even culture—which we either appreciate or adopt. But what we see and how we perceive what is before us is what distinguishes us one from another. The crises—the hurricane, its aftermath, our response—have blown the cover off my barely buried distrust in this nation's active principles. And I was born here. This is my country. As a child of slave lineage, I am fully aware that roads were cut here by my ancestors, that lumber was felled and rolled and stacked and houses were built by my forefathers. The pale and the privileged were fed by the breasts and the kitchen sweat of my foremothers. Train tracks laid by the brothers of my uncles and their uncles' older brothers—some of them in jail, just because. The hard work and incredible heat of building this nation from a stolen Native wilderness rode the axe blades swung by the parents of my parents' parents. Work forced on them, labor forced from them.

I may be five steps—or one misstep—away from a roof in New Orleans. I am three generations away from being on a list of possessions. I am not far from a posse in Gretna. I am not too far from a time when the only way inside for me was to be obsequious at a Southern back door. Yet and still, this is my country. By right of birth, and blood, and building, and ancestry, I too call this country home.

Generations

I know that it is by the grace of God that my family has survived long-term trauma and neglect here. I know that my shaking suspicion, my trembling and terror at watching people left to float, or die, or claw their way to higher heights in New Orleans, is a natural feeling. I am of course entitled to suspect this nation and its treatment of people who look like me. Healthy psychology requires this protective response.

If people like me saw poverty the way this nation seems to, if we let poverty trip us up, we would all be either abject or dead. I was raised to not even consider poverty, whether or not it surrounded me. To consider money was to become a slave to cash. With my short three generations removed from ownership, I cannot willingly become a slave, to anything.

Nonetheless, we are the children of generations legally and fairly relentlessly constrained to poverty. Hundreds of years of pennilessness were forced on us. Our earning power is both narrow and recent.

My great-grandfather was a cook on the Southern railroad. President Eisenhower once tipped him a silver dollar and it was one of the proudest and richest single moments of my great-grandfather's life. His name was James Franklin Williams. No one but his loving family knows his name, though he cooked on the affluent train line for fifty-two years. We had a silver plated tray given to testify to the many mornings of eggs cooked to requested perfection, and evenings of steak. His food served in white-only dining cars, replete with starched white table linens. Loads of work, loads of excess to feed wealthy white passengers riding in comfort and style. My Papa cooking day in and day out, on a moving train. My great-grandmother benefitted; she could ride the train free, but only in the colored section. She could not sit and don a table napkin and eat the food her husband cooked. Viola Moore Williams is who she was. No one except those of us who loved her knows her name, either. Every African-American name we know, we know in spite of poverty. To be black and have survived in America, you have had to crawl through the dark tunnel of poverty, on your belly, on your knees. This is the American way—for us. We are all Louis Armstrong, we are all Oliver Twist. All we have accomplished here, we have made with poverty yoked across our shoulders, carrying buckets of water to quiet some owner man's thirst. Poverty is how this country contained us, dismayed us, delayed us. Awful, racist weights to carry on.

What Remains at Stake

No doubt the business of the Mississippi ports and the slick work of the refineries will command attention and be restored to power. No doubt these bastions of industry and money creation will even survive the drenching spill. New Orleans' cultural capital, however, her cultural intelligence, needs attention and nurture and hothouse respect. Who knows whether it is possible to seed and tend and water a uniquely American cultural memory that thrives by a black beating heart? Can we nurture New Orleans' jazz and brass and rhythm, restart an interrupted future? Can we practice those phrases again? Can the social and artistic landscape be retouched after such devastating floods and malevolent neglect? Will Black Indians return, and chant? Do you know how long you can sustain a twelve-bar blues? Whose Krewe you are on? Will people who have been the real New Orleans stand up, be free blacks, be proud, be demanding, be counted? Will survivors band together to shake down some make-up for this massive catastrophe? Or, will limited resources and fake color-blindness make this forced migration a permanent and culture-bending shift . . . ? There is an outcome to being in a post-traumatic state of disorder: the stress and strain of fury, the heat and hale of memory are dispersed.

The stakes are incredibly high now. The future is long. The past is deeply rich, roux. Can we go more intelligently forward? Can we build levees that have structural strength, and integrity?

311

In some cities, you can dial this number to request city services. Establish this. Establish city services. Do what makes sense in the new New Orleans.

The Battle for the New New Orleans

I hope there is a battle. I hope the light of day blares into the backest rooms, even if we have to break through and go *in* through rooftops. I hope we refuse to be ignored. I hope we stand outside in the ninth ward, repopulate the Treme, and point our accusing finger toward every slave quarter. I hope we shout, rooftop to rooftop: *This is where we live.*

My daughter's birthplace has been so diminished. Decimated? Wiped out? Neglected, neglected, neglected. This travesty—unacceptable, untenable, unthinkable. She deserves to know the city that swings, that sings, that she was born to. It is New Orleans that makes her able to hear and to say "horricane." She deserves to know the kiss of that sweet swamp, the same weather she experienced her very first, unsuspecting, spring. Each child, every one, deserves a well-built and well-considered place to grow up on. In this case, a protected, and not neglected, new, New Orleans.

How to Help

We all need to stay in the lane. Stand up. Speak. Apply pressure. Refuse to ride high horses. Refuse to buy into lies. Refuse to give up, refuse to relinquish. Barge into back rooms. Be sure you have an emergency readiness kit for your family. Be sure you have an evacuation plan. Do not plan to wait for FEMA. Pretend. See yourself standing on a roof for five days. Contemplate rising water. Imagine yourself without, without.

Decry poverty. Support education. Fight for a new New Orleans that revives its old swing. Visit. Look underneath the surface. Chant. Don't be persuaded to change the city's color. Stand in Congo Square. Learn its history. See if Marie LaVeaux is still buried.

Go to New Orleans. Pick up a hammer. Use your vacation to help build your nation. Habitat for Humanity, New Orleans, is building houses, one at a time, under the leadership of a former, elected president. Give money. Help the new city grow up around its longstanding cultural wealth. Arrange to see Harry Shearer's *"The Big Uneasy."* Learn the true story of this catastrophe through his revealing documentary film. Do not be afraid of rhythm. Have no fear of swing. Stop pretending to be color blind, but put down your wariness of black people. Keep your eye on this prize—the great American city, cultural icon, and teacher—stand by for a new New Orleans.

Meet me. Let's all work together, let's all think together. In the dry outdoors, not in a back room. I'll be waiting at the corner of Independence and Humanity Street. Or, if you'd like we can meet at the corner of Flood and Onward. If you'd rather meet uptown, I'll wait at the corner of President and Prytania; let's hope the streetcar's running.

One last word. I have not been a person who believes rumors, in my life. As a writer, I can research, I can often find the facts. But if the rumors about the new New Orleans are true, if the theft of the city for blonder purposes is true, if there is no intention to rebuild the city that once was New Orleans, I only have this to quote: *Do you know what it means to miss New Orleans?*

HEADLINE: Swamps regenerate.

DARK WATERS

Yusef Komunyakaa

> Our civilization poisoned river waters, and their contamination acquires
> a powerful emotional meaning. As the course of a river is a symbol of time,
> we are inclined to think of a poisoned time. And yet the sources continue
> to gush and we believe time will be purified one day.
> —*Czesław Miłosz, from "Rivers" in* Road-Side Dog

I grew up in the Green Empire. Magic City. The place was there, brimming
in its mossy quietude, before the axes began to swing—cutting down the virgin pine forest on July 4, 1914, when the town was incorporated. The name
comes from the Native American–named creek, "Bogue Lusa," where smoke-
dark waters flow through the city.

The Great Southern Lumber Company was established by someone from
Buffalo, New York, connected to Goodyear, in 1906. By then, the presence
of the Native American had been virtually erased; now there was a killing to
be made from the great, towering pines.

During the 1950s Bogalusa seethed, a hotbed for racism. Segregation,
enforced by a minority, imposed inequality upon the majority of this city's
population. There were no black doctors, lawyers, postal workers, police

officers, firefighters, bank tellers, salespeople, machine operators, et cetera. Those who did go off to college returned as public school teachers to segregated schools. Everyone else faced making a living some other way, and no matter the skills, the work involved perpetual hard labor.

As a matter of fact, a metaphor for the daily realities of life in Bogalusa was manifested in the graveyards of the black and white inhabitants. Whites lavished monuments of granite and marble on their dead over acres of plush, green cemeteries. The graveyard for African Americans, half-hidden near the city dump, was visited by vultures and scavengers that lingered between the smoldering hills of garbage and the graves, whose keepers fought off the constant encroachment of saw vines and scrub oak.

This hellish symbol was analogous to the town's psyche. It reflected an attitude that had been cultivated over many decades. It was the law—social and legal—a way of thinking that ran so deep that it went unquestioned each generation. Bogalusa was frozen in time.

The same attitude that allowed settlers to produce smallpox-infected blankets for Native Americans seemed alive in the psyche of our city. One could almost hear Sweet Medicine of the Cheyenne lamenting: "Someday you will meet a people who are white. They will try always to give you things, but do not take them. At last I think you will take these things that they offer you, and this will bring sickness to you. . . ."[1]

The first known settlers in the area were Scottish and Irish pioneers from the British colonies of Georgia and Virginia, as well as North and South Carolina. The Treaty of Paris, which briefly created British West Florida in 1763, also attracted Loyalists fleeing the American Revolution. By 1906, when the Great Southern Lumber Company was established—and before it was to grow into what was boasted to be the world's largest sawmill, the Native Americans had been suppressed to near extinction.

Their ghosts remained evident in some faces as my poem "Looking for Choctaw" suggests:

> we dared him to fight,
> But he only left his breath
> On windshields, as if nothing
> Could hold him in this world.[2]

I grew up with the feeling that the Choctaw lived in our presence, in a half glimpse, somewhere among the trees as elusive, nocturnal souls.

Many Bogalusan blacks believed that "a good education" would lift them out of poverty and make their lives more equal to those of whites. They saluted the flag and trusted the Bill of Rights. Some had returned from World War I, World War II, and the Korean Conflict, but they were still waiting for things to change. Some were counting the decades and years, making promises on their deathbeds, getting restless. A few were dreaming aloud.

In January 1964 the KKK burned crosses throughout Louisiana. Also, fifteen black people registered to vote in Tensas Parish, the last parish to enforce total disenfranchisement of blacks. In November the Deacons of Defense and Justice was founded in Jonesboro, Louisiana. The group advocated armed self-defense against the Klan. In December KKK members from around Natchez, Mississippi, burned a shoe-repair shop in Ferriday, Louisiana, owned by fifty-one-year-old Frank Morris. He died in the blaze. In January 1965 black protesters picketed Columbia Street stores in Bogalusa, a Klan stronghold. In May the Klan held a large rally in the Magic City, their Green Empire. On June 2, O'Neal Moore, African American and a sheriff's deputy in Washington Parish, was murdered by a white man who drove by in a pickup truck near Bogalusa. Ernest Ray McElveen, a forty-one-year-old Crown Zellerbach labor technician and member of the Citizen's Council of Greater New Orleans and the National States' Rights Party, was arrested not far from the murder scene. In July protests by the Voters League and the Deacons for Defense implored the Justice Department to enforce the Civil Rights Act through suits against city officials and the Klan. In 1966 Clarence Triggs, a bricklayer, was found dead after he left a civil rights meeting sponsored by the Congress of Racial Equality.

I have a love-hate complex with Bogalusa. The place still affects how I live and think. Its beauty and horror shaped the intensity of my observations, prompting my father to say, "Boy, you have a mind like a steel trap." Now, years after my book *Magic City*, I realize that I had attempted to present how toxicity taints the social and natural landscape. For me, the millpond— a hundred or so yards from our house—was always a place of ritual. We fished there. And sometimes we even swam in the dark water. But in the back of my mind, I was always suspicious of this slow-running pond. I think the poem "The Millpond" attempts to focus on my apprehensions:

Gods lived under that mud
When I was young & sublimely
Blind. Each bloom a shudder
Of uneasiness, no sound
Except the whippoorwill.
They conspired to become twilight
& metaphysics, as five-eyed
Fish with milky bones
Flip-flopped in oily grass.[3]

I was aware of the hard splendor of this small, semirural city. I knew about cutting and hauling pulpwood because I had done it, as I attempt to describe in "Poetics of Paperwood":

We pulled the crosscut
Through the pine like a seesaw
Of light across a map
Of green fungus.
We knew work
Was rhythm,
& so was love.[4]

Well, at least, I knew I loved nature—I sought so many hours in its solitude. It was the engine of my imagination. Maybe this is what Sophie Cabot Black projects in "Nature, Who Misunderstands" when she writes, "Nature loves and makes you love."[5] Perhaps we haven't learned nature's greatest instruction: we are connected. Everything's connected.

When it comes to wishing a "divine paradise" or an earthly Eden into existence, human history and imaginative literature are a web of contradictions and bloated wishful thinking, as when Saint John of Damascus says, "In truth, it was a divine place and a worthy habitation for God in His image. And in it no brute beasts dwelt, but only man, the handiwork of God."[6] Following this line of thinking—does God invent God's own death through humans? Is commerce the death of God, since humans seem more deadly than so-called brute beasts?—a deacon might ask, "Doesn't God give people dominion over everything?"

Everything adds up to capital. Living from birth to death involves commerce. The poor, disenfranchised people I grew up with couldn't afford fancy tombstones and divine-looking burial plots for their loved ones. Some seemed born diminished—cogwheels of flesh in a monumental system that stole and sold even the airspace overhead as if they were part of an experiment that had gone wrong.

Or, as I listen to Don Byron, an experimental jazz clarinetist, I read again from the notes that introduce his CD:

> And the album title "Tuskegee Experiments" refers to two experiments conducted on Black American men at the Tuskegee Institute.
>
> In 1932, the U.S. Public Health Service, with generous assistance from local Black medical professionals, initiated the longest human medical experiment in American history. More than half of the four hundred men chosen had syphilis, while the rest formed a non-syphilitic control group. None were informed of their condition, and they were observed for over 40 years, but NOT treated, just to document the physical effects of syphilis left unchecked. In the Tuskegee Aviation experiment, over-qualified and under-compensated Black men endured unnecessary indignities simply to "prove" they could be trusted to fly military aircraft.
>
> To me, these two experiments are metaphors for African-American life. In one, we see once again that black life is cheap, and that a person of color can be enlisted to work against the best interests of his group, for nothing more than a brief "vacation" from the pain of invisibility or the pressure of being seen as part of an "inferior" group.[7]

In essence, Byron points out that it takes a cultivated, sanctioned attitude to design a project that dehumanizes and kills people. It is the same attitude that prompted certain settlers to distribute smallpox-infected blankets to Native Americans. It is an attitude of war. A few decades ago, the same kind of stance advocated that the United States should bomb the Vietnamese into the Stone Age. A similar attitude drives the marketplace: the so-called Third World countries often function as a dumping ground for numerous products that are harmful or banned in the United States and Europe. Some of the brainiest among us serve as reckless juggernauts geared up for another margin of profit, as if a capitalist must always sell his or her soul, that he or she isn't capable of compassion and morality. After all, by using simple deductive logic, since the civil rights movement occurred less than four decades ago, with institutionalized injustices as a way of life, as law and custom, it should be no surprise that there are people in positions to whom minorities cannot entrust their lives and well-being. Hate mongers are still among us; some wield power and make decisions as to where harmful chemicals are stored and toxins dumped. All of this may be done with an almost unintentional malice—a way of thinking linked to the imperatives of an unjust history—without second thought.

We don't have to think of Nazi Germany to know that some humans have experimented on others for insane reasons. In my mind, all this connects. What about South Africa's Dr. Death: Dr. Wouter Basson? As I read the article "The Poison Keeper," this exposé grew even more frightening:

> We nonetheless know that, at Roodeplaat, Basson's scientists were working with anthrax, cholera, salmonella, botulism, thallium, *E. coli,* ricin, organophosphates, necrotizing fasciitis, hepatitis A, and H.I.V., as well as nerve gases (Sarin, VX) and the Ebola, Marburg, and Rift Valley hemorrhagic-fever viruses.[8]

Chet Raymo says in *Skeptics and True Believers* that:

> Some of the new criticism of science has come from inside the scientific community and is informed by a thorough understanding of scientific process. As such, it is especially welcome and useful. For example, Dai Rees, secretary and chief executive of Britain's Medical Research Council, writing in *Nature,* makes a startling claim: "Science has contributed massively to human misery" by undermining traditional stable societies without offering any compensating vision of what human life might be. It is time for scientists to pay their dues, he insists. . . . Scientists must accept responsibility for the application of their discoveries—for good or ill.[9]

Like a true American pragmatist, Raymo attempts to chastise Rees, and goes on to conclude that,

The conflict is not between science and society, as such, but between the two segments of society which I have labeled Skeptics and True Believers. . . .

Certainly, it is not the sole responsibility of scientists to show the way to accommodation of empirical knowing and spiritual longing. This is a task that must occupy scientists, philosophers, theologians, poets, and artists.[10]

We must pay dues to ourselves and each other. Perhaps this is why Robert Oppenheimer questioned his heart and mind in the creation of the atomic bomb. I agree with Raymo's insistence that the larger intellectual community should pose questions and create a dialogue about ethics and technology.

It is scandalous, but often citizens have to create organizations to protect themselves from the vicious practices of businesses going beyond the bounds of free enterprise. When we look at the preamble established by the delegates to the First National People of Color Environmental Leadership Summit held October 24–27, 1991, in Washington, D.C., the gravity of the problem is telescoped:

We, the People of Color, gathered together at this multinational People of Color Environmental Leadership Summit, to begin to build a national and international movement of all peoples of color to fight the destruction and taking of our lands and communities, do hereby re-establish our spiritual interdependence to the sacredness of our Mother Earth; to respect and celebrate each of our cultures, languages and beliefs about the natural world and our roles in healing ourselves; to insure environmental justice; to promote economic alternatives which would contribute to the development of environmentally safe livelihoods; and, to secure our political, economic and cultural liberation that has been denied for over 500 years of colonization and oppression, resulting in the poisoning of our communities and land and the genocide of our peoples, do affirm and adopt these Principles of Environmental Justice. . . .[11]

For me, the first and last of the seventeen principles underline the overall importance of the summit:

1. Environmental Justice affirms the sacredness of Mother Earth, ecological unity and the interdependence of all species, and the right to
be free from ecological destruction. . . .

17. Environmental Justice requires that we, as individuals, make personal and consumer choices to consume as little of Mother Earth's
resources and to produce as little waste as possible; and make the conscious decision to challenge and reprioritize our lifestyles to insure the
health of the natural world for present and future generations.[12]

When I was growing up in Bogalusa I could taste the chemicals in the
air. It was something we accepted as a way of life, but it is also something one
never forgets. I have tried to recapture an image of my hometown in "Fog
Galleon":

Horse-headed clouds, flags
& pennants tied to black
Smokestacks in swamp mist.
From the quick green calm
Some nocturnal bird calls
Ship ahoy, ship ahoy!
I press against the taxicab
Window. I'm back here, interfaced
With a dead phosphorescence;
The whole town smells
Like the world's oldest anger.
Scabrous residue hunkers down under
Sulfur & dioxide, waiting
For sunrise, like cargo
On a phantom ship outside Gaul.
Cool glass against my cheek
Pulls me from the black schooner
On a timeless sea—everything
Dwarfed beneath the papermill
Lights blinking behind the cloudy

Commerce of wheels, of chemicals
That turn workers into pulp
When they fall into vats
Of steamy serenity.[13]

One cannot miss Bogalusa's acid smell, but Louisiana State University
Medical Center's *Bogalusa Heart Study* seems to suggest that overall health
concerns are limited in a town that has been, for the most part, silent in its
demands for industry to clean up toxic sites. Here are two troubling items in
the *Bogalusa Heart Study:*

• Autopsy studies show lesions in the aorta, coronary vessels, and
  kidney relate strongly to clinical cardiovascular risk factors, clearly
  indicating atherosclerosis and hypertension begin in early life.
• Environmental factors are significant and influence dyslipidemia,
  hypertension, and obesity.[14]

The disparity in economics is at the center of the racial and cultural divide that influences environmental politics. Unfortunately, this is doubly true
in places such as Magic City where the economic distance between black
and white citizens is immense, and this chasm encapsulates and underscores
history's imperative. For instance, statistics from the 1990 census verify the
situation: the highest percentage of African-American residents lives in north-
central and southeast Bogalusa, with an annual income of five thousand to
seventeen thousand dollars; northeast Bogalusa has the highest white population, boasting an annual income of forty to fifty-one thousand dollars.

Even food products can be measured with dollar signs: poor communities usually pay more for their inferior food products. Also, it is more likely
that chemical- and pesticide-free products are sold in high-income areas. An
attitude permeates the relationships between merchants and certain communities, as is the case of American companies marketing questionable products
in parts of the so-called Third World (tobacco products distributed in Asian
countries and the former Soviet Union). Or, we only have to look at the proliferation of billboards and other advertisements in minority communities
for alcohol products—with the help of celebrity endorsements. Such things

aren't accidental; everything is planned and perfected with the same attention as is given to any weapon. An argument can be made, as many have done previously, that the availability of drugs in certain communities is no accident; to the degree that it is planned, this offers yet another example of how communities are violated.

Our fears become our worst enemies. We need to trust each other. Otherwise, the mental health of the society wears to a fragile state. Distrust diminishes our emotional lives on a personal level and further deepens the chasm of misunderstandings among our communities.

I grew up in a climate of distrust. Blacks didn't trust whites, and it was sometimes difficult to disentangle truth from myth and folklore. For example, no black person could sell illegal, homemade liquor, but there was a white man who sold his brew to blacks. Not only did he sell "stoopdown" under the nose of the law, but it was rumored that he doctored his corn whiskey with pinches of Red Devil lye. We believed that some among us were slowly being poisoned. This is the kind of thing that fosters mistrust, when one doesn't know where the truth begins, similar to a *Sixty Minutes* scenario. Since many of the white citizens of Bogalusa have kept blacks economically disadvantaged for generations, during the 1970s and 1980s, some blacks believed that well-off white families were redeeming food stamps at the local supermarkets, that some even paid their black domestics with government food stamps. "There's nothing a white man won't do to keep a black man down," they'd say, "If he can't legally keep you in chains, he'll connive some way to keep his foot on your neck."

This was the folk wisdom from my community. So, when it came to the politics of pollution and dumping of hazardous waste in the black community, many of us understood it was business as usual—a reflection of the national psyche. When we learned that white families were draining their toilets into Mitch Creek, we assumed that it was done only because blacks swam downstream on Sunday afternoons; we weren't allowed to swim at the Y.

"Bogalusa? It seems familiar. Where have I heard that name? It's on the tip of my tongue."

Oftentimes, that's the reaction I'll hear to the word "Bogalusa." Sometimes I'll add, "The nineteen-sixties?"

"Yeah, that's right. The civil rights movement."

Most times, I'd leave those words hanging in the air.

Louisiana has a bad record when it comes to civil rights and protection of the environment. But Jim Motavalli's article "Toxic Targets" in *E: The Environmental Magazine* suggests that there's a deeper problem. He writes:

> On September 10, 1997, Environmental Protection Agency (EPA) head Carol Browner issued a simple but unprecedented order: She disallowed the state of Louisiana's approval of an enormous polyvinyl chloride (PVC) plant in Convent, a small, mostly African-American community already inundated with 10 other toxic waste producers.[15]

One can see that a pattern had been already established, that the Japanese-owned Shintech plant must have been surprised by the federal government's directive. Motavalli states:

> The term "environmental racism" wasn't in the vernacular until it appeared in a 1987 study by the United Church of Christ's Commission for Racial Justice entitled *Toxic Wastes and Race in the United States.* Ben Chavis, the commission's director, stated simply that "race is a major factor related to the presence of hazardous wastes in residential communities throughout the United States," and a new field of study was born.
>
> The pillars that allow pervasive environmental racism are beginning to crumble. In April, the Nuclear Regulatory Commission denied a license to a uranium enrichment plant impacting the African-American communities of Forest Grove and Center Springs, Louisiana. . . .[16]

I cannot stop thinking of these two lines from Antonio Machado's "He andado muchos caminos": *"Mala gente que camina / y va apestando la tierra . . ."* ("Evil men who walk around / polluting the earth . . .")[17] Sooner or later, our cultivated attitudes force all of us to pay our dues. Agriculture Street

Superfund site, where houses sit atop a polluted landfill. South Memphis's highly toxic Defense Depot, suspected of causing a cancer cluster among the African American residents. But there are stories that garner even more news coverage, because the dream isn't half buried, a slow kill.

In *Dispatch,* Shirley Ayers writes:

When a city's fire chief is the very first casualty of a hazardous materials explosion, you can be pretty sure that it is going to be a bad day. Such was the scenario in Bogalusa, Louisiana, last fall when a railroad tank car holding nitrogen tetroxide (rocket fuel) exploded at the Gaylord chemical plant, releasing a mushroom cloud of poisonous gas that sent thousands of people, including the Bogalusa Fire Chief, to an area hospital.[18]

When people from across the country called me and asked, "How's your family down in Bogalusa?" I said that I had my fingers crossed. I didn't say that my fingers have been crossed since the late 1960s, since the civil rights movement, and since the 1970s, when I became aware that I had grown up across from a millpond filled with chemicals that "seasoned" logs.

I have never been sentimental about nature. I have accepted it in the same way as these lines by Emily Dickinson:

A Bird came down the Walk—
He did not know I saw—
He bit an Angleworm in halves
And ate the fellow, raw,

And then he drank a Dew
From a convenient Grass—
And then hopped sidewise to the Wall
To let a Beetle pass—[19]

Nature teaches us how to see ourselves within its greater domain. We see our own reflections in every ritual, and we cannot wound Mother Nature without wounding ourselves. She isn't a pushover.

MUJERES DE MAÍZ

Women, Corn, and Free Trade in the Americas

Maria Melendez

I grew up in the era of Save-the-Blank conservation. As a teenage member of the Sierra Club, I was routinely sent mailings exhorting me to Save the Whales, Save Our Coastlines, Save the Rain Forest, Save the Redwoods. By contrast, the task of opposing the North American Free Trade Agreement during the early nineties, the years of its signing and ratification, must have seemed a sloganeer's nightmare: save us from a rich-getting-richer-and-poor-getting-poorer-world-of-greed-and-destruction was the "liberal" message that reached me, if only dimly, through the political noise being made against NAFTA here and there. But the whole thing just seemed confusing to me. I was suckered by the use of the word *free*. I was raised to think that *free* is, always and everywhere, equal to *good*. Even more confusing, I knew my early twenties self to be a staunch liberal, politically speaking, but proponents of NAFTA were said to support "liberalized trade," and soon their "neoliberal agenda" was being criticized in what I'd call "liberal" publications. So which was it: liberal equals good or liberal equals bad? And besides, you couldn't hug an ideal of economic justice, like you could a tree. In November 1993, when NAFTA was ratified by the United States Congress, my reflections on the matter could be summed up by the dismissive phrase that is the hallmark of political apathy: What! Ever!

A decade and a half later, I'm still dismissive of many things I probably can't afford to ignore, but thanks to ecofeminism and, oddly enough, corn, talk of "free trade" in the Americas is finally firmly in my view.

The most beautiful corn I've ever seen grows behind the home of Adelina Santiago, a shopkeeper in the Sierra de Juárez of Oaxaca, Mexico. In a rectangular plot about one hectare in size, her corn thrives, greener than the brightest suburban lawn, taller than any man, with bone-colored tassels that splay out from the tops like sparklers. I traveled to Oaxaca in June 2004 to learn more about the relationships between women and corn. I'd recently lived across the street from an industrially farmed cornfield that was off-limits, No Trespassing, untouchable. Because I have always loved touching plants—as a girl, I trolled the aisles of Navlet's Nursery for hours, stroking pansy petals, running my hands through the feathery needles of Norfolk pines—this field filled me with a tactile sense for the loneliness of industrial corn. In Oaxaca, I stepped into the rows between señora Santiago's corn plants, felt the fine maroon hairs on the stalks, rubbed the shiny leaves bigger than a boot print. Drunk on the mountain sunlight, beside the alive and breathing cornstalks, I felt like I was greeting a long-lost sister.

(Such instances of personal fulfillment occurred repeatedly during my travels in Oaxaca. It's embarrassing to note that through my sense of fulfillment, I enacted a familiar neocolonial tourist gesture, in which the wounds of sensory deprivation suffered by inhabitants of an industrialized country are balmed and soothed by contact with the perceived sensuality and sensory stimulation located in a "less-developed" country. The fact that the goal of this essay extends beyond an account of personal eco-fulfillment to an effort at understanding larger global processes may or may not compensate for my problematic position, depending on what response it elicits to the matters at hand.)

Both the state of Oaxaca and the species *Zea mays* (corn or maize) are hot-button issues for conservation biology in the Americas these days. Although the stories science tells about the origins of maize are varied and contested, the most credible theory, at present, posits that seven to twelve thousand years ago, maize developed (through selection by Mesoamerican people) from a wild teosinte grass. Recent genetic evidence suggests this domestication process took place in the highlands of what are today Mexico's southwestern states, including Oaxaca, and archaeologists have found the oldest-known remains of early maize ears in a cave in the Oaxaca Valley. Today, the mountains and valleys of the state of Oaxaca bear the world's greatest maize diversity.

In 2001, the world's first instance of transgenic contamination of a native race of corn was discovered by University of California–Berkeley researchers Ignacio Chapela and David Quist . . . in Oaxaca. They found "transgenes," meaning genes from another species (a cauliflower bacteria, in this case), introgressed into the DNA of native corn. Though a smear campaign brought their methodology into question, the researchers' data indicating the presence of transgenes in native varieties of corn was not disputed. Further studies by American and Mexican researchers have verified additional instances of transgenic contamination in native Mexican maize. In a sense, NAFTA can be seen as the cause for this contamination, because corn is wind-pollinated, and the native species in question "caught" pollen from transgenic U.S. corn imported under the agreement.

Because the Oaxaca region could be considered the evolutionary birthplace of corn, and because the state itself has been "ground zero" for transgenic contamination issues, I wanted to do some poetic research on the implications, for women's lives, of transgenic contamination in maize. As a Chicana poet, I'd been reading contemporary Chicana poetry with an eye toward shared themes, and had noticed the recurrence of powerful images of corn in poetry by Chicanas from all over the United States. It seemed logical to me that rural Mexican women's connection to corn might represent the historical and psychological roots of contemporary urban and suburban Chicana poets' connections to corn. When I sat down with the head of an organic market in the capital city of Oaxaca and said, "I'm here to learn more about the relationships between women and corn," he said "Oh, you mean tortillas, in which this relationship lives!" Yes! In my abstract, academic fixation on the concept of "relationships," I had been sorely in need of someone to point me in just this direction: toward the "things" that embody ideas—in this case, tortillas.

In rural Mexico, the tortilla is a communicative body, a treatise, a *testimonio* proclaiming a woman's expertise and skill, care for her family and community, and, yes, her relationship to corn. It speaks in the subtle dialects of flavor and nourishment.

During my travels in Oaxaca, I visited nine rural households for *platicas* (chats) with women about tortillas and maize. Most women generously showed me how they made tortillas and where their family grew its corn, and most visits ended with a delicious snack of tortillas with cheese or meat. The North American Free Trade Agreement, and its ongoing effects, hung around the edges of all of the conversations.

As I entered the tortilla-making hut (a small wooden building common to rural households in Oaxaca) of María Antonieta Gigón in the Sierra de Juárez mountains, she asked to see my passport. The request was startling and vaguely alarming to me; as a mixed-race Chicana, I'm very experienced with intercultural encounters in the United States, but in the rural pueblos of Oaxaca I was *gringa* as *gringa* could be, and the Lonely Planet guide had warned travelers to relinquish their passports only if absolutely necessary. I thought about it for a minute, taking in my surroundings and noting how un-threatening my hostess seemed—a mother, probably in her early forties, wearing a modest navy-blue circle skirt, intent on baking her tortillas—and offered to show señora Gigón my passport in exchange for her allowing me to try and bake a tortilla or two.

As we laughed together at my attempts to move the sticky, delicate tortilla dough from the *prensa*, a metal press which converts a mound of masa into a flat circle, to the *comál*, a pre-Columbian wood-heated hot plate where tortillas are baked, she told me more about why the passport fascinated her. She wanted to learn what they looked like and how to obtain one because she wanted to visit her eldest son, who had been working in San Diego for the last several years. The way she looked past me as she told about her desire to see him, and the urgency in her voice when she asked how much a passport cost, pointed to an unspeakable sense of loss. This same sense of loss came through again and again as women spoke of their sons or brothers, uncles or spouses in the United States. By flooding the Mexican market with grossly over-subsidized U.S. corn, NAFTA's "liberalized trade" has displaced millions of commercial corn growers in Mexico, causing increased male immigration to the United States and a tandem increase in women's poverty, as the women left behind must act as de facto single heads of household. Today, impoverished Mexican and Central American women make the dangerous journey north "across the line" in increasing numbers, in the hopes that the money they'll send home will make up for the economic hardship suffered in the absence of husbands, fathers, brothers. These women carry memories of wrenching good-byes with their children and loved ones. The domino effect of their poverty falls hardest, perhaps, on their children, as demonstrated by a new generation of child immigrants who ride the tops of trains through Mexico and risk their lives crossing into the United States to find their mothers.

Although I never probed deeply enough to determine if NAFTA could have been at the root of the emigration accounts from the particular women I spoke with, the knowledge that an agreement pushed along by the United States has led to dramatic increases in family fragmentation and women's poverty should weigh heavily on further considerations of the expansion of trade liberalization in the Americas.

Real power to address poor and/or rural women's priorities is entirely absent from the history of NAFTA's creation and implementation. Here one of the most basic ecofeminist lines of logic can easily be drawn, a line connecting the treatment of women to the treatment of the environment. NAFTA accords the same disempowered status to the environment as it does to rural women. The only international NAFTA-related body that has sought any input from rural women is the Commission for Environmental Cooperation, a NAFTA board that can only provide "encouragements" and "suggestions," rather than fines and enforcement, on matters of environmental concern attendant with the implementation of the agreement. While it is written into NAFTA that a corporation can take legal action against a state in which environmental regulations hamper that corporation's business, NAFTA limits the Commission for Environmental Cooperation's official realm to that of toothless "cooperation." Thus the CEC becomes the environmental equivalent of the angel in the house for NAFTA; a beneficent body whose role is to provide gentle guidance on eco-right and -wrong, while wielding none of the economic power of a head of household, a roll in this case played by the few wealthy men of the signatory nations whose stock investments have swelled as a result of NAFTA.

The reverse of the old ecofeminist equation, in which the trampling of women's rights is contemporaneous with the trampling of environmental rights, remains to be explored: if the architects of international trade agreements kept rural women's needs more centrally in view, would wiser environmental stewardship and greater biodiversity ensue? In the case of maize, the answer may well be yes.

The contamination of native races of maize in Mexico with transgenes (human-engineered genes containing genetic material from another species) is considered a threat to Oaxaca's celebrated maize diversity, in that there is a possibility that maize with transgenes, created to be extra pest- and fungus-resistant, could dilute the genetic vigor of local maize races, cultivated over multiple millennia. Some varieties of Oaxacan maize have been so carefully bred as to now be considered evolutionary "specialists" for an *individual hillside*. What's wrong with fungus-resistant corn, you ask? In some rural Mexican areas, a certain species of corn fungus is considered a culinary delicacy! What's wrong with pest-resistant corn? Some women I spoke with reported that they believed transgenic corn to have smaller ears, with kernels that didn't dry well for masa-making. The larger point: scientists engineered transgenic corn to serve the interest and convenience of big agribusiness, but rural Oaxacans bred indigenous varieties of corn over countless generations to serve localized tastes, customs, preferences, and climates.

Where do women fit in to all of this? As head cooks in their households, rural Latin American women retain significant knowledge about desirable qualities in their food items, and their experienced selectivity influences seed saving and swapping practices. Some suggest this has been true even from the invention of the *Zea mays* species: that it was women who patiently bred corn from wild grasses those thousands of years ago. With this in mind, we can see the ancient sisterhood, still alive and evolving today, between women and corn. Corn is a key part of a rural Mexican woman's sustenance from birth to the world beyond death: nursing mothers are often given a corn and cocoa drink to increase their milk, and corpses buried in traditional Zapotec ceremonies are sent to the afterlife with handfuls of cornmeal to nourish them on their souls' long journeys. Conversely, women as "maize processors" and seed savers play a key role in the sustenance of local maize races. The transgenic pollen now loosed onto Mexican winds enters these women's cornfields without their consent, and it modifies the biodiversity and physical characteristics of their corn in unpredictable ways. Given rural Mexican women's exceptional level of intimacy and expertise with maize, I'm betting that if they had been included in the initial discussions, conceptions, drafting, and implementation of NAFTA, they would never have allowed the one to two *million* tons of transgenic maize to enter their country, *unlabelled,* as the fathers of NAFTA have allowed each year since the agreement's ratification.

I don't wish to paint rural Mexican women as mere poster children for the rape of the global south by the north; they are, after all, whole people with whole lives and complex concerns, many of which have nothing to do with the United States. These women do not pass their time huddled in corners discussing, in trembling voices, the latest oppressive policy to come across the border. No, they have better things to do: tortillas to make, daughters to raise, mothers to bury, seeds to sort. I simply wish to highlight aspects of liberalized trade, as practiced post-NAFTA, that were invisible to my younger, more dismissive self. The Central American Free Trade Agreement, basically a version of NAFTA applied to Central America and the Dominican Republic, barely squeaked by its July 2005 ratification in the United States House of Representatives, passing by just two votes. This points to a growing American unease with a brand of liberalized trade that benefits a few and harms many.

In order to work for justice, both environmental and feminist, American activists cannot keep a narrow focus on domestic issues while proponents of "neoliberal trade" continue to work toward a Free Trade Area of the Americas. Some activists have dubbed the FTAA "NAFTA on steroids," since it applies most of NAFTA's provisions to all the products, people, and biomes from Canada to the tip of Chile. The über-male connotation of this "on steroids" claim is right in step with George W. Bush's own stock phrases for promoting his trade agenda in the Americas. When he spoke of "knocking down" trade barriers and "opening" new markets, he sounded eerily like a teenage boy making cherry-busting brags.

I call on American thinkers, writers, and activists to put on ecofeminist goggles and give the two paeans to greed—NAFTA and CAFTA—a thorough read. (The government has posted the full texts of both agreements online.) Then together, in front of our lawmakers' offices, in streets, in magazines, with our dollars and our sense, let's practice sisterhood and fellowship with all residents of the Americas, particularly those residents, human and otherwise, that big-business-favoring transnational agreements attempt to ignore.

HAZARDOUS CARGO

Ray Gonzalez

My car idles on the shoulder of the two-lane road, about one hundred yards from the entrance to Caldwell-Briseno Industries, a thriving solid-waste disposal facility in Sunland Park, New Mexico, ten miles northwest of downtown El Paso. I can't see what lies behind the metal fence, its threads tightly wound together, barbed wire running along its top for hundreds of feet. I think I see mounds of dirt beyond the barrier and warehouse buildings spread throughout, but the long row of diesel trucks blocks my view. Eight of them are lined up at the gate, waiting to be checked off and allowed to enter and deposit whatever hidden cargo they are carrying. The entrance is reinforced by a guardhouse, three men in uniform standing inside the glass, watching the slow-moving parade of vehicles.

I sit in my car with the windows closed because the exhausts from the trucks spread fumes everywhere. The plant is near the Rio Grande, and Cristo Rey, the mountain with the statue of Christ at the top, looms over the area, its brown slopes two miles away. A friend in El Paso told me about this place and mentioned that the company had found a good location—surrounded by acres of cottonwoods, salt cedar, and other river vegetation. Most people don't know it exists or what is left after empty trucks roar away. As I count the vehicles, two more pass me and get in line, and I wonder if anyone ever questions why so many loud trucks turn into this area off the main highways on the west side of the city.

I want to see how a waste dump so close to town operates, perhaps even talk to some residents of Sunland Park, but my plans are cut short when a white four-wheel-drive van screeches to a stop next to my car, the blue and green Caldwell-Briseno logo painted on its doors. The uniformed driver, decked out in sunglasses and a blue baseball cap with the logo on it, stares at me until I lower my window. He lowers his passenger-side window, and I see he is Mexican American.

"I'm sorry, sir, but you can't stop your car here," he says politely.

"I was just driving through and wanted to see all the trucks," I tell him above the roar of the waiting line down the road.

"You can't stop here." He looks over his shoulder as a radio squawks inside his van. "Turn around right here and you can get back to Doniphan."

"Isn't this a public road?" I point toward the street that goes past the gates.

He looks at me without answering, his brown face with its thin, well-trimmed mustache glistening under his cap. "Turn around right here, sir. No unauthorized vehicles are allowed to stop here."

"Okay," and I wave good-bye. He pulls forward so I can make a U-turn before another truck arrives and blocks me on the shoulder. I spin around and head back toward town. Four more lumbering, weighed-down trucks churn toward the facility before I reach the main road out of Sunland Park. Before I get on Doniphan, it hits me. None of the trucks in the long line or the ones approaching have company logos, lettering, or signs on them. Every truck is anonymous, and I can't tell to whom they belong or what they carry. It can't be a coincidence that none of them is marked, though some have New Mexico and Texas license plates, while others carry Chihuahua, Mexico, plates.

These trucks remind me of the black helicopters in *The X-Files* television series. Once you realize that "the truth is out there," you can't help but spot the trucks on the highways. There is no way to keep an accurate count of how many of these highly visible, yet invisible, trucks carry millions of gallons of toxic chemicals from U.S. plants and maquiladoras across the border into Juárez. In a way, it is a silent operation, an invisible network that basically runs unimpeded. Since these diesel trucks and rigs blend into normal business traffic, no one is going to ask them to stop and find out what time bombs are riding in the back. Despite laws regulating these border factories, hazardous waste gets dumped on the border every day.

These trucks supposedly appear at waste facilities by following designed routes marked by HC signs. The signs are everywhere I look in the southern New Mexico and El Paso area. White, diamond-shaped highway signs with the big, green letters "HC" on them. Hazardous Cargo. HC signs point the way—the lawful stops, turns, and streets to get out of one area and show up with your chemical mess in another. I don't know when they first went up; they were not posted on highways and roads when I was a boy in El Paso. These warnings are a recent response to government regulations on shipping materials that have probably been sent through the area undetected and unregulated for decades. Now, I spot dozens of HC signs on main streets in El Paso, entry ramps to the freeway, and on Interstate 25 heading north toward Las Cruces. Some of the key places to find them are on the international bridges between Juárez and El Paso. If you look closely among the hundreds of cars and trucks lined up to cross each way, you will spot an HC sign.

The Southwest is the most nuclear-polluted and chemically ruined area of the United States. It is the location for top-secret military installations and radioactive waste sites. Interstate 25 is the route to White Sands Missile Range, Los Alamos Nuclear Laboratory, and Cheyenne Mountain in Colorado. Secret cargoes are shipped, transferred, and secretly shifted on huge trucks every day across Arizona, New Mexico, and west Texas; I-25 the main artery that sends government and industrial waste toward its final resting place. One of the newest dumping sites is the Waste Isolation Pilot Plant, mined 2,150 feet below an ancient salt formation thirty miles southeast of Carlsbad, New Mexico. Los Alamos National Laboratory had the honor of being the first to dump what is called "transuranic waste" at the Carlsbad site. Transuranic wastes are generated primarily during the research, development, and production of nuclear weapons. This waste includes everything from laboratory clothing, tools, glove boxes, and rubber gloves to glassware and air filters. Trucks rumbling south on I-25, and passing through El Paso, carry the waste in Transuranic Packing Transporters—reusable shipping casks, three to a truck, and each filled with fifty-five-gallon steel drums of matter to be buried under the desert.

There are daily hazardous cargo caravans no one knows about, with most of the people living in the area not paying attention to the growing business of dumping dangerous materials and leftovers from a region undergoing tremendous economic and industrial changes. When state or city governments do find out, there is little they can do to stop the dangerous materials from passing through their area, though the Western Governors' Association, made up of several western state government offices, spent ten years preparing regulations to oversee dangerous shipments, but they have not stopped the increasing tide of waste or new companies making money by taking care of the sludge. Flooding the landscape with HC signs and keeping the trucks on these designated routes are victories from long-fought legislative and economic battles between federal and state agencies. Decorating the El Paso landscape with HC signs also means these designated routes are here to stay, bringing the risk of chemical spills and public endangerment with them.

Hazardous cargo has become big business because the passage of the North American Free Trade Agreement (NAFTA) years ago meant more trade and more factories having to get rid of their manufacturing messes. In January 1997, Mexican president Ernesto Zedillo inaugurated what he called the "NAFTA highway" to boost further trade between the United States and Mexico. He dedicated sixty-two miles of a highway running through the state of San Luis Potosi, about halfway between Mexico City and Laredo, Texas, and promised thirty-eight million dollars to complete it. By 1998 trucks were moving 160,000 tons of products daily along the partially finished highway, about half the cargo weight moved between the two countries in a twenty-four-hour period. When it signed NAFTA, Mexico insisted that any dangerous materials generated by the maquiladoras, U.S.–owned factories in Mexico, must be transported back to the country of origin, even though a 1997 report by Mexico's National Institute of Ecology claimed that only 12 percent of eight million tons of hazardous wastes receives adequate treatment. Thus, more HC signs sprang up all over the El Paso area and literally hundreds more trucks and vans began clogging the freeways. In public documents, Caldwell-Briseno estimates three hundred vehicles pass through its gates per day. Of those, it reports that 250 are commercial disposal trucks full of cargo directly from Juárez maquiladoras. These carriers dump six thousand cubic yards per day or eighteen hundred tons of waste every twenty-four hours. Sunland Park is ten miles northwest of downtown El Paso. The roads around El Paso, and other areas along the United States–Mexican border, are packed with heavy trucks and vans, though many local citizens might say it is part of becoming a major city.

One of the few encouraging steps taken in an attempt to control these hazardous materials happened in 1996. The Mexican city of Nogales, on the Arizona border, conducted a hazardous-waste worker training program. They gathered one hundred Mexican workers from maquiladoras in the San Luis and Mexicali areas. The five-day program consisted of lectures on the marking, packaging, and filling out of shipping forms, placarding, and driver training. As one of the few training programs on either side of the border, it received media attention and promises by the Daewoo Electronics maquiladora in San Luis that it would increase its programs for workers and encourage other industries to do the same.

Five years later the only media stories you hear are the ones about the increasing number of workers with medical problems caused by working conditions, the murdered Mexican girls who work in the factories, and the growing level of contamination in the Rio Grande. In the meantime, the HC signs shake in the hot wind of a desert summer. How many truck drivers that know these marked routes have been trained in moving industrial waste, hydrocarbon affected soils, and radioactive sludge? New Mexico passed a law in 1986 requiring that all hazardous waste be exported out of the state. Chances are they are not dropping it in the El Paso area because that is too close to home, so the growing number of trucks on border highways mainly come from U.S. companies producing industrial trash right across the river in Mexico.

The white diamond signs that guide these trucks to the landfill blend into the thousands of billboards, traffic lights, and highway directional signs. They have been erected to make sure the risky fallout from thriving border commerce does not wander from the plotted path and into "safe" parts of neighborhoods. Their drivers must know the routes from memory by now but, as I count the HC markers, I realize the only freeway in El Paso is a legal route and so is every major street in town! I have never heard about any toxic spills in the El Paso area, yet the proliferation of the white signs on city streets and its lone freeway says the legal route is the only route. It should be evident to any El Pasoan who has noticed the former sleepy town now has heavy rush hours and gridlock that a good portion of the traffic causing these problems are long parades of large diesel trucks carrying their secret cargoes from a thriving border industrial revolution.

I walked around Paisano Street and asked a few people if they knew what the HC sign down the block stood for. Not one out of eight people I stopped knew what it meant. Five said they had never noticed the sign before; one of them, a young comedian with a smirk on his face, answered, "Doesn't that mean Hispanic Culture?" The other three thought they were directional signs to Juárez.

In 1999 an environmental group working with state officials managed to keep a radioactive-waste site from being constructed in Sierra Blanca, about a hundred miles southeast of El Paso, though the fight to stop the Carlsbad site failed. The underground dump in the salt flats of southeastern New Mexico is only a few years old and is being watched and regulated by a number of state and federal agencies. The volatile issues these facilities raise come and go in the media, though the inadequate highways being used to truck NAFTA waste are starting to get some attention as more stories about dangerous breakdowns by Mexican trucks keep appearing.

HC. I drive the streets of my hometown in the hundred-degree heat of June searching for more signs. They start to appear as I move across town. The white diamonds are everywhere because I am looking for them, their green letters on white rather unnoticeable, if you think about it. While I drive around town counting HC signs, the radio reports that in northern New Mexico, the Los Alamos fire is out of control. It has destroyed dozens of houses and rolled over parts of the nuclear laboratory compound. Government officials claim there is no danger of the fire reaching concrete-covered storage sites. I drive the streets of El Paso and find what I have been looking for in the furnace of the afternoon.

I am back on Paisano, one of the streets closest to the Rio Grande channel, and a quick route to Caldwell-Briseno, a few miles away. There are two HC signs close to each other near the last exit before downtown El Paso. Both are spray-painted in graffiti, the only defaced ones I have found all day.

The first diamond glows in orange letters that turn the HC into AO, perhaps an attempt to abbreviate "asshole." The second is more creative. Someone has used black paint to change the green H into two black crosses—††—and the O into a black peace sign from the sixties—☮. I had no idea today's taggers knew that old symbol. At the red traffic light, my car waits in the middle of a three-lane side road leading to the freeway. The lanes on either side of me are filled by several diesel rigs, their long, sleek bodies humming quietly as their drivers wait for the light to change, black smoke from their exhaust pipes swirling toward the blue sky of a busy, working day.

SILENT PARROT BLUES

Al Young

Environmental racism forces people of colour, in the words of
Rev. Ben Chavis Jr.,[1] "to bear the brunt of the nation's pollution
problem." Examples of environmental racism abound. Called by some
"human sacrifice zones," these are areas where mining occurs, where
pesticide use is rampant, and of course where the pollution of the military,
the biggest source of pollution on earth, accumulates and is stored.
—*Myrla Baldonado, Statement Coordinator,*
People's Task Force for Base Clean Up (in the Philippines)

Whenever anybody says he's struggling to become a human being
I have to laugh because the apes beat him to it by about a million years.
Struggle to become a parrot or something.
—*Jack Handley, from the* New Mexican, *1988*

Even I, who knew next to nothing about parrots, understood that this parrot
was exceptional. He didn't curse, he didn't sing, he didn't even speak. Nor
did he look well. His coat of many colors was listless and raggedy. Not only
did he look as though he'd been plucked and picked on, he looked as though

he had been "buked and scorned," as the faithful Negro spiritual would have it. This sad-faced, underground parrot looked as if he had just been sprung from solitary confinement. And so he had. My mouth fell open when Valve, the parrot's owner, told me the story.

"He's from South America," Valve said, "from Bolivia."

"What kind of parrot is it?"

"A macaw."

"And where do you keep it?" I asked.

"I keep him in there." Valve pointed to the opened door at the end of a row of washing machines that led into a grim and usually padlocked supply closet.

"But," I sputtered, "there are no windows. You mean, you keep him locked up in there in the dark?"

"Look," Valve said, "there's air he can breathe, and what does he need with light? There's really nothing in there to see, is there?"

"But why do you keep him at all?"

Valve turned on his one good leg and said, "Do you know what this bird is worth? He'll fetch me five thousand dollars if he'll fetch a nickel."

"Wow, that's pretty good money."

"Damn right, it is. So now do you understand?"

"No," I told him, "I still think it's cruel to keep any bird locked up in a room with no air and no light."

Indignant, Valve said, "Well, that's *your* problem. He's going right back in the supply room. I feed him, I give him water. That's all he really needs."

"You got a name for him?"

"Nope, not yet. I bought him off a guy who brought him from South America. You're a writer. You got any good ideas for names?"

Again I stared at the poor creature whose straight-ahead gaze was as stark and as fixed as some of the broken inmates I'd met during visits to prisons, where I sometimes get invited to teach or talk about poetry or storytelling or to lead workshops. Because my things were almost ready to come out of the dryer, I decided to stay there in the laundry room and read. Shaking my head, I watched in silence as Valve placed clean newspaper, the local tabloid, around the bottom of the cage. For a moment it occurred to me to write a letter to the *Daily*.

When I stepped off the elevator, my arms piled high with warm, folded clothes, sheets, and towels, there stood Briscoe, my neighbor. An intellectually curious veteran of the American War in Vietnam, Briscoe, a fellow Mississippian, was carrying *The Sirius Mystery,* by Robert K. G. Temple, the out-of-print book he'd recently loaned me about the Dogon people of Mali, West Africa. We shared an admiration for the Dogon. Secretive about their religion, these people know as much and more than contemporary astronomers and astrophysicists about the virtually invisible star Sirius B, companion star to Sirius. Their knowledge of Sirius B predates its modern discovery in 1970 by at least thirty-two hundred years. From ancient times the Dogon have claimed this star as their ancestral homeland. They also knew about Saturn's rings and Jupiter's four major moons millennia before Galileo invented his telescope. Briscoe and I shared an interest in at least a dozen such subjects. We had a rapport.

"You look upset," he said.

"I am upset."

"What about?"

"Just now, downstairs in the laundry room—"

"What happened, man?"

"Valve had a bird, a parrot. And he keeps him locked up in—you know that little room off the laundry room where they keep supplies?"

"The one that's always got the padlock on it?"

"That's the one."

"Wait," said Briscoe. "You're telling me Valve's got some kinda bird locked up in there?"

"Not just any bird, Briscoe. It's a fancy parrot from Bolivia. It looked awful. I mean, he had feathers missing, and you could tell he wasn't doing so hot."

"Damn!" Briscoe's face lit up. "And it's probably illegal."

"Illegal?" I said. "What it is, is inhumane."

"Inhumane like a motherfucker," said Briscoe. "But why does that surprise you? Somewhere down the line, there's probably some money in it for Valve. I just wish I could get him to come up here and fix my stove."

"And there's stuff I need repaired, too."

"Tell you what you need to do," said Briscoe. "Look, man. You are articulate, and people around here respect you as a writer."

"You flatter me, Briscoe. Do you really think people in Silicon Valley still read anything except tech manuals and how-to books?"

"No, here's what I'm saying. . . . You need to write this up and take it over to City Hall."

"City Hall?"

"Take it straight to the mayor and to the city council."

"Briscoe, what good is that gonna do?"

"Al, you know as well as I do—white people don't like that shit. They hate it—mistreating birds and animals, messing over whales and owls and eagles. They won't stand for it. They care more about a missing cat or a dog than they care about you or me. In fact, they're prepared to make your ass extinct in a minute before they'll let anybody fuck with a timberwolf."

"So you're saying—"

"Blow Valve out of the water—that's what. Expose his tacky, cold-blooded ass."

Stunned for the moment at Briscoe's suggestion, I let it roll around in my head until it made me laugh. I laughed so hard I almost dropped my clean laundry.

"That's some funny shit, ain't it?" Briscoe boomed. "Now, they came over here, wiped out the Indians, chopped down the forest, dumped everything they could think of into the rivers and the lakes, buried radioactive shit in places we still to this day don't know about. They got rid of public transportation and put everybody in cars. They got me all messed up with this Agent Orange, tore up those people's country with chemicals and land mines, and now here they come, talking about 'Save the Planet.' Sheee-it, the black male—we're an endangered species, too, you know."

"Hey, Briscoe, I'll have to think about your city hall idea."

"You tell the city what you just now told me. Before you know it, I guarantee, they'll have some kinda special animal rescue squad over here to handcuff Valve and haul him away, and then some organization will up and nurse that parrot back to health."

"Yeah," I said, "if only that parrot would speak up."

The incident inspired me to do some reflecting. Early in the last century, and the century before that, most Americans—my grandparents, for example—

who knew anything about nature, knew it through work. They hunted and trapped or fished for food; they farmed and preserved. I am now old enough to remember the Mississippi woods and farmlands I roamed and explored with other kids in the 1940s: the creeks we swam, the mineral springs and wells we drank from, and all the farm procedures. We milked cows, churned our own butter, made our own soap, planted and harvested, and picked fruit from trees. We literally lived off the land. Growing up that way, without running water or electricity, using mules and horses for transportation and plowing, we might as well have inhabited the nineteenth, eighteenth, or seventeenth centuries. Agribusiness might have been going strong in California, but it hadn't yet run small farmers off the land in the South.

By the late twentieth century, Americans experienced nature largely through recreation: hiking, skiing, surfing, scuba diving, mountain climbing. And yet few realize that it was colonialism in general (and British colonialism in particular) that popularized the notion that nature was something to be tamed or conquered. "The Conquest of Everest," "The Conquest of Space"—such phrases still express relatively recent attitudes toward the natural world.

The capitalist view of nature as an endless source of raw materials and material riches persists. We now know that the present rate of runaway manufacturing and consumption will exhaust and shut down the rain forest in less than fifty years. Does it matter? Does it matter that the crack in the ozone layer, reported some years ago, has grown into a hole the diameter of several midwestern states? One of my buddies now quips that once Americans tire of sport utility vehicles, they'll start driving buses. They'll start passing bills to widen the streets and driveways to expand parking space.

"Can you picture it?" he says. "One or two people to a bus—their own individual, private, *personal* bus—hogging up traffic and talking on a satellite phone? Or maybe, by then, they'll be looking at their talkmate on a videophone."

In the middle of Europe's eighteenth century, when romanticism—an artistic sentiment, a predisposition—grew legs and developed as a full-fledged, walking, talking art movement, it traveled quickly to the colonies. Jean-Jacques Rousseau, coiner of the phrase "noble savage," had kicked off romanticism in France. The individual was *it* and not only *it* but all that mattered. Literary life alone in England and America thickened with romantic spirit. Rejecting city life and the spread of industrialism, the English romantics—Shelley, Byron, Keats, Thomas Gray, Samuel Coleridge, and William Blake, among others—did their part to exoticize nature.

Nature, in the romantic scheme of things, stood apart from humans; romantics viewed it as some kind of "objective reality." Traditional societies, on the other hand, have always regarded humans as an inseparable part of the natural world. In America, the prose of Ralph Waldo Emerson and Henry David Thoreau (who, the whole time he was over in Walden, getting close to nature, brought his dirty laundry home for his mother to do), Nathaniel Hawthorne, James Fenimore Cooper's "noble savage" redskins, Washington Irving, and the poetry of Edgar Allan Poe and Walt Whitman came down hard on the side of romanticism.

In what we like to think of as the postmodern world, romanticism—with its obsessive focus on the individual—is alive and thriving. All you have to do is pick up a mass-market magazine, snap on the TV or radio, or surf the internet to see how deeply we remain under its spell. Advertisements are all about *my* dandruff, *my* running shoes, *my* personal computer, *my* thirst, *my* four-wheel-drive Jeep.

How would an audience react to a shot that slowly pulls back from a tight close-up on a glamorous model to gradually reveal everything that has gone into the making and disposal of a given product? If in some way we were forced to visualize all the people (workers and marketers), all the fuel (and I would not overlook human nourishment), all the vehicles, all the raw materials, and all the natural resources (including sunlight, rain, and wind)? When you add to this the decades it has taken to produce the raw materials, and the generations of human beings it has taken to produce all of the people whose brain, muscle, and blood have gone into manufacturing this product, then we've journeyed from *a* picture to *the* picture. Connectedness or interconnectedness is what I'm talking about here.

Vietnamese Buddhist Thich N'hat Hanh includes in his list of the Five Aggregates the idea of interorigination, which he terms "the interdependence of all events." *This* couldn't have happened if *that* hadn't happened. It sounded like heady stuff until I pulled back and started noticing how intimately I was hooked up to everything around me. With everything I could see, feel, touch, smell, taste, remember, imagine, or make up, I was connected and involved. Often the connections were shocking or hilarious. They helped me understand at a grown-up level why my grandmother would shift from calm to fury whenever she saw me or any of her other grandchildren fouling the slop pail of food scraps we saved to feed the hogs. You didn't fool around with chicken feed or well water, either. Everyday she and the other oldsters found some reason to tell us: "What goes around comes around."

What connects me to Valve and that sad macaw he was sequestering? Several months after I first saw him with the bird, Valve was fired as building super-intendent. Natasha, another tenant, who was as outraged as I was about the silent parrot, reported to me that the poor bird died in that supply-room closet. One day I went down to do laundry and found a large green feather with streaks of yellow, blue, and coral in it.

When I showed Briscoe my keepsake, he said, "Ain't that a bitch? You know, man, we got to learn to be more like the American Indian."

"How so?"

"The Indian, you know, knows all about the Great Spirit. The Indian knows we are one with the earth. Shit, our people back in Mississippi knew that, too. If all you got to believe in is this white man's stuff, I feel sorry for your ass."

"But, Briscoe," I said, knowing I would get his goat. "I thought you were a good Democrat."

"Uh-uh, look out now! You know I don't play that Democrat-Republican shit. I figured that one out while I was over in Vietnam."

"Figured what out?"

"It was the Republicans *and* the Democrats, both, had my ass over there. And it's the Democrats *and* the Republicans that's got me messed up now. And on top of that, the government still won't admit they did anything wrong. At least we get a little medical attention now. The poor Persian Gulf Syndrome vets don't get shit. It's like my boy John Oliver Killens was say-ing when he wrote that novel—what's the title of that book we were talking about?"

"And Then We Heard the Thunder?" I said.

"That's it, yes! *And Then We Heard the Thunder.* Man, that's a bad book. I loved it. I'm talking about pure-dee bipartisan ignorance. *Multi*partisan, where that shit be coming at you from all sides. I used to read that book in

Vietnam, and then I'd lie down on the ground to catch a nap. I used to get in some good naps over there. But then one of those damn grenades or explosions would go off and wake you up."

This was the very way Briscoe and I conversed—that is, on his good days.

"Native peoples believed the earth was alive," I said.

"That's right," said Briscoe.

"The earth was alive, the river was alive, trees were alive, the sky was alive, fire was alive . . ."

"Amen, brother."

"And the earth was sacred. The earth didn't leave off over here, then human beings picked up and began someplace else. They believed we were a part of the whole picture."

"That's right," said Briscoe, "but you know you're preaching to the choir, don't you? The earth knew how to take seeds and make 'em grow into whatever that seed was intended to become. Now you got the man fucking with the seeds and fucking with the earth and fucking with the water and fucking with the air and—"

"Hold on, Briscoe. The original meaning of the word 'fuck' is 'to plow.'"

"Oh, yeah? Is that Greek or Latin or something?"

"No, Anglo-Saxon."

Briscoe considered this. "Well, some kinda way, that figures, too, doesn't it? Because they have really fucked over everything and everybody."

"So," I said, "if you believe the earth is alive, and the waters, and the trees and the sky, and you're related to it all—then you treat all of it with respect."

"The Indians did," said Briscoe. "And the Africans did, too."

"But if you don't believe those things are alive, and if you don't believe they have anything to do with you—"

"Except," Briscoe broke in and said, "*except* provide you with the means to turn a quick buck, like your boy Valve with that pitiful-ass parrot he had holed up down there . . ."

"In which case," I said, picking up where I imagined he'd trailed off, "it's okay to dump pesticides and nuclear waste and PCBs and anything at all into the earth."

"Right," said Briscoe. "Dump it round where black people and Mexicans and Indians live."

"And poor whites," I added.

"Thank you, brother. You know, Little Charlie—Bubba, like they call him down home—he's so busy believing that bad propaganda they put out about us—hogging up all the welfare, dealing all the drugs, taking all the drugs, committing all the crimes—until he forgets they're messing him over, too. Now, you take Valve with his raggedy self . . ."

"Wait," I said. "I want to come back to something you said."

Briscoe threw up his hands. "Both of us have said so much, I can't remember half of what I just now said."

I said, "But I do. You were talking about ignorance."

"Ignorance, yeah, it's plenty of that everywhere you go. Even right here in Silicon Valley. You ought to hear some of the ignorant stuff I have to listen to when I go out on these computer programming jobs."

"Well," I said, "to clean silicon requires some heavy chemical solutions, you know. Here in the valley they send up hundreds of tons of chemicals everyday. People think it's a clean industry, but that's only because they can't see what's happening."

Briscoe, a habitual sniffler, was always trying out holistic treatments for his drastic sinus condition, which was Agent Orange related. He said, "You don't have to tell me. I'm walking proof. That shit is doing a number on me, on you, on all of us."

"So, Briscoe, tell me, what do we do about all this?"

"I already told you. But since you didn't go down to City Hall, and since you didn't write no letter to the editor of the paper, you still got to tell this story. It takes somebody like you to tell this so people can understand. The average person can't understand what these Green Peace people and ecology people are driving at. I used to didn't understand it, either. Far as I was concerned, that was white yuppie stuff, part of all them protests I missed out on in the sixties and early seventies because I was over there fighting communism, making the world safe for democracy."

Briscoe grinned his sly, coy grin. "At least that's what they told me I was doing. And now China and the United States are tighter than Dick's hatband. Tell you, after this Agent Orange started kicking my ass, I woke up in a hurry. You got to write about this, man. And when you do, be sure and put in there about how crack and heroin, which the CIA put on us, how that's a hazardous waste substance, too.

"And put in about all this plastic the government lets big companies package stuff in, then we're the ones supposed to figure out how to recycle it. And get in something about the way they're locking up all the black people and Mexicans in jail, and making it a cheap labor source, business you can invest in on the stock market—work some of that in, too."

I brought the parrot feather upstairs to my kitchen, where I attached it to the hanging wire storage basket of onions and apples and oranges and bananas. I didn't want to forget what had happened.

Remembering the pens people used to fashion from feathers, and that big captive bird's last frozen gaze, I knew I would one day follow Briscoe's suggestion and get some of it down in black and white.

THE ART GALLERY

Elmaz Abinader

The house was filled with light, the kind that flattens itself in squares against the wall; framing the plain green paint, the embroidered textiles; handprints. A white early evening, and I was at a party in the east end of Jerusalem—on the Palestinian side. The guests were in tight, urgent conversations with one another. Most people were smoking; no one seemed to be eating, although a table along one wall of the room offered small dishes with shiny olives, stacks of Arabic bread, smooth-surfaced dips, and rounds of crisp-looking cucumber. I held a glass of warm ginger ale and introduced myself to no one, just wandered around, glancing at a painting of an old Moroccan market, running my finger along the mother-of-pearl shaped into a diamond on the lid of a mosaic box. Many of the things on the shelves were familiar: etched brass plates, blue glass bottles, a brass incense burner. This could be a house in Jordan or Lebanon, with its stone exterior, cold floors, and brocade furniture. But it was not. Rather it sat on a slight hillside in Palestine, where I couldn't sleep, where I couldn't write; where my thinking became frantic. My starling wings were stilled and immobile. I counted my steps, closed my ears, smoothed my feathers. I was happy not to be noticed.

I loved this house. It was modest, bright, and simple. No maids lingering around, no guests dressed with a sense of high fashion. It could be my house with high bookshelves—rows of books in English, their paper backs curled and pages frazzled at the sides. Yellow walls, a table that holds six, one easy chair, and an assortment of other chairs pulled out to accommodate guests. Rooms opened to one another, offered continuous space.

The party was for a consulate official who was retiring. It had nothing to do with my visit, and I was relieved. My country host, Dena, brought me along, and my presence here was unexpected and a little insignificant. I assured her I was fine alone taking everything in, the room, the guests. She offered me more to drink and introduced me to some people whose names I didn't remember a few seconds later. We spoke for a minute about the party, my impressions of Palestine, then went our separate ways—they to friends, me to walking along the tile of the house, drifting in and out of small groups.

I wandered into the small enclosed porch where several men were speaking in Arabic. Two were facing the approaching twilight through the window. A man with a beard greeted me in Arabic, asking the question that prompted me to give my name and to apologize that I didn't speak Arabic.

The only man in a suit responded, "Yes, the writer, Dena told us you would be here." He introduced himself as Nabeel and presented his three companions.

Their names passed in a small breeze above my head, but I stayed there, caught in their solace, the meditative mood that filled the air. Nabeel pointed to the other men who were standing together. "These are the greatest Palestinian artists, and we're talking about their new show."

I turned to them, one bearded with romantic eyes, the other quite tall and almost sandy-haired, and the last bald and older than the other two. "It's such a pleasure to meet you. A real pleasure. I am so excited." Words crashed all over each other as I spoke; I was not sure they understood me. The greatest artists in Palestine attracted me more than all the literati, consulate officials, journalists, escorts, or professors I met on these trips. Art has no "official line" or rehearsed rant. I moved in closer. "Tell me about your work. Please."

The bearded one turned to his friends and translated. He shifted his eyes back to me and they spoke quite quickly but softly. He nodded his head once. "I used to paint with oils and do some sculptures, but the three of us agreed to only use materials that comes from here." He poked two fingers toward the ground. "Here from Palestine."

I looked at the floor, the flat ceramic tile in a sandy shade. My inner voice repeated what he had said about using Palestine in their work. There was a life under this floor, I remembered, a land that was perpetual even in the midst of the battle. Stones, rock, soil, subsoil, grass, weeds, fallen leaves, mulch, dirt, flowers, dead or growing. Using their country to create art— their country, occupied and invaded. Beneath my feet, as I walked from one end of Jerusalem to another, were the grains of multiple histories, stones of many memories; earth that grew hate, anger, protection, and possession. I toured Jerusalem with my head lifted, examining the architecture of the past, the icons of each legacy that built this city. This artist traveled head down, targeting materials among the scrub of Palestine. I tried to imagine his hands scooping up the dirt underneath.

"Do you mean you make clay from the earth of Palestine?"

He rubbed his forefinger and thumb together then pulled them back quickly. "We do. We takes plants and makes colors." His arms opened. "And, and . . ." His gaze fogged a little.

"Just natural things or salvage too?"

He turned toward Nabeel who shrugged his shoulders, moved a hand side to side.

I shifted—not sure.

Nabeel asked, "Explain again?"

"I understand how natural things from the plants and dirt of Palestine are used. I was asking if there are other things, like old things, thrown-away things."

Nabeel nodded and interpreted for the artist. What pieces of Palestine constructed the canvas or the figure and form? Whose footprints were in the colors of his paintings? Did they manifest in a terra-cotta tone, muted and as dried as the earth, or is there a brilliance drawn from the flowers, seeds, and grass?

The bearded artist shook his head. "Not me, no." He pointed to the taller artist. "He use pipes and wires and bombs pieces and bullet . . . things."

"Shells," I offered.

The sculptor pantomimed wire bending with his hands.

"How big are the sculptures?" I flattened my hand beside me as if I was measuring the height of a child.

He touched my hand gently and raised it until it was stretched above my head.

"I understand."

The sculptor spoke to the painter and then left the room. We stood alone near the window. Outside, the air was graying and the lights from the nearby houses went on. I wished I could remember his name, talk to him in Arabic, artist-to-artist, imagination-to-imagination, cause-to-cause. How long have I taken what's beneath my feet for granted—walking, hiking, running the long trails in the hills near my home. So then when the earth becomes the fight, how could I give up ownership or steal pieces of it like these men do?

The artist continued. "Yes, we use nothing artificial at all. Not for color, not for frame."

I pictured his hands plucking leaves from bushes growing from the gravelly earth, smelling them, putting them in a pot. The reds were pushed from flowers and extracted from seeds; the greens from grass and stems; the yellows swiped from bushes and weeds. He offered me a filterless cigarette, took one himself, and in the glow of the flame, his eyes burned too. He picked a piece of tobacco from his tongue. The fingers that scooped up the earth. This was ownership; this was distilling the land of occupation. Transforming it. Grain by grain he was gathering Palestine in a way it could not be taken from him.

"May I see your work?"

"It is very close by," he threw his hand toward the window. "At a very good gallery."

I mentally reviewed my schedule. I could borrow a driver and maybe go on an afternoon free of other events. I would invite the artists to come and I might take pictures of them beside their pieces. We would have dinner and I would memorize their stories; remember them like poetry, take them back with me. This would be a great gift to receive while I was here—rather than another book, another manuscript, a promise to try and translate someone's work, I could carry the sense of Palestine through the eyes of this painter and his colleagues. The other guests were a low hum and seemed to be far away. I was excited. The air outside the porch was gray and quiet; rows of houses marched up the hill. Where could the gallery be?

"I would love to come to the gallery, but I would like to come when you are there. It would be a pleasure to talk to you about your work. Is it possible? When could we meet?"

He dropped the cigarette onto the floor and stomped on it while he translated to his friends. They snorted some response that involved hands and head shakes.

The bearded artist stared out the window, his face now in profile. "I cannot join you."

I was stricken for a moment. "I'm sorry; I didn't mean to impose." My hands were sweaty and I watched a small white car climb the stone street. "You must be very busy and in high demand."

His face did not shift. "You see, the gallery is on the other side of the border."

"But I thought you said it was nearby."

Every place I traveled, short or long distances, I was surprised by the number of checkpoints, the inspections, and the interrogations of my driver or of me. The borders became familiar, and when I saw a group of soldiers standing along the road, I automatically pulled out my passport.

"Yes," he nodded and pointed up the street. I followed his fingers to the top of the hill. The road crested next to a jumble of a playground with a slide and some swings. "The border is there."

Suddenly, near the playground next to houses that resembled the house where we were standing, I could make out, as plain as the moon, a small guardhouse. Sitting in the entrance, a sentry was smoking and blowing long streams that were caught by the streetlight. His M16 was on his lap, angled toward the sky.

Although I had spent most of the night watching the dusk arrive, the street turn from white to gray, I had missed this detail—this signpost reminding me that the mosaic boxes in this living room weren't the ones on my coffee table in California, or that the brass plates weren't the set hanging on the walls of my mother's family house in Lebanon. That a road was not a road, but a line that boxed us in this moment of time. The artist understood this. He recognized the intangible lines in the dark, the ones that divided standing at a dinner party from being handcuffed on the roadside. I did not have the eyes of the Palestinian who knew where he could step and move, whose foot on one block, which resembled another block that could be home, was actually across the parallel of safety, was over the DMZ, was forever in prison, was suspicion of terrorism, was the end to a house, or school, or the wholeness of his family.

I withdrew from the window as if I was about to step on a land mine. I was so lucky. My writing was portable, could be folded and tucked in my back pocket. My books could be printed and copied, distributed and read. They didn't depend on place, here or there. His paintings were confined not only to the small audience that viewed them, but they were also kept from the artist, from their fatherland. The water around my heart was rising, the tide was in.

I turned back to the artist. Sifting through the words that would say . . . the sorrow I wanted to express, I found myself muted. We stood in silence and kept our eyes on the road. I was anxious seeing a playground, a border, a rifle. This was occupation. Not just political rallies, disturbed funeral parades, border checks, artillery, and stones. It was also a rifle next to a child's swing. A soldier outside the bedroom window, his smoke rings rising toward invisible stars. I felt defenseless. This was everyday for the artist, his family, his friends, his town. He could not move forward or across; so he went down to the earth and through it. Palestine was not only Palestine, but also the colors of a boat, the sky, water; of imagination and of freedom.

I was learning everything I needed to know just standing here, next to him, watching a car slow at the top of the hill, the soldier talking to the driver, papers passing through the window. But I imagined the artist was not seeing this—he was searching in the night for the gallery where his paintings hung—just out of his reach.

TOUCHING ON SKIN

Kimiko Hahn

All depends on the skin you're living in
—*Sekou Sundiata*

Container, wrapper, largest tissue, permeable line between inside and remote; as porous/boundary, lovely dialectic. And in the context of an exchange with Meena and Jessica, gendered and colored.

A few weeks ago, we three talked about borders, a subject so complex that we could only give way to its complexities—rather than attempt immediate distillation. (Plus, complexities are more fun—)

A distinct yellow, for instance, might translate into community and/or market. When neither is the case, the aesthetics that remain Asian American in my mind are passed. Passed up instead of passed along. (What happens to a *zuihitsu* on necrophilia? To the asymmetry in a piece on premature burial?)

Aesthetics? For me, what Japanese call *kotoba*—i.e., *words* (such as wordplay or literary allusion) and, for immigrants and their offspring, a relationship to at least two languages that makes both speech and the self anxious about expression.

The companion aesthetic is *kokoro,* literally *heart.* In that conversation, we spoke about home, real and symbolic. The real is real: whether Jessica's Manila or Meena's Kerala. Both *kokoro* and *kotoba* engender my deepening interest in Japanese forms. Not as an Experiment, but as a given. I am not being Experimental with *zuihitsu* and *tanka*—I am working within a tradition, albeit in the English language in America in the twenty-first century. So my heart resides in a real and idealized, say, Maui *or* Ground Zero, as well as *haibun.* And what are forms but boundaries for the subjective?

Which brings me back to the epigraph and to the word *depend.* We all depend on borders—to protect us as well as to cross and double-cross. In William Carlos Williams's famous usage, there are at least three meanings: *to be affected or decided by other factors; to vary according to the circumstances; to hang down or be suspended by something.*

I depend on my skin. On this wall. This pigeonhole. This frontier.

I am always this skin. I am always *not two-halves, not two-wholes,* but *two three-quarters,* in feeling. An incompletion, a wealth, a lack, a home, a diaspora, et cetera. At times, an Asian American version of *high yellow.* Mongrel. Hybrid.

Such skin is also a kind of room where I can work freely. Take risks in subject and craft. *(Kokoro, kotoba—)* Be an artist. That margin.

Boiled milk, drum, peach, flick, et cetera.

But what is defined as protection can transform into the site for torture. *Threshold.* Or the possibility for identification and exclusion. *Or* various kinds of inclusion, some exhilarating.

I look at my face: not exactly white. Or the color of my mother's face. I look at color. Like I don't belong. But this tissue *houses me,* holds my heart inside. I belong to my own color. My daughters, to their own colors. Meena and Jessica's children, to their own colors. The color belongs to me.

(Even as there is traffic in flesh—)

Strange, how an object that is defined as protection, inspires so much terror. And passion.

Priests say that a church is not *the church*; it is merely the building. And especially because I am not religious, so, too, my skin is where I belong. So too, this is the point from where we, idealistically enough, determine that we all have skin; ergo—wherever you are, Sekou, as ever, I depend on your words as the skin I'm living in.

3

ENCOUNTER

THE THINKING MEN

For the builders of Old Main, circa 1856

Nikky Finney

"Tradition has it that the workmen were Negro slaves; but whether that
applies to only the common laborers or to skilled workmen I cannot say."
—*David Duncan Wallace,* History of Wofford College, 1854–1949

We were more than blue fingers & endless backs.
To teach us was against the law. Our math, mind,
and muscle could see beyond what they thought
they had enslaved.

We knew more than we could say.

In the middle of a cow field every heart hammered
purpose, nailed a learning floor, poured tower one
and two, one hundred feet high,

arms & legs ballooned and sweltered in the endless
daily march & task, holding close okra soup,
waist beads, and the old, old names
back across the water.

We slid and nagged adze & auger, laid roof & wall
from east to west, all progress depending upon
weather, twenty-pennies, and architect's disposition.

We were thinking men. Our hands were living blackboards.

A true and readable account is what we wanted left
behind. The toil and task of character planted
in the soft stew of oak, dirt, rain, tar, & longleaf pulp.

From can see to can't see, in between the pegging
and plugging of labor, a man can sign his name to his
grindstone task with or without budget or permission.

With or without quill or lead a signature
can still be minted in vermilion mud.

Who he is and the thing done, melded
into his own cash & coin, as long as the walls

themselves stand tall. This was no simple field fence,
some easy throw of dung, sod, & sop, meant to keep
hog & mountain lion out. We raised this place

in the name of the new day coming, how we would,
one day, be counted, along with the day-to-day blight
of life equally wormed out. We carved out

these doors and hallways for the long grasp and bright
understanding that one day would arrive, realizing
all the while that those who entered might not only

fish for answer, root and dive for more than heads
or tails, but also memorize for the sweet curve and
curl of the words themselves, even if

we could not join in the lifelong hunt for any of it
ourselves. In every arch & swirl of ruby brick
there is a mix of Bantu and Gambian oil, fingernail,
and spit. Tin cups of elder chokecherry blood
run along 226 feet & cord.

In every whorl of mud a print of our day to day
has been made great and permanent. Math, mind,
and muscle plied deep into each and every dark seam.

The part of us they could see was tethered
like a mule's back. The part they could not: our levitation
into one whole sky of black & beating wing.

It took math and muscle, mortise and tenon, to build
ten plus one recitation rooms, to cut chapel (forty-eight by eighty),
laboratory, office, and one museum (thirty by thirty-seven).

I stood, many a day, in the shadow of the next day
coming, just before the big bell had finished sounding,
just after the shout to line and circle up, testing my

mind against the tired muscle of my spine,
walking the plank before myself, thinking plain,
and in the loud, with reaching, outstretched hands.
Once done, I would bow

to the eyes of that nearly finished room, where I had
cut the floor and windows through myself,
making certain with rule & plane that the good sun

could bounce here and there and high enough,
to reach the precious printed page. This light
and learning floor was the way forward
through the wilderness. Why else keep it from

us with such force and might? They would like
us to believe that some men are born to read
and turn pages, while other men are born to walk
on nails and turn the earth.

Our hands were living blackboards. Math, mind,
and muscle, the long-drawn fingerprints
of thinking men, left behind for good. Here:
in every wall.

All this can leave a clear mark upon a world.

LEARNING THE GRAMMAR OF ANIMACY

Robin Wall Kimmerer

To be native to a place we must learn to speak its language.

I come here to listen, to nestle in the curve of the roots, in a soft hollow of pine needles. To lean my bones against the column of white pine, to turn off the voice in my head until I can hear the voices outside it. The *shhh* of the wind in the needles. Water trickling over rock, nuthatch tapping, chipmunks digging, beechnut falling, mosquito in my ear and something more, something which is not me, for which we have no language, the wordless being of others in which we are never alone. After the drumbeat of my mother's heart, this was my first language.

I could spend a whole day listening. And a whole night. And in the morning, without my hearing it, there might be a mushroom that was not there the night before, creamy white, pushed up from the pine needle duff, out of darkness to light, still glistening with the fluid of its passage. *Puhpohwee.*

Listening in wild places, we witness conversation in a language not our own. I think now that it was a longing to comprehend this language I hear in the woods that led me to science, to learn over the years to speak fluent Botany. Which should not, by the way, be mistaken for the language of plants. In science I did learn another language, of careful observation, an intimate vocabulary that names each little part. To name and describe you must first see, and science polishes the gift of seeing. Science is a beautiful language, rich in particulars, revealing the intricate mechanisms of the world. I honor the strength of that language, which has become a second tongue to me. But, beneath the richness of its vocabulary, its descriptive power, it feels like something is missing, the same something that swells around you, and in you, when you listen to the world. The pattern of its surface hides an empty center, like a gorgeous tapestry over a scarred wall. Science is a language of distance, which reduces a being to its working parts, the language of objects. The language we speak, however precise, is based on a profound error in grammar, which seems to me now a grave loss in translation from the native language of these shores.

My first taste of the missing language was the word *puhpohwee*. I stumbled upon it in a book by the Anishinaabe ethnobotanist Keewaydinoquay, a treatise on the traditional uses of fungi by our people. *Puhpohwee,* she explained, translates as "the force which causes mushrooms to push up from the earth overnight." As a biologist, I was stunned that such a word existed. In all its technical vocabulary, Western science has no such term, no words to hold this mystery. You'd think that biologists, of all people, would have words for *life*. But, I think in scientific language, our terminology is used to define the boundaries of our knowing. That which lies beyond our grasp remains unnamed. In those three syllables I could see an entire process of close observation in the damp morning woods, of the mystery of their coming, the formulation of a theory for which English has no equivalent. The makers of this word understood a world of being, full of unseen energies which animate the world. I've cherished that word for many years, as a talisman, and longed for the people who gave a name to the life force of mushrooms. The language that holds *puhpohwee* is one that I wanted to speak. That word for rising, for emergence became a signpost for me when I learned that it belonged to the language of my ancestors.

Had history been different, I would today likely speak *Bodéwadmimwen* or Potawatomi, an Anishinaabe dialect. Like many of the 350 indigenous languages of the Americas, Potawatomi is threatened. The powers of assimilation have done their work. My chance of hearing that language, and yours too, was washed from the mouths of children in Indian boarding schools where speaking your native language was forbidden. Children like my grandfather, who was taken from his family, just a little boy of nine years old.

This history has scattered our people, and I live far from our reservation; so even if I could speak the language, I would have no one to talk to, except perhaps at our yearly tribal gathering. A few summers ago, a language class was held there, so I slipped into the tent to listen.

There was a great deal of excitement about the class because for the first time, every single fluent speaker in our tribe would be there as teachers. When called forward to the circle of folding chairs, the speakers moved slowly—with canes, walkers, and wheelchairs, only a few under their own power. I counted them as they filled the chairs. Nine. Nine fluent speakers. In the whole world. Our language, millennia in the making, sits in those nine chairs. The words that praised creation, told the old stories, lulled my ancestors to sleep, rests today in the tongues of nine very mortal men and women. Each takes their turn to address the small group of would-be students. A man with long gray braids tells of how his mother hid him away when the Indian agents came to take the children. He escaped boarding school by hiding under an overhung bank where the sound of the stream covered his crying. The others were all taken and had their mouths washed out with soap, or were punished in worse ways, for "talking that dirty Indian language." But, because he alone stayed home and was raised calling the plants and animals by the names Creator gave them, he is here today, a carrier of the language. The engines of assimilation worked well. The speaker's eyes blaze as he addresses us. "We're the end of the road," he says. "We are all that is left. If you young people do not learn, the language will die. The missionaries and the U.S. government will have their victory at last."

A great-grandmother from the circle pushes her walker up close to the microphone. "It's not just the words that will be lost," she says. "The language is the heart of our culture, it holds our thoughts, our way of seeing the world. It's too beautiful for English to explain." I thought of *puhpohwee*.

Jim Thunder, the youngest of the speakers at seventy-five, is a sturdy, brown man of serious demeanor, who spoke only in Potawatomi. He began solemnly, but as he warmed to his subject, his voice lifted like a breeze in the birch trees and his hands began to tell the story. He became more and more animated, rising to his feet, holding us rapt and silent although almost no one understood a single word. He paused as if reaching the climax of his story and looked out at the audience with a twinkle of expectation. One of the grandmothers behind him covered her mouth in a giggle, and his stern face suddenly broke into a smile as big and sweet as a cracked watermelon. He bent over laughing, and the grandmas dabbed away tears of laughter, holding their sides while the rest of us looked on in wonderment. When the laughter had subsided, he spoke in English at last. "What will happen to a joke when no one can hear it anymore? How lonely those words will be, when their power is gone. Where will they go? Off to join the stories that can never be told again."

So, now my house is dotted with sticky notes in another language, as if I were studying for a trip abroad. But, I'm not. I'm coming home.

Ni pi je ezhyayen? asks the little yellow sticky note on my back door. My hands are full, but I switch my bag to the other hip and pause long enough to respond. "*Odanek nde zhya,*" I'm going to town. And so I do, to work, to class, to meetings, to the bank, to the grocery store. I talk all day and sometimes write all evening in the beautiful language I was born to, the same one used by 70 percent of the world's people, a tongue viewed as the most useful, with the richest vocabulary in the modern world. English. When I get home at night to my quiet house, there is a faithful sticky note on the closet door. *Gisken I gbiskewagen!* And so I take off my coat. I cook dinner, pulling utensils from cupboards labeled *emkwanen, nagen.* I have become a woman who speaks Potawatomi to household objects. When the phone rings I barely glance at the sticky note there as I *dopnen* the *giktogan.* And whether it is a solicitor or a friend—they speak English. Once a week or so, it is my sister from the West Coast who says *Bozho. Moktthewenkwe ndaw*—as if she needed to identify herself, who else speaks Potawatomi? To call it "speaking" is a stretch. Really all we do is blurt garbled phrases to each other in a parody of conversation. How are you? I am fine. Go to town. See bird. Red. Fry bread good. We sound like Tonto's side of the Hollywood dialogue with the Lone Ranger. Me try talk good Injun way. On the rare occasion that we actually can string together a halfway coherent thought, we freely insert high school Spanish words to fill in the gaps, making a language we call Spanawatomi.

Tuesdays and Thursdays at twelve fifteen Oklahoma time, I join the Potawatomi lunchtime language class, streaming from tribal headquarters via the Internet. There are usually about ten of us, from all over the country. Together we learn to count and to say pass the salt. Someone asks, "How do you say '*please* pass the salt'?" Our teacher, Justin Neely, a young man devoted to language revival, explains that while there are several words for *thank-you,* there is no word for *please.* Food was meant to be shared, no added politenesses were needed. It was simply a cultural given that one was asking respectfully. The missionaries took this absence as further evidence of crude manners.

Many nights, when I should be grading papers or paying bills, I'm at the computer running through online Potawatomi language drills. After months, I have mastered the kindergarten vocabulary and can confidently match the pictures of animals to their indigenous names. It reminds me of reading picture books to my children. "Can you point to the squirrel? Where is the bunny?" All the while, I'm telling myself that I really don't have time for this and what's more, have little need to know the words for bass and fox. And since our tribal diaspora left us scattered to the four winds, who would I talk to anyway?

The simple phrases I'm learning are perfect for my dog. Sit! Eat! Come here! Be quiet! But since she scarcely responds to these commands in English, I'm reluctant to try and train her to be bilingual. Once an admiring student asked me if I spoke my native language. I was tempted to say, "Oh yes, we speak Potawatomi at home. Me, the dog, and the sticky notes."

Our teacher tells us not to be discouraged. He thanks us every time a word is spoken, he thanks us for breathing life into the language, if we know only a single word. "But I have no one to talk to," I complain. "None of us does," he reassures me. "But, someday, we will."

So, I dutifully learn vocabulary, but find it hard to see the "heart of our culture" in translating "bed" and "sink" into Potawatomi. I found learning nouns to be pretty easy, after all, I'd learned thousands of botanical Latin names and scientific terms in my life. I reasoned that this would not be too different. It's just a one-for-one substitution, a job of memorization. At least on paper, where you can see the letters. Hearing the language is a different story. There are fewer letters in our alphabet, so the distinctions among words for a beginner are often subtle. With the beautiful clusters of consonants of *zh* and *mb* and *shwe* and *kwe* and *mshk,* our language sounds like wind in the pines and water over rocks; you really have to listen.

English is a noun-based language, somehow appropriate to a culture so obsessed with things. Really speaking of course requires verbs and here is where my kindergarten proficiency at naming things leaves off. Only 30 percent of English words are verbs, but in Potawatomi that proportion is 70 percent. Which means that 70 percent of the words have to be conjugated, and 70 percent have different tenses and cases to be mastered.

European languages often assign gender to nouns, so that one has to learn *la mesa* and *el perro.* Potawatomi does not divide the world this way, into masculine and feminine. Nouns and verbs both are classified not as male and female, but as "animate" and "inanimate." You "hear" a person with a completely different word than you "hear" an airplane. Pronouns, articles, plurals, demonstratives, verbs, and all those syntactical bits that I never could keep straight in high school English are all aligned in Potawatomi, so that we have different ways of speaking of the living world and of the lifeless. You use different verb forms, different plurals, different everything depending on whether what you are speaking of is alive. It's very complicated. These verbs nearly halt my efforts.

In frustration I think to myself, "No wonder there are only nine speakers left." I'm trying, I really am, but this complexity makes my head hurt and my ear can barely distinguish between words that mean completely different things. One teacher reassures us that this will come with practice. But another elder concedes that these close similarities are inherent in the language. Stewart King, a knowledge keeper and great teacher, reminds us that the Creator meant for us to laugh. So people deliberately built humor into the syntax, so that a small slip of the tongue can convert "We need more firewood" to "Take off your clothes." In fact, I learned that the mystical word *puhpohwee* is used not only for mushrooms, but for certain other shafts which also rise up mysteriously in the night.

My sister's gift to me one Christmas was a set of magnetic tiles for the refrigerator, in Ojibwe or Anishinabemowin, a language closely related to

Potawatomi. I spread them out on my kitchen table looking for familiar words. The more I look, the more worried I get. Among the hundred or more tiles, there was but a single word that I recognize. *Megwech*—"Thank-you." The small feeling of accomplishment that the months of study had yielded evaporated.

I remember paging through the Ojibwe dictionary she sent, trying to de-cipher the tiles, but the spellings didn't always match and the print was too small and there are way too many variations on a single word and I was feel-ing that this was just way too hard. The threads in my brain were all knotted and the harder I tried the tighter the knots became. The pages blurred and my eyes settled on a word—a verb of course: "to be a Saturday." *Pfft*—I put down the book with the anger of frustration. Since when is Saturday a verb? Everyone knows it's a noun. I flipped more pages. All kinds of things seemed to be verbs . . . my finger finds: "to be a hill," "to be red," "to be a long sandy stretch of beach," and my finger rests on *wiikwegama*: "to be a bay." Things I know with considerable scientific certainty to be nouns and adjectives are presented here as verbs. "Ridiculous!" I rant in my head, "There is no reason to make it so complicated. No wonder no one speaks it. What a cumber-some language, impossible to learn, and more than that—it's all wrong. A bay is most definitely a person, place, or thing; a noun and not a verb." I was ready to give up this struggle. I'd learned a few words, done my duty to the language that was taken from my grandfather. Oh, the ghosts of the mission-aries in the boarding schools must have been rubbing their hands in glee at my frustration. She's going to surrender, they said.

And then I swear I heard the zap of synapses firing. An electric current sizzled down my arm, to my finger and practically scorched the page where that one word lay. In that moment I could smell the water of the bay, watch it rock against the shore, and hear it sift onto the sand. A bay is a noun, only if water is dead. When "bay" is a noun, it is defined by humans, trapped be-tween its shores and contained by the word. But *wiikegama*, to *be* a bay, the verb releases the water from bondage and lets it live. "To be a bay" holds the wonder that, for this moment, the living water has decided to shelter itself between these shores, conversing with cedar roots and a flock of baby mer-gansers. Because it could do otherwise—become a stream or an ocean or a waterfall—and there are verbs for that, too. To be a hill, to be a sandy beach, to be a Saturday . . . all are possible as verbs only in a world where everything is alive. Water, land, and even a day. The language is a mirror for seeing the animacy of the world, for the life that pulses through all things, pines and nuthatches and mushrooms. This *is* the language I hear in the woods, this is the language that lets us speak of what wells up all around us. And now those vestiges of the boarding schools, those soap-wielding missionary wraiths hang their heads in defeat.

This is the grammar of animacy. Imagine seeing your grandmother standing there at the stove in her apron and then saying, "Look, it is making soup. It has gray hair." We might snicker at such a mistake, but recoil from it also. In English, we never refer to a member of our family as "it," or indeed any other person. Such grammar would be a profound act of disrespect. "It" robs a person of selfhood and kinship, reducing a person to a mere "thing." So it is in Potawatomi and most other indigenous languages, we use the same grammar to address the living world as we do our family. Because it is our family.

To whom does our language extend the grammar of animacy? Not just our human relatives, but all our relations. Naturally, plants and animals are animate, but as I learn vocabulary, I am also discovering that Potawatomi understanding of what it means to be animate diverges from the list of attributes of living beings we all learned in Biology 101. In Potawatomi 101, I learn that rocks are addressed as animate, as are mountains and water and fire and places. Those beings imbued with spirit deserve their own grammar— our sacred medicines, our songs, drums, and even stories are animate. The list of the inanimate seems to be smaller—objects which are made by people often fall in this category. Of an inanimate being like a table we say, "*What* is it?" And we answer *Dopwen yewe*. Table it is. But of apple, we must say "*Who* is it?" And reply *Mshimin yawe*. Apple he is.

Yawe—the animate "to be." I am, you are, s/he is. To speak of those possessed with life and spirit we must say *Yawe*. By what linguistic confluence do Yahweh of the Old Testament and *yawe* of the New World both fall from the mouths of the reverent? Isn't this just what it means, to be, to have the breath of life within, to be the offspring of creation? The language reminds us, in every sentence, of our kinship with all of the animate world.

English doesn't give us many tools for incorporating respect for animacy. In English, you're either a human or a thing. Our grammar boxes us in by the choice of reducing a non-human being to an "it," or if it must be gendered, inappropriately a "he" or a "she." Where are our words for the simple existence of another living being? Where is our yawe? My friend Michael Nelson, an ethicist who thinks a great deal about moral inclusion, told me of a woman he knows, a field biologist whose work is among others than humans. Most of her companions are not two-legged. Her language has shifted to accommodate her relationships. She kneels along the trail to inspect a set of moose tracks . . . "Someone's already been this way this morning." "Someone is in my hat," she says, shaking out a deerfly. Someone, not some thing.

When I'm out in the woods with my students who are learning the gifts of plants and to call them by name, I try to be mindful of my language, to be bilingual between the lexicon of science and the grammar of animacy. Although they still have to learn their scientific roles and Latin names, I hope I am teaching them to also know the world as a neighborhood of non-human residents, an animate world. Through our days in the woods together, the most important thing I hope that they come to know is, as Thomas Berry has written, that the "universe is a communion of subjects, not a collection of objects."

One afternoon, I sat with my field ecology students by a *wiikegama*, and shared with them this idea of animate language. One young man, Andy, splashing his feet in the clear water, asked the big question. "Wait a second," he said as he wrapped his mind around this linguistic distinction. "Doesn't this mean that speaking English, thinking in English, somehow gives us permission to disrespect nature? By denying everyone else the right to be persons? Wouldn't things be different if nothing was an 'it'?" I wanted to give him Awiakta's poem, "When Earth Becomes an It".

Being swept away with the idea, he says, feels like an awakening to him. More like a remembering, I think. The animacy of the world is something we already know. But, the language of animacy teeters on extinction, not just for native peoples, but to everyone. Our toddlers speak of plants and animals as if they were people, extending to them self and intention and compassion— until we teach them not to. We quickly retrain them and make them forget. When we tell them that the tree is not a "who" but an "it," we make that maple an object, we put a barrier between us. We set it outside our circle of ethical concern, of compassion. "It-ing" another being absolves us of moral responsibility and opens the door to exploitation. Saying "it" makes a living land into "natural resources." If maple is an "it," we can take up the chain saw. If maple is "she," we have to think twice.

Another student counters his argument. "But, we can't say *he* or *she*; that would be anthropomorphism." They are well-schooled biologists, who have been instructed, in no uncertain terms, to never ascribe human characteristics to a study object, to another species. It's a cardinal sin that leads to a loss in objectivity and, as Carla points out, "It's also disrespectful to the animal. We shouldn't project our perceptions onto them—they have their own ways, they're not just people in furry costumes." Andy counters, "But, just because we shouldn't think of them as humans, they are still beings. Isn't it even more disrespectful to assume that we're the only species that count as persons?" The arrogance of English is its underlying assumption that the only way to be animate, to be worthy of respect and moral concern, is to be a human.

We Americans are reluctant to learn a foreign language of our own species, let alone another species. But imagine the possibilities.

A language teacher I know explained that grammar is just the way we chart relationships in language. Maybe it also reflects our relationships with each other. Who would have guessed that grammar could be a tool of global transformation? A grammar of animacy leads us to whole new ways of living in the world, as if other species were a sovereign people, as if the world were a democracy of species, not a tyranny of one. Where we extend moral responsibility to water and wolves. When we can conceive of a legal system which recognizes the standing of other species. It's all in the pronouns.

Maybe Andy is right. Learning the grammar of animacy could well be a restraint on our mindless exploitation of land. But, there's more to it. I have heard our elders give advice; you should go among the standing people. Or go spend some time with those Beaver people. Reminding us of the capacity of others as our teachers, as holders of knowledge, as guides. Imagine walking through a richly peopled world, none of whom are human. Birch people, bear people, rock people. Persons whom we think of and therefore speak of as beings worthy of our respect, of inclusion in a peopled world. Imagine the access we would have to different perspectives, the things we might see through other eyes, the wisdom that surrounds us. We don't have to figure out everything by ourselves, there are intelligences other than our own, teachers all around us. Imagine how less lonely the world would be.

I still struggle mightily with verbs and can hardly speak at all. I'm most adept with my kindergarten vocabulary. But, I like that in the morning I can go for my walk around the meadow, greeting neighbors by name. When a crow caws at me from the hedgerow, I can call back "*Mno gizhget andushukwe!*" I can brush my hand over the soft grasses and murmur "*Bozho mishkos.*" It's a small thing, but it makes me happy.

I'm not advocating that we all learn Potawatomi or Hopi or Seminole, even if we could. We came to these shores as immigrants speaking a legacy of languages, all to be cherished. But to become native to this place, if we are to survive here and our neighbors too, our work is to learn to speak the grammar of animacy, so that we might truly be at home.

I remember the words of Bill Tall Bull, a Cheyenne elder. As a young person, I spoke to him with a heavy heart, lamenting that I had no native language with which to speak to the plants and the places that I love. "They love to hear the old language," he said, "it's true." With fingers on his lips, he added, "You don't have to speak it here," then patting his chest, "if you speak it here. They will hear you."

LISTENING FOR THE ANCIENT TONES, WATCHING FOR SIGN, TASTING FOR THE MOUNTAIN THYME

Gary Paul Nabhan

"Look where you're walking, cousin!" Shibley shouted to me from upslope. "You're walking through sign!"

I glanced down at my feet, which were for the first time planted on a ridge in the Anti-Lebanon Mountains, the geographic boundary between contemporary Lebanon and Syria. One foot was sinking into a bit of mud, the other more firmly resting on a limestone ledge.

"Sign," I said to myself. Sign. No scat. No tracks. No browsed thyme, thistles, mallows, or mouse tips indicating that wild or domestic animals had passed this way.

"Sign, cousin? What sign?" I asked Shibley, who unlike me had walked this slope ten thousand times since childhood. Shibley Nabhan, who still lived on the outskirts of Zahle in Kfarsibad, the village of our grandparents. Herbalist, hunter, water witcher, and mineral diviner, Shibley had ambled these slopes with shotgun, hoe, or olive-branch witching stick in tow. Field archaeologist, vernacular architect, Shibley had no fancy credentials other than his architect's license, but he did have a lot of street smarts about what this land could say to someone. He hustled downslope to make sure I was getting the message.

"What sign?" I asked again, in case the arid breeze had blown my earlier question away from his ears. This time he was there by my side, leaning his elbow on my shoulder, twisting his salt-and-pepper mustache. We both faced the same direction, looking down at the ground, intent on finding something that I had yet to even imagine.

"What kind of sign?" I whispered to him, conceding my cluelessness.

"This is a sign," he said, pointing downslope with his foot. "This is a sign . . . maybe for treasure. But where they put it, I don't know. The people do it sometimes, these cut marks in the rock, other times, my God does it. *This one?* Not by God, maybe someone out here. . . ."

As he spoke, I began to see. A serpentine shape cut into the limestone. A snake's snout facing downhill.

"It's pointing to the place . . ." and as he shaped vision into words, he scrambled downslope and then up onto a slight rise, smack-dab in the midst of our great grandparents' field.

"See, cousin?" he said, panting, as I caught up with him and caught my breath as well. "See? Big foot of the camel, that's what the snake was reaching for. There, you see?"

I saw: deep in a limestone outcrop, the impression of camel tracks. As vivid as my own shoeprint left in the mud some dozen yards upslope. These signs were hand-carved yesterday; they were perhaps from our nomadic clan's yesteryear.

"They might tell the secret of what is buried for us," Shibley smiled, hopeful.

"Buried beneath this limestone? Isn't this outcrop rather thick?" I asked, as if his hope were based on an incredulous assumption.

"No, not right here on the bedrock . . ." Shibley said, pointing. "Where the camels are walking, you know. Somewhere right before us, here in the earth."

Earth. By that I guessed he meant the shallow lens of limy soil that had somehow remained upon this slope despite ten thousand years of grazing, farming, and foraging. I looked out into the Biqaa Valley far below us; still rich with topsoil, it formed the curve of the Fertile Crescent, where some archaeologists claim that agriculture began. But here in the Anti-Lebanon Mountains, soil a foot and a half deep was a treasure in and of itself.

"Treasure . . ." Shibley murmured.

"Treasure buried under so little soil?" I asked, half in doubt, half in wonder. I hoped that he would read in my voice only the latter.

"Well, maybe not gold, or old-time bronze. Maybe ancestral-ground boundary marker. Maybe where some miracle happened long time ago, marked by our forefathers, those who took camel as their sign. I can never tell what it is, first time. I come back here, over and over and over, trying to know: Which signs from my God, which from Man . . ."

As we continued our descent toward the village, I could not take my eyes off the patches of exposed bedrock beneath my feet. Impressions of the hooves of goats, sheep. Human footprints. A bear claw, which Shibley pointed out to me, though it stood just before where the toes of my shoes touched the ground.

"We still have bear up above our highest pasture, sleeping in caves right now. They don't come down into the pastures much, except when it's too dry. Then they get thirsty, they get hungry."

We hear bells above us. I keep looking down at the bear claw in the bedrock until Shibley nudges me. He has turned to gaze upslope, high into the mountains. He touches my shoulder. I pivot, and realize that he is looking for where the sounding of bells is coming from.

"It's the Bedu," he sighs. "Returning from our highest pasture with a few sheep and goats. We let them graze up there all summer, they give us milk for making yogurt and cheese. The *luban,* the yogurt, you know, it tastes different each week of the summer. That's because the sheep eat different medicines, the wild herbs. If they eat *zaa'tar,* the *luban* tastes like *zaa'tar.*"

Zaa'tar. The wild mountain thyme of the Mediterranean. I had recently learned that it is a witch's brew of aromatic oils. Some chemicals in the thyme arsenal are so potent, they deflect or destroy insect pests. Others are pungent enough to deter browsing by larger animals; after a while, they must move on to the next bush. And there are other aromatic oils exuded onto the leaf surfaces of thyme that slow the loss of water from the plant as a whole, a worthy adaptation for an herb of arid climes.

The most peculiar characteristic of thyme, my colleague Yan Linhart discovered, was that different plants in the same mountain patch each had a different mix of these aromatic oils. Some were better at repelling insects, other at deterring browsers, while others excelled at surviving drought. Collectively, a patch or population of mountain thyme could endure a panoply of stresses, thanks to the heterogeneity of its membership.

As with the camel print held in the rock, if you open yourself to its presence, you could read a patch of thyme in different ways. A treasure, a boundary marker, a little miracle.

The same winter I visited my grandfather's village for the first time, I spent some time where other desert dwellers still live a seminomadic existence halfway around the world from Lebanon. I had invited my Seri Indian friend, Adolfo Burgos, and his wife, Amalia Astorga, to come with me to the now-abandoned village of his own grandfather, at Tecomate Well on Tiburón Island in the Sea of Cortés. They had not visited there for some time, in part because the Mexican government had tried to sedentarize the Seri on the mainland, away from their island home.

As soon as we arrived, Adolfo began to pray and sing while Amalia danced around the well, evoking the spirits of those who had been born, lived, and died there in the past. After two hours of showing us details of this coastal encampment, describing each with great emotion, they felt drained and tired; we headed back toward the beach. But as we did, I noticed a giant sprawling cactus on the edge of the camp with sticks stuck into the ends of its arms. Suddenly, I realized that this multiarmed cactus, known in Spanish as *pitahaya agria,* could not be found at all in the surrounding natural vegetation. It was, in fact, altogether rare on the north side of the island.

I had heard that plunging miniature harpoons into the tops of giant cacti was boys' play in Seri villages, but I had also heard that it was part of a sacred rite. Although I knew that Amalia was pretty exhausted, I took her hand and walked over to the cactus with her, hoping that she might have enough reserve to at least comment on the wood rods stuck high in the arms of this rare cactus. When we arrived at the base of the cactus, she looked up at it for a moment, saying nothing. Then she looked all around us, and back toward the well, as if to gauge where it was placed.

"See," she said, pointing to one of the hand-carved rods stuck horizontally into an upper branch of the spiny cactus, "this was inserted when a baby was born here. Since then, the cactus has grown upward from the height of the rod," and she pointed to the length of cactus stem rising above where the stick had pierced the flesh of a younger cactus. Then, she added matter-of-factly, "Many of us have a plant like this, which our parents used to mark our birthplace, the very day we were born."

I did not fully fathom what she was saying. "The rod was put into the cactus when that spot was at the tip of the branch?"

She looked at me kindly, realizing that I couldn't understand it all. "The very day a child was born here, this cactus was transplanted to the very place where the child's placenta was buried."

"You mean the cactus was planted here and the rod was stuck into it the same day?" My mind reeled.

"Yes, so that later on, they could show the child where he was born and how much the cactus had grown since then. Many of us know where our plants still grow. I know my saguaro cactus, it's over at Campo Onah. When I was a newborn, they hammered a stick into a cactus that they brought there from a place nearby. The plant belongs to me, the person born the same day. That's where they buried my placenta."

The Seri have a phrase to describe the place and time of birth, of burying your placenta back into the earth: *Hant Haxp M-ihiip. Hant,* they say, means "time, place, world, earth." *Haxp M-ihiip,* they say, means "birth." A cactus to commemorate when and where you hit the ground, coming out of your mother, when and where your placenta went back into the earth.

I can no longer imagine Seri territory without envisioning thousands of cacti and elephant trees transplanted across the desert, marking spots where babies first broke into light, where their grandparents and godparents hammered or harpooned small sticks into plant flesh so that they could later show the children how much they had grown. I cannot imagine my grandparents' own natal grounds without remembering the ancient camel, sheep, and snake prints that will always surround them. Whatever I viscerally felt as my sense of place before last winter, it has been indelibly changed by touching transplanted cactus, deepened by walking among bedrock carvings of animal tracks, and flavored by mountain thyme overwhelming the other wild fragrances in sheep milk. If I had not learned from my grandparents, uncles, aunts, and cousins how to look at, walk across, and taste the world, I would not have an inkling how to do that among other cultures, and my own meager life would be far poorer. But as it stands, I have the scent of thyme on my hands, and cactus thorns have been tattooed into my memory.

Ever since I worked as a student intern at the first Earth Day's headquarters in 1970, I have wondered why the so-called environmental movement is so clumsy at reaching out to speak to folks like my cousin Shibley or to my Seri Indian friends like Adolfo and Amalia. Or more to the point, it can hardly hear their voices or see their signs. Conference after conference of nature literature, meeting after meeting of environmental activists, we receive group photos that largely look as though they are underexposed, as if they consist of monotones, not the range of colors, characters, and communities that collectively inhabit the earth. When I worked that spring of 1970 in Earth Day headquarters, I often slept on the mailbags in the headquarters office, a floor above a coffee shop where African, Caribbean, and Latin Americans would congregate late at night after the jazz and blues clubs had closed up their bars. Why did it seem, at the time, that those two floors of the same building represented divided worlds? Why was there no jazz flowing into our ears as we worked? Why were there so few people of color, people of the soil, among our ranks?

That gap has shrunk some since 1970, but few folks I know are content that it has shrunk enough. More than anything else, I want to imagine a dialogue between cultures living in the same homeground, I want to hear a bunch of nature writers swapping tales the way musicians in a jazz band swap riffs. I want us to find a groove where sounds from all around us, a wide range of natures, a wide range of cultures, play off one another, rising and diving, blending, diverging, skipping across the surface like perfectly thrown stones across a pond. I want to watch the ripples they make, as they spread out and stretch and take on new shapes in every little cove they flow into. I want to see them as they each begin to read one another's sign, as they hear the ancient ringing in the mountain echoing down to where they stand together, grateful to be in one another's presence.

EARTHBOUND

on solid ground

bell hooks

Kentucky hills were the place of my early childhood. Surrounded by a wilderness of honeysuckle, wild asparagus and sheltering trees, bushes shielding growing crops, the huge garden of a black landowner. Our concrete house on the hill, a leftover legacy from oil drilling, from the efforts of men to make the earth yield greater and greater profit, stood as a citadel to capitalism's need for a new frontier. A child of the hills, I was taught early on in my life the power in nature. I was taught by farmers that wilderness land, the untamed environment, can give life, and it can take life. In my girlhood I learned to watch for snakes, wildcats roaming, plants that irritate and poison. I know instinctively; I know because I am told by all-knowing grown-ups that it is humankind and not nature that is the stranger on these grounds. Humility in relationship to nature's power made survival possible.

Coming from "backwoods" folks, Appalachian outlaws, as a child I was taught to understand that those among us who lived organically, in harmony and union with nature, were marked with a sensibility that was distinct, and downright dangerous. Backwoods folks tend to ignore the rules of society, the rules of law. In the backwoods, one learned to trust only the spirit, to follow where the spirit moved. Ultimately, no matter what was said or done, the spirit called to us from a place beyond words, from a place beyond man-made law. The wild spirit of unspoiled nature worked its way into the folk of the backwoods, an ancestral legacy, handed down from generation to generation. And its fundamental gift, the cherishing of that which is most precious— freedom. And to be fully free, one had to embrace the organic rights of the earth.

Humankind, no matter how powerful, cannot take away the rights of the earth. Ultimately nature rules. That is the great, democratic gift the earth offers us—that sweet death to which we all inevitably go—into that final communion. No race, no class, no gender, nothing can keep any of us from dying into that death where we are made one. To tend the earth is always then to tend our destiny, our freedom, and our hope.

These lessons of my girlhood were the oppositional narratives that taught me to care for the earth, to respect country folk. This respect for the earth, for the country girl within, stood me in good stead when I left this environment and entered a world beyond the country town I was raised in. It was only when I left home, that country place where nature's splendors were abundant and not yet destroyed, that I understood for the first time the contempt for country folk that abounds in our nation. That contempt has led to a cultural disrespect for the farmer, for those who live simply in harmony with nature. Writer, sometime farmer, and poet Wendell Berry, another Kentuckian who loves our land, writes in his book *Another Turn of the Crank* that "communists and capitalists are alike in their contempt for country people, country life, and country places."

Before the mass migrations to northern cities in the early nineteen hundreds, more than 90 percent of all black folks lived in the agrarian south. We were indeed a people of the earth. Working the land was the hope of survival. Even when that land was owned by white oppressors, master and mistress, it was the earth itself that protected exploited black folks from dehumanization. My sharecropping granddaddy jerry would walk through neat rows of crops and say, "I'll tell you a secret, little girl. No man can make the sun or the rains come—we can all testify. We can all see that ultimately we all bow down to the forces of nature. Big white boss may think he can outsmart na-ture, but the small farmer know. Earth is our witness." This relationship to the earth meant that Southern black folks, whether they were impoverished or not, knew firsthand that white supremacy, with its systemic dehumaniza-tion of blackness, was not a form of absolute power.

In that world, country black folks understood that though powerful white folks could dominate and control people of color, they could not con-trol nature or divine spirit. The fundamental understanding that white folks were not gods (for if they were they would be able to shape nature) helped imbue black folks with an oppositional sensibility. When black people mi-grated to urban cities, this humanizing connection with nature was severed; racism and white supremacy came to be seen as all-powerful, the ultimate factors informing our fate. When this thinking was coupled with a break-down in religiosity, a refusal to recognize the sacred in everyday life, it served the interests of white supremacist capitalist patriarchy.

Living in the agrarian south, working on the land, growing food, I learned survival skills similar to those that hippies sought to gain in their back-to-the-earth movements in the late sixties and early seventies. Growing up in a world where my grandparents did not hold regular jobs but made their living digging and selling fishing worms, growing food, and raising chickens, I was ever mindful of an alternative to the capitalist system that destroyed nature's abundance. In that world I learned experientially the concept of interbeing, which Buddhist monk Thich N'hat Hanh talks about as that recognition of the connectedness of all human life.

That sense of interbeing was once intimately understood by black folks in the agrarian south. Nowadays it is only those of us who maintain our bonds to the land, to nature, who keep our vows of living in harmony with the environment, who draw spiritual strength from nature. Reveling in na-ture's bounty and beauty has been one of the ways enlightened poor people in small towns all around our nation stay in touch with their essential good-ness even as forces of evil, in the form of corrupt capitalism and hedonistic consumerism, work daily to strip them of their ties to nature.

Journalists from the *New York Times* who interviewed Kentucky po' rural folk getting by with scarce resources were surprised to find these citizens ex-pressing a connection to nature. In a recent article titled "Forget Washington.

The Poor Cope Alone," reporter Evelyn Nieves shared: "People time and again said they were blessed to live in a place as beautiful as Kentucky, where the mountains are green and lush and the trees look as old as time." Maintaining intimacy gives us a concrete place of hope. It is nature that reminds us time and time again that "this too will pass." To look upon a tree or a waterfall that has stood the test of time can renew the spirit. To watch plants rise from the earth with no special tending reawakens our sense of awe and wonder.

More than ever before in our nation's history, black folks must collectively renew our relationship to the earth, to our agrarian roots. For when we are forgetful and participate in the destruction and exploitation of the dark earth, we collude with the domination of the earth's dark people, both here and globally. Reclaiming our history, our relationship to nature, to farming in America, and proclaiming the humanizing restorative of living in harmony with nature so that the earth can be our witness is meaningful resistance.

When I leave my small flat in an urban world—where nature has been so relentlessly assaulted that it is easy to forget to look at a tree, a sky, a flower emerging in a sea of trash—and go to the country, I seek renewal. To live in communion with the earth, fully acknowledging nature's power with humility and grace, is a practice of spiritual mindfulness that heals and restores. Making peace with the earth, we make the world a place where we can be one with nature. We create and sustain environments where we can come back to ourselves, where we can return home. Stand on solid ground and be a true witness.

THIS WEIGHT OF SMALL BODIES

Kimberly M. Blaeser

To see a World in a Grain of Sand,
And Heaven in a Wild Flower,
Hold Infinity in the palm of your hand,
And Eternity in an hour.
　　—*William Blake, "Auguries of Innocence"*

I

Apologies to Blake, but last summer, deep in the heat of the Southern Hemisphere, I saw the world in a banana leaf. More. Standing in a dinner line, holding the frondlike green sheaf, the evening feast suddenly seemed touched with a symbolic light.

That August evening, a patchwork of international writers, architects of voice and page, we gathered as part of the Utan Kayu literary festival with regional Indonesian writers and artists. Stepping outside from a particularly smoky reading and welcomed by the humid Magelang night, we mingled and moved—perhaps more quickly than is strictly polite—toward the drinks and refreshments awaiting us.

I repeated to myself the lengthy food cautions meant to keep me healthy during my travels. They involved a litany of avoidance: avoid anything but bottled water; avoid anything that might have been washed in water, not boiled; avoid unpasteurized products; avoid uncooked meats, et cetera, et cetera. In simplest terms: peel it, boil it, cook it, or forget it. But by this time, I was craving a green salad, and perhaps for this reason the largesse of the banana leaves immediately caught my eye.

Over the previous week, we had visited various sites—embassies, galleries, colleges, high schools—and I had begun to anticipate with trepidation the arrival of our meals. Not for the foods themselves, which I invariably enjoyed, but for their presentation. In a country with no infrastructure for dealing with waste, the Western packaging influence had run amuck. Lunch at one of our stops was presented to us as a small cardboard box on top of a paper plate with a paper napkin accompaniment. The box contained plastic utensils and several tasty cellophane-wrapped items. As I ate, I watched the waste pile up and remembered the view from the back of my Jakarta hotel.

The front of the luxury hotel was landscaped, had elaborate lights, fences, and guards. A look out the back window, however, showed three-sided corrugated-metal structures, shanties, behind which lay piles of garbage—all the way down to the river that was presumably the water source. The water that flowed out of the pipes in my twelfth-floor room was not pleasant to smell or to bathe in. No one had to remind me not to drink it.

Several times on my journey, I recalled a smartly worded critique I once heard from my fellow tribeswoman Winona LaDuke. Speaking of garbage, packaging, and recycling, she asked, "Where is 'away?'" as in, "I'm going to throw it *away.*" I had now seen the "away" that Americans for a large part will never view up close.

And so, the banana leaf. Thick and smooth, it graced the palm of my hand, and upon its emerald body I placed rice, meat in peanut sauce, and vegetables. Then some local sweets followed. Everything edible or biodegradable. If portents do reside in the everyday—fortuitous markers, or nature's hieroglyphs like the animal signs in which I was instructed as a child—that twilight encounter with the banana leaf shimmered as a symbol for the challenges we face in sustaining our fragile world.

I see myself in the puzzle of its transport, wondering what of my own past causes me to finger the green leaf edges as if in comprehension. Why does this night remind me of a night twenty years earlier, driving into the dusky woods south of Twin Lakes, coming upon my uncle after he has just killed and skinned out a small buck? I see him as he stands with the still steaming deer heart skewered on a stick. Why does the simple Indonesian food taste of memory? Of childhood evenings sitting with relatives as we undressed the wild hazelnuts we had picked, removing the brownish bract, pooling our small bounty of nuts. What forsaken rhythm of heart do I feel in the beat of that night, in my memories of camp suppers, of berry picking, of bounteous green gardens?

I think what beats at the center of these moments has something to do with earth community, with labor and reciprocity, rather than simple abundance. *Aseema.* Tobacco placed in solemn offering. A supplication to ancient gods or a simple gesture of connection. Harvesting has long involved seasonal rituals and complex celebrations that symbolize our engagement with place, our immersion in a cycle of belonging. Tribal gatherings always involve both relationships and foodstuffs. The Tohono O'odham of the American Southwest travel together to gather the cactus fruits, extended families of Great Lakes Anishinaabeg set up spring sugarbush camps, tribal peoples everywhere come together to harvest—fish, clams, wild rice, all earth's sustenance. And the ceremonial and practical respect they pay to the land source enhances the continuance of their community as well as the stability of the food products themselves.

We always leave a little behind, I was told. Berries. Fish. Rice. Nuts. Indeed the very methods used to gather wild rice in my Ojibwe community— bending the plants and pounding with a flail to knock the ripened kernels into the canoe bottom—guarantees that some will fall into the water and accomplish reseeding. Indeed many families still "plant" rice for later generations of relatives, deliberately sowing part of their harvest. Customs that limit harvesting or accomplish renewal might originate from spiritual teachings— *Leave some for the animals. For the manidoog and little people.* These practices become ritualized in song, story, or pattern. As ritual, they are sustained or prescribed through the communal history of repetition, renewed as each generation takes up tasks tightly entwined with beliefs.

And, if we come to knowledge through our bodies as much as through our minds, then clearly the habit of labor, too, looms large here. We enter into a process through our own reaching limbs, our scratched and pierced hands that pluck the riches from protective thorns. Holistic methods become embodied memory through the physical acts of tradition. We search, paddle, place offerings, set net, catch, clean, cook; we lift, dig, plant, cut, fill, haul, build, peel, preserve, and repeat all in endless cycles of remembrance. Perhaps this explains why two-thirds of the words in the Ojibwe native language are actions—verbs. *Nandawaabam. Jiime. Biindaakoojige. Bajida'waa. Debibidoon. Bakazhaawe. Minozan.* Indeed contentment, too, may reside in the body as well as the soul. How many times have we lingered, flushed, spent, in the afterglow of a day's toil? *Now we rest while the stars sing songs for workers.*

Standing in the Indonesia night, I know the upturned green palms hold the labor of many brown hands. They hold land knowledge. Somewhere else they might be corn husks or lotus fronds. In my own past, they might be the filleted bodies of fish.

II

Nearly every winter weekend of my Minnesota childhood, we went ice fishing. Though such expeditions might not appeal to some, we went for pleasure as well as for food. Preparations for the season might begin weeks or months before as my brother and I made fish-house candles with my mother, pouring the layers of colored wax into cream cartons or tin cans of various sizes, carefully adding a string wick. And waiting. Meanwhile my dad repaired a portable canvas fish house or designed and constructed the homemade sled on which we would haul all that we needed. I see the sequence of activities, the seasonal preparations and the day outings, as ritualized only in hindsight. To us, it was simply our everyday.

In the dark of the winter morning, we collect our cold-weather clothes, perhaps haggling a little over a particular pair of mittens. I remember proudly layering wax paper on the table (or when I grew taller, on the kitchen counter) and with great ceremony I inquire of each person what they would like spread on their bread, what meat they want, and how many sandwiches. I pack dill pickles, fish-house candy, coffee in the thermos, water in the dented red jug. We gather wood decoys (carved, weighted, and painted by my dad, my brother, or my uncles), a heavy pronged spear, ice-fishing rigs, bait, buckets, an auger, chisel, ice scoop, playing cards, a cribbage board, ice skates, fishing gear, metal stringer, blankets, towels—an endless array of fish-house necessities. Among the most important in the northern climate: matches in protective tin, a lantern, and firewood.

Laden and dressed in warm layers, we set out first by car, then on foot from the landing. The walk is joyous, often rowdy as we crunch through the crust of snow on ice, check in on others already fishing, call out warnings about still-open holes. Our heavy-booted feet lift easily as we journey into the infinity of a northern lake—sun snow-sharpened, light on white on ice.

We arrive slightly breathless from the cold and the excitement, set immediately to preparing outside holes. At first we queue for turns at chiseling, lifting the heavy tool and bringing it down to chip away at the ice in ever deeper and widening circles. The repetitive motion gradually becomes hypnotic until the fatigue of our still small arms breaks the rhythm and, reluctantly, we pass the chisel to other hands. Still we each hope that it will be with our magical downward thrust that the water arrives. Miners after summer's gold, we always shout when the first moisture seeps up from the dark spiral, pools, then in a gush breaks through and splashes onto the sides of the hole, gracing the frozen ice surfaces with water, with a fluid, wet rush of memory.

Anticlimactic in contrast, more tasks follow: clearing the ice, checking depth, placing the bobber, baiting the hook with a shiner, a chub, or a crappie minnow, and securing the rig's metal tip in the small round mound of chipped ice that now surrounds the fishing hole. Then renewed anticipation. An upturned bucket for a seat. And winter waiting.

Meanwhile fire has been set in the barrel stove and belongings unpacked in the small windowless fish house, our six-by-eight destination. So we barter our positions—inside or outside, spearholder or watcher. Outside we might skate while the fish make up their minds, or lose ourselves in ice layers, follow intricate visual patterns across the canvas of frozen water.

Inside we will settle in, darkness secured by a tattered army blanket at the door. Minutes tick into hours as we sit crowded and hunch-shouldered over the rectangle cut into the floor of the fish house, cut into the ice beneath. Water, the only light in our darkness. We take turns puppeting the fish decoy through the green tinted lake world, make it swim, dip, and dive. We hope the flash of tin fin, the lure of its painted scales will call the fish from the weeds, from the edges of our longing.

As schools of minnows and curious perch swim in and out of our vision, we whisper stories like they were ancient incantations. Of how you once dipped your hand, rinsed and lifted only seconds before the smart snap of a muskrat might have taken your finger for a fish. Of the lurker—*the length of your arm*—that Ike watched and finally outwaited over the long days of January. The soft slow looping of language pairs with the smooth lengthening swim of the decoy. Motion told and repeated while the four-prong spear rests just there on the edge of the ice as it has for decades in one hand or another. Soon patience and the stories work their enchantment. Something always rises to the bait. The white belly of fish may flash as it meets the quick spear thrust. Or the northern, turning in the silt black bottom, that rudders just out of reach, heightens our every hunger.

And the day bears on, dusk creeping, inching towards its destiny. While we fish. And dream. Our stare now sees deeper into winter water. Beyond fish. Beyond the dark edges of the ice.

Finally, as if into another age, we emerge again from the fish house, where we have been lulled by the womblike darkness. We are thrust anew into the sudden cold, the startling blue-white winter. And fish spots, mirages, flash before our eyes as we stretch and shake awake tingling limbs.

Outside, anglers jig their bait. They wait. The lines we have pulled from these mysterious waters seem endless as every day of childhood. The filament that flails like live electric wire in our stiff hands wakens us from winter reverie. Grasping the line, we could simply haul our catch in hand over hand, but now and then in excitement we run gleefully from the holes, carrying the line away with us and our hooked fish up from the small water center.

Fishing routines turn, repeat, like the simple looping of decoys. Each dusky evening we depart, leave with empty sandwich wrappers and frozen bodies of fish. With tired steps we set out, align ourselves by distant tree patterns or follow twinkling cabin lights, and move in arcs toward the far-off shore.

Soon cheeks flush hot and red in the warmth of the car, eyes shutter, nearly closed as we sketch word-fish on the drive home, these swimming more swiftly and larger in the lake of our contentment.

In the late-night fish cleaning that follows, we try our hands at scaling and filleting. Then, mesmerized by the mastery of our parents' knives, we watch each deft move as the bellies spill their secrets: yellow masses of eggs, air sacks, sometimes a still beating heart, and the mysterious digestive sacks. Opening the thin membranes, we see again the cycles of feeding of which we are a part. Sometimes minnows are found whole, as yet undigested within the larger fish. Worlds within worlds, cycles overlapping other cycles—as children, through the simple seasonal activities, we pressed our noses against the windows to these realities.

III

What nourished us then was more than the fish, the rice, meat, nuts, berries, and other gathered foods. And the symbolism in the Magelang night rose from the coalescence of more than sugarbush camps and Javanese custom. What do we fathom in regional ceremony or a seasonal harvest ritual? What symbol of infinity is the weight of these small bodies—the northern pike, the lotus, the banana leaf? Deep in the skewered heart of deer, buried some-place in the gestures of every subsistence activity, beats belief. Belief that we live entwined in intricate sets of relationship. Because we gather these natural gifts for food, tools, shelter, medicine, we believe with our bodies as well as our minds that we must pay attention to their survival. Some among us hold them as relatives to whom we owe a portion of care. What shimmers in my memory of that Indonesian night is a certain kind of belonging, not be-longing to a mass of assembly-line consumers, but belonging to a committed, native, local economy.

If I measure the distance between my own early immersion in just such a community and my present longing, it might equal the steps between the poorest Jakarta dwelling and the city's dark polluted river. But I know that distance is neither temporal nor merely physical. Somewhere in our under-standing of economy as a distribution of wealth, industrial escapism has fixated on the wealth of product—fast food and Hello Kitty are mimicked around the world. Questionable Western ideals of progress wield influence in more and more remote places with disastrous economic and ecological results. Nation after nation has constructed governments built on various false notions of independence, on belief in separate realities. Church from state. Third world from first world. Human from all else. *Away* from the everyday. What we need are experiments in return.

In my journey last summer, I also visited a rural high school seminary. Their "auditorium" was a roofed, open-sided space, relying on air currents rather than air conditioning for cooling. In their complex, the school kept pigs to help deal with waste products, kept chickens for eggs, had a garden for produce. Each of the boys worked at chores to keep the community running. They slept three-high in bunk beds, hung their hand-laundered shirts on lines to dry. Perhaps they would live in luxury air-conditioned rooms if such were available. Or perhaps someone there sees links between things such as faith, community, responsibility, and ecology, between lifestyle and the wealth of spirit. This one tiny pod.

Can you see the distance, the chasm we must cross? We can get there without Blake. Without the grain of sand. The banana leaf. Or the dark thunder of regret. We can even begin the journey in the midst of material excess. Vision itself is not linked to circumstance. Something that is before you now will do. Silver body of fish. The ancient patterned sky. A child's palm. Just look closely. Some remembered light might shimmer and ignite.

SHARING BREATH

Some Links Between Land, Plants, and People

Enrique Salmon

The Earth speaks in many languages, but only in one voice. It is a voice of compassion, and of pain. It is a voice of trust, and of the unknown. It is a voice of life, and of natural death. It is a voice of our ancestors, and of those who will inherit our legacies. But it is also a voice that emanates in unison from every living thing on Earth. It binds our breaths, and nourishes our integration. The loss of only the tiniest member of the union weakens the voice, which may soon become a whisper unless we begin to speak for those whose languages are not heard. The unheard includes not only plants and animals, places or open spaces, streamsides or oceanscapes: they include people. More specifically, the cultures of people who maintain a sustainable and enhancing relationship with their land are at risk.

Relationships with the land are generated from and enhanced through cultural histories, stories, and songs. Through my family, I encountered and gathered my Rarámuri cultural history through morals, ecological lessons, and observations. Cultural history is more than a story; it's a way of perceiving ourselves as part of an extended ecological family of all species with whom we share ancestry, origins, and breath; a way of acknowledging that life in our environment is viable only when we view the life surrounding us as family. This family, or kin, includes all the natural elements of the ecosystem. My people, the Rarámuri are affected by, and affect, the life around us in the Sierra Madres of Chihuahua, Mexico.

Cultural history and family-centered ecological lessons are woven into the fabric of our daily lives. Sitting in the sun with my grandfather in his small cornfield, I learned how corn and chiles were our parents and protectors. He told me about the beginning of the world as he whittled. He taught me to respect the trees as relatives when he caught my cousins and me swinging from the rubbery limbs of his huge fig tree. I remember the pungent and savory smells of grandma's plant arbor. I would sit and watch her grinding chiles and herbs in her old metates and mortars while she talked about our origins and about our plant relatives.

The cultural history of the Rarámuri expresses how the world began, how the animals emerged, and how the first Rarámuri found their way to their homeland. The history explains also how plants are direct relatives to people. For me, as an indigenous ethnobotanist, cultural history serves as a conduit through which I can explain my culture's perceptions of and experience in the natural world. It also provides metaphors and models through which I can interpret actions and interactions between people and plants.

One afternoon I visited the government classes at a boarding school in Nararáchi, a small mountain village of Rarámuri people located in the Sierra Madres of Chihuahua, Mexico. The students arrive early Monday mornings from their scattered *rancherías* (small multifamily agricultural communities) and return home on Friday afternoons. On this particular afternoon, they were learning history. The lesson focused on the Mexican Revolution. The young instructor, on a six-month government assignment to teach in a rural area, was from Mexico City. He spoke in Spanish, discussing the glories of Pancho Villa, Zapata, Carranza, and the despotism of Díaz. He did not mention Rarámuri involvement in the revolution, nor did he discuss the effects the revolution had on the Rarámuri.

The revolution suspended agriculture in some areas, as revolutionaries raided Rarámuri *rancherías* for food and sometimes young girls, whom they forced into servitude. My grandmother used to tell us how her parents would hide her in the corncrib when Pancho Villa's men came looking for food. Often the young men were "volunteered" into military service, either by the Mexican Army or by the revolutionaries. One reason my Rarámuri grandfather ended up in the United States was to escape serving in the military.

During the week of government classes, these children are engulfed in an alien culture. They are indoctrinated into the Mexican way of perceiving history, which will influence their perspectives of the land. After the Mexican Revolution, the land became something to dominate. The Green Revolution of the 1960s launched the notion that the land and the people who worked it were there for the good of the continuing revolution. When the children go home, however, their history differs, along with their perceptions of the land.

Heroes are the focus of Western cultural history. Those people who influence events usually dominate, lead, and conquer. In contrast, the focus of Rarámuri cultural history is the landscape—the trees, plants, animals, and children, which share the landscape, rather than dominate it. Our origin story offers an example of this understanding.

In the beginning, matter and *iwígara,* the breath of life, met. From this meeting Onorúame, the creator, was conceived and born. After he matured, Onorúame created the land. On the land Onorúame placed many animals, including deer, rabbits, turkeys, owls, eagles, fish, bats, and bears. He made insects fly in the air and crawl on the ground. At first the land was flat and featureless, so Onorúame asked Ohí, the bear, to shape the land with his claws. Ohí shaped the Sierra Tarahumara, other nearby mountains ranges, arroyos, and the deep barrancas. Plants were created next. The Rarámuri considered many of these plants to be human; some of them were believed to have become plants after they first lived as humans.

According to the Rarámuri chronicle, the first people were corrupt and lazy. They had been created by Onorúame and sent to Earth, falling from the sky like raindrops. Their lives were short, so they ran everywhere in order to accomplish their daily tasks. But they did not appreciate the lives given to them by the creator, and gambled constantly, neglecting their fields, each other, and the land. Out of disgust, Onorúame brought a huge rainstorm, flooding the entire region and killing the people.

On a hilltop in the mountains two children, a boy and a girl, survived the flood. The children were scared at first. Onorúame consoled them. The children then became lonely, missing all their friends and relatives. Onorúame assured them that they would not be lonely for long. He asked them to be patient, and he would find a way to alleviate their situation. On the third day of their isolation, Onorúame appeared before the children and gave them some corn seed. He instructed them to wait for the waters to recede, then to go about scattering the seeds. From the seeds, he said, new life will emerge. In three days the waters began to dry up, and the children walked about scattering the seeds. As Onorúame said, new life began to sprout.

At first the corn plants grew as expected. Their stalks were strong, and their leaves reached all the way to the ground. Eventually ears sprouted from the intersections of stalk and leaf. Corn silk appeared. But one day the children noticed human heads emerging from the ears. They could see black hair on top of the heads, then the foreheads, and soon the entire heads and bodies sprung forth and sprawled out onto the ground. This was happening everywhere the corn plants grew, and in a short time, the land had been repopulated. The reason the Rarámuri live in small scattered and isolated communities is traced back to this scattering of corn seeds, which also scattered the people. Today many Rarámuri continue to think of themselves as the children of corn.

The world outside the Sierra Tarahumara is one of relative uncertainty and perhaps danger. Rarámuri tales of giants from the north and east and of Chabochi, the bearded ones (nonindigenous people), from the south reveal this anxiety. The Rarámuri word for north, *michu*, is similar to the name of the Nahuatl god of death, Mictlanticutli. The perception of the direction of north is one of danger. The word for west, *tobuku*, also means to submerge, suggesting the path of the sun each evening. *Ori* is the word for east. It means to return. South is expressed with the word *tugeke*, which is very close to the word *tuga*, meaning to roast. But *tu* is also an old Uto-Aztecan word for south.

Through Rarámuri eyes, the world outside the Sierra Tarahumara appears relatively unsafe. We would prefer to remain within the mountains and canyons that comprise Gawi Wachi, the place of nurturing. In a very real way the mountains and canyons have always protected us from disease and European encroachment. Our cultural history reveals the protective nature of the Sierra. In order to escape the flood, the two children fled to the safety of a high place. People still live in the numerous caves and canyons of the Sierra. Caves act also as Rarámuri expressions of safety. A Rarámuri story recounts how, when the sun came too close to Earth, it burned everyone except those living in caves. Mountains, caves, and canyons are not only symbols of safety, but also rebirth. And these symbols carry over to actions as well. Peyote ceremonies, rituals of rebirth, and journeys to the other reality take place in caves. The Rarámuri dead are buried in caves. Mountains remain symbols of strength and of refuge.

The mountains of the Sierra Tarahumara support the levels of the universe as well as Rarámuri culture and cosmology. The mountains and barrancas are directly connected to the creation of the world and offer an unbroken continuity to the creation of the people, as well as the familial connection between Rarámuri origins and the creation of other living things such as plants.

Some plants living today were originally created by Onorúame, and some once existed as plants but were later transformed by Onorúame into humans. As a result there are many Rarámuri understandings of plants that include gendered plants, plants identified as Chabochi, plants who are indigenous, and plants who are Rarámuri. The categories of plants are indistinguishable from the Rarámuri categories of humans and, to a large extent, mirror human social categories. In addition, the moral and behavioral attributes of these human social categories are projected onto the corresponding categories of plant people.

The Rarámuri are at the first level of a hierarchy. At the next level below, Chabochis are contrasted with indigenous people. At the next level, indigenous people are divided into Rarámuri and other indigenous people. Rarámuri often separate themselves into Cimarronis, the wild ones, and Gentiles, those who converted to Catholicism. The category of other indigenous people includes Apache, Yaqui, Opata, Guarijio, Tepehuan, and Mayo.

Sunú (corn) is female. Many of the terms associated with corn suggest mother's milk and breasts. *Wásia (Ligusticum porteri)* is female as well. The word *wasi* also means mother-in-law. *Sitákame (Haematoxylon brasiletto)* is a female plant whose characteristics note special attention. A story from the eastern Sierra says that:

> *Sitákame* was at one time a human who quarreled with everyone. She got angry when she lost gambling, and started fights at *tesguinadas*. She quarreled with *wásia*, tobacco, and even squash. Onorúame eventually lost his patience with *Sitákame* and changed her into a plant.

But *sitákame*'s female associations do not end there. *Sitákame*'s inner heart wood is red. It is used for several remedies, but especially for excessive bleeding during menstruation and after childbirth. In the story, *Sitákame* is afforded human characteristics, emotions, failings, and personality. She has a sister and acquaintances but loses her human lifestyle due to an addiction to gambling.

Male plants include piñons and junipers, oaks, tobacco, beans, squash, peyote, and datura. All these plants, except *sitákame*, were originally created in their plant form. In the minds of Rarámuri, they are not anthropomorphized. They are human but with different features.

My grandfather used to mention how Bawákawa, Tobacco, and Baka-bu bahi, Corn Husk, used to drink corn-beer together. In his husky voice he imitated the voices of Tobacco and Corn Husk as they asked for the drinking gourd, and he told stories of other plants. Before, when plants talked with Rarámuris, Tobacco and Corn Husk were drinking friends. They drank together at *tesguinadas* (ritual corn-beer drinking gatherings) and gambled together. A friend of theirs was Drinking Gourd. He would meet them at *tesguinadas*. Together they became beautifully drunk. This is why it is good to smoke at *tesguinadas*. The story illustrates the human qualities applied to plants but also offers a cultural explanation for a particular tradition by applying what is expected to be proper human actions to plants.

But tobacco, smoke, and fire carry additional weight in Rarámuri ritual and prayer. The Rarámuri only smoke at night to avoid confusing the creator, who might mistake the smoke for clouds, and not produce real clouds for making rain. Both smoke from tobacco and from pine resin incense are employed as healing agents. Smoke is a visible aspect of breath that permeates all life. Some healers strengthen their patients' breath by blowing smoke into them. Fire is an element of every Rarámuri gathering, ceremony, dance, and ritual. Semana Santa (Holy Week) ceremonies do not begin until the first evening when fires are lit atop the mesas and high points surrounding the communities. Evil characters associated with Diablo are scared of fire and will not visit the dance and ceremony.

Food plants and many other plants are female because they take care of us and feed us. Female plants tend to be domesticated food plants or plants used for general healing and for female ailments. Male plants tend to be ceremonial, used by experienced healers, potentially dangerous, and are often not related to the Rarámuri.

A healer from the Sierra was telling me about *híkuli,* peyote, being a Rarámuri. I asked him how he knew that *híkuli* was a human. He said, "*Híkuli,* and other plants, talk to me. I hear them when I walk near them. Sometimes they talk to me in dreams." To the healer and to other Rarámuri, the plants exist at the same level as humans. They speak to us.

Plants are also broken down into indigenous groups. Although some people consider *bakánawi* to be Chabochi, it is sometimes considered to be Apache because of their fierceness and unpredictability. Some *híkuli* are Apaches as well due to the unpredictability of the species.

It is not surprising that the Apache are singled out as relations of dangerous plants as they often raided Rarámuri stores of corn and animals, stole children and women and killed our warriors. The animosity between the two peoples revealed itself when Rarámuri warriors volunteered to scout for the Mexican army during the 1880s when Apache raids were especially virulent. It is reported that a Rarámuri named Mauricio single-handedly killed the war chief Victorio in 1880.

Many important plants are Rarámuri, including some hallucinogenic plants, but not those that are fatally toxic. *Sunú* (corn) is Rarámuri, as are the domesticated plants *muní* (beans), *bachi* (squash), and *kori* (chiles). *Sitákame* is a Rarámuri. The wood of this small tree is prized for making staffs of office for community leaders and is carved for the rasping sticks still used in ceremonies. The true peyote, *híkuli (Lophophora williamsii),* is not consumed by all Rarámuri. Some fear the plant, saying that it will make a person go crazy. Nevertheless, many Rarámuri continue to consume *híkuli.*

There is a false peyote called *híkuli cimarroni (Ariocarpus fissuratus).* It is also a Rarámuri but is, as the borrowed Spanish name implies, one of the "wild ones." During the time of the Jesuits, many Rarámuri never converted to Catholicism. They were either rebellious or were situated so deep in the far reaches of the barrancas that they never encountered the missionaries. Many Cimarronis, as they are called by other Rarámuri, still live in the far corners of the canyons and are said to still carry bows and arrows.

One warm afternoon I was sipping *cokas* (Pepsi) with some Rarámuri friends in the small one-room *conasupo* (small government-sponsored general store and trading post) at the edge of Norogachi. In walked three traditionally dressed Rarámuri. I noticed they were leaner and darker than the Rarámuri around Norogachi. Their dress was cut slightly different and they wore leather–soled sandals as opposed to sandals with soles made out of car tires. I also noticed that they carried water gourds and bows and arrows. When they entered, everyone quickly became quiet and cautiously stared at the newcomers. The three asked for *cokas,* which they quickly and quietly sipped. Their eyes darted around at the contents of the room and at us. We must have looked like the timid rabbits that they, no doubt, hunted with their bows. One of them traded some herbs for some colorful cloth. They finished their drinks and quickly left. No one spoke for a moment. Finally a friend broke the silence and whispered, "Cimarronis."

Bakánawi, for the most part, is categorized as Rarámuri. The uncertain classification of *bakánawi* is most likely a result of the three species of plants that share the name. There are several uses of the *bakánawi*. The disproportionately large tuber of the species of *Ipomoea purpurea* is carefully collected and used to help people who are crazy or have lost parts of their soul.

Wásia (Ligusticum porteri) is a plant who possesses both medicinal and magical qualities. *Wásia* has always been a Rarámuri; she just looks like a plant. She is one of Onorúame's favorite beings but is hated by Diablo and sorcerers. Many Rarámuri carry a piece of *wásia's* hairy root around their neck or in a small pouch in their waist sash. It is said to repel the evils and spells of sorcerers, to bring good luck, and to ward off rattlesnakes. It is used in nearly every healing ceremony in the form of a tea, which is consumed to treat several ailments.

Kori (chile) was once a Rarámuri, who was transformed into a plant by Onorúame. *Kori* was changed into a plant for fighting with two other

Rarámuri plants, *sitákame* and *habiki*. Like *wásia, Kori* is also attributed with the power to repel sorcery. One eats *kori* to scare away sorcerers. It is a part of nearly every meal throughout the Sierra Tarahumara and is used as a medicine for both people and animals.

Other plants that are Rarámuri include *okoko* (*Pinus* spp.), *aorí (Juniperus deppeana), bisíkori (Pinus edulis), seréke (Dasylirion simplex), sokó (Yucca decipiens), ruyá (Nolina matapensis),* and *rohísawa* (*Quercus* spp.).

Plants are human to the Rarámuri, but plants make up a small segment of the entire ecosystem of the Sierra Tarahumara, which is seen as tied directly to Rarámuri identity.

The Rarámuri are part of an extended ecological family that shares ancestry and origins. We share an awareness that life in any environment is viable only when humans view the life surrounding them as kin. The kin includes humans as well as all the natural elements of the ecosystem. We are affected by and, in turn, affect the life around us. The interactions that result from this "kincentric ecology" enhance and preserve social structure and the ecosystem. Interactions are the commerce of social and ecosystem functioning. Without human recognition of their role in the complexities of life in a place, life suffers and loses its strength to carry on.

I call this sphere of thought kincentricity because it encompasses several senses: the way in which plant names are learned, the ecological roles of plants, and the perception that plants are kin that are linked through *iwígara.*

One evening I went to Cusarare to watch the *matachine* dances. I stood in the doorway at the old adobe church and watched the dancers, arranged in two lines, reel back and forth to the repetitive music of the violins. After several repetitions, the colorfully attired dancers whooped, then whirled, interlaced the dancing lines, and continued. Along the walls of the church many Rarámuri stood or sat on the floor. They watched the ceremony in silence, although their eyes reflected their concentration on the dancers. Some tourists were there, including a group of Europeans.

After many whoops and whirls the *chapeon,* or dance leader, signaled for the music to stop. The dancers left the church and went to a patio across the church square to drink *suwi-ki.* During the break, one of the tourists approached me and asked why only a few Rarámuri were dancing. I said, "They are all dancing, some dance with their breath." At all Rarámuri dances there will be nondancers sitting nearby, leaning upon a church wall or a railing, standing with their arms crossed against the cold. They might have their blankets draped over one shoulder with stern faces and eyes intent on the events. These people are not spectators; they are dancing with their breath. This means that they, like supporters at a healing ceremony, offer their thoughts and energy toward the dancers as a way to strengthen their actions. In this way they boost the dancers' intention of keeping the land strong. It is important to dance with your breath and to concentrate on the dancers and the event. In this way one's being, spirit, and breath are strengthening the dancers and the ceremony.

The Rarámuri believe that human breath is shared by all surrounding life, that our emergence into this world was possibly caused by some of the nearby life forms. From this awareness we understand that we are responsible for the survival of all life and are cognizant of human kincentric relationships with nature similar to those we share with family and tribe. A reciprocal relationship has been fostered, with the realization that humans affect nature and nature affects humans. This awareness influences Rarámuri interactions with the environment. These interactions, these cultural practices of living with a place, are manifestations of kincentric ecology.

At *yúmari* ceremonies, dances and songs are performed to heal people as well as animals and the land. During the ceremony the women dance in a continual *iwí* (circle), while the male singers and chanters dance within the counter-clockwise moving circle. The songs ask that the land be nourished and that the land nourish the people. As the songs are performed, the *iwí* continues to turn. The *iwí* represents the fertility of the land. *Iwí* also conveys other meanings. It translates roughly into the idea of binding with a lasso, but it also means to unite, to join, to connect. Another meaning of *iwí* is to breathe, inhale/exhale, or respire. *Iwí* is also the word used to identify a caterpillar that weaves its cocoons on the madrone trees (genus *Arbutus*). The dance is a metamorphosing caterpillar, suggesting a whole morphological process of change, death, birth, and rebirth associated with the concept of *iwí*.

Alone, *gara* means good, well, virtuous, and lawful (as in just). In use, it often is expressed when people wish to affirm an event or statement. After songs and dances are performed, one will hear from the watching crowd affirmations of *"gara, gara,"* "it is good."

Iwigá means soul. Soul can be an elusive concept, even among the Rarámuri, to whom it means different things depending on who is talking. It can mean life force but also breath. Generally, however, it is the soul, or *iwigá,* that sustains the body with the breath of life. Everything that breathes has a soul. Plants, animals, humans, stones, the land, all share the same breath.

On the surface *iwigá* and *iwígara* are different concepts. But *iwigá* is an essential aspect of the larger concept of *iwígara.* The spectrum of *iwígara* would diminish without the notion that there exists a force, breath, an *iwigá* emanating through all life. Each concept requires the other in order to be fully understood.

I was once watching a logging operation near the heavily forested mountain community of Pahuachique. After the trees were cut by hand, the Rarámuri laborers wrapped the huge tree trunks with chains and watched the logging truck drag the trunks to the back end of the truck. Once there, the laborers, aided by the small crane and winch on the truck, loaded the heavy trunks onto the bed of the truck. The process is dangerous and the workers are open to many possible injuries. As I watched, one of the trunks slipped from its chain and careened into the fleeing workers. One did not move quickly enough, and his leg was severely injured. His companions quickly wrapped him in a blanket and loaded him onto the truck to be taken to the nearest clinic. I noticed that as the men cared for the victim and loaded him into the truck they continued to whisper to the victim *"mu chapi iwigá,"* "hold onto your soul."

Injury is not the only time for the Rarámuri to be concerned about losing their breath or soul. When a Rarámuri child becomes sick, the parents offer food to a creek or pond, hoping this will attract the child's lost soul back to the child. Rarámuri parents are often afraid to move a sick child to a hospital that is so far away from home because it will be difficult for the child's soul to find its way back to the child.

Iwígara is the soul or essence of life everywhere. Therefore, *iwígara* is the idea that all life, spiritual and physical, is interconnected in a continual cycle.

We are all related to and play a role in the complexity of life. To the Rarámuri the concept of *iwígara* encompasses many ideas and ways of thinking unique to the place with which the Rarámuri live. Rituals and ceremonies, the language, and, therefore, Rarámuri thought are influenced by the lands, animals, and winds with which they live. *Iwígara* is the total interconnectedness and integration of all life in the Sierra Madres.

Iwígara becomes most clear with regard to managing the land. It is *iwígara* that guides Rarámuri agriculture, medicine, and foraging. The use of plants for healing and for food becomes a window through which to see Rarámuri participation in the natural community. The origin stories and those of the plant relatives show how we are a part of a land onto which we were placed to serve as caretakers. We are also directly responsible for the health of the creator, who works hard each day to provide for the land and its inhabitants.

In return for Rarámuri care, the land provides a cornucopia. *Sepé,* wild greens, are collected by nearly all Rarámuri to augment the daily diet of corn, beans, potatoes, squashes, wheat, and a variety of other products, both Old and New World in origin. The land also permits the raising of goats, sheep, chickens, and pigs. Some Rarámuri raise cows and horses. Nondomesticated plants are available from the land as well.

This rich area offers many wild plant medicines, most of which are exploited by the Rarámuri. The Rarámuri also utilize many natural materials from the forests and barrancas. They include *basíkori* (piñon) for building and fuel. For household use and as a way to supplement their meager incomes they weave baskets of sotol leaves, pine needles, and yucca leaves. Many baskets and other crafts are sold to the exploding tourist industry.

Most Rarámuri still collect edible greens, which are dried and stored to be eaten later. They recognize and harvest many plants that are used for colds, arthritis, baskets, stomachaches, corn-beer, bruises, the blood, and headaches. Collecting trips are not special fractions of time, nor are they specifically planned. Plants are collected as one walks to the *conasupo* (trading post), as one comes over to visit, or in-between times when one enjoys stopping by the creek to toss rocks into the water.

When the people speak of the land, the religious and romantic overtones so prevalent in Western environmental conversation are absent. To us the land exists in the same manner as do our families, chickens, the river, and the sky. No hierarchy of privilege places one above or below another. *Iwígara* binds and manages the interconnectedness of all life. Within this web there are particular ways that living things relate to one another. All individual life plays a role in the cycle. One elder mentioned, "It is the reason why people should collect plants in the same way that fish should breathe water, and birds eat seeds and bugs. These are things we are supposed to do."

Rarámuri land management and resource use are harmonized with ecological ethics that positively affect the local environment. It is understood by the Rarámuri that cultural survival is directly linked to biological survival of the Sierra. Over the centuries methods of land use were developed that adhered to this understanding. Horticultural and agricultural techniques included selective coppicing, pruning, harvesting, gathering, cultivation, transplanting, vegetative propagation, sowing, discriminate burning, and weeding.

Gathering techniques, such as that of collecting basket materials, have enhanced the functioning of ecosystems for centuries. These actions have influenced the diversity of species at an ecological and even evolutionary level. Through intentional and incipient plant dispersal, alteration of the forest with controlled burning, and selective pruning and coppicing, the Rarámuri have contributed to the quality and functioning of the environment. The practices affect the reproduction of plant populations, modifying genetic compositions and species interactions. This is logical and easy to comprehend when it is understood that Rarámuri cultural priorities are also ecological and, therefore, hold the world together for the people as well as for animals and plants.

There has been very little of the North American continent that was ever untouched by humans. Except for some of the loftiest peaks and hottest desert locations, the land has been managed just like a garden. And in most places where people have lived sustainably, the diversity of the place has been enhanced by the practices of the people. Today this wild sort of mutualism lives on. In the Sonoran Desert, sand food and the HiaCed O'odham have sustained a pleasant symbiosis. Where willow and sumac abound, indigenous basket makers have found a way to assure that their materials will always be there through careful pruning. Juniper trees across the Southwest provide bow staves without having to be killed. Camas root in British Columbia offers an example of mutualism that increases the wild crop. Traditional salmon weirs in northern California enhanced the species. Native Californians burned the understory of oak groves, which decreased competition and increased the harvest. The Rarámuri carefully select the middle-sized onions to save the old ones for new propagation and young ones for future bulbs. Pine needles are collected for basket weaving in a way that sustains the yield, while yucca leaves are cut from the center of the plants to sustain the plant and its harvest.

Rarámuri land management represents a tradition of conservation that relies on a reciprocal relationship with nature, where the idea of *iwígara* becomes an affirmation of caretaking responsibilities and an assurance of sustainable subsistence and harvesting. It is a realization that the Sierra Madres is a place of nurturing that is full of relatives with whom all breath is shared.

Cultural survival can be measured by the degree to which cultures maintain a relationship with their bioregions. Ecologists and conservation biologists today recognize an important relationship between cultural diversity and biological diversity. Cultural evidence for these relationships includes land-influenced language patterns that can be found in normal speech or in song and oration. In addition, ceremony and ritual drama intended to honor the land and to increase its abundance are an important part of the land/human relationship. Specific religious beliefs, such as land-based entities and forces, are equally important. Folklore, stories, and cultural history intimately describe specific bioregions as places to which the culture relates. The interior landscape reflects the indigenous relationships to their lands. The maintenance of that cultural landscape is an essential part of cultural survival.

When the language disappears, the sum of cultural cognition of the landscape is lost. In the Rarámuri language, images of nature are prompted by words and phrases. References to the process are heard in names of plants, songs, oratory, and metaphors. Encoded in the language is the Rarámuri inclination to seek nurturing relationships with nature.

The knowledge passed through a generation is practical knowledge that will eventually become sacred. During the intergenerational discourse the metaphors and cultural models of plants, as relatives and as humans, develop and are intuitively understood. At this time the younger ones will begin to comprehend the link between the notion of *iwígara* and the interaction of all life. The scope of Rarámuri ecology is only reinforced through ceremony, land management practices, and language. Ceremonies are performed expressions of Rarámuri ecology.

Cultural histories speak the language of the land. They mark the outlines of the human/land consciousness. Under my grandfather's fig tree I learned not only our cultural history but also the centuries of practical and spiritual knowledge that have evolved over a vast stretch of time and acknowledge our relationship to a place.

BURNING THE SHELTER

Louis Owens

In the center of the Glacier Peak Wilderness in northern Washington a magnificent, fully glaciated white volcano rises over a stunningly beautiful region of the North Cascades. On maps, the mountain is called Glacier Peak. To the Salishan people who have always lived in this part of the Cascades, the mountain is Dakobed, the place of emergence. For the better part of a century a small, three-sided log shelter stood in a place called White Pass, just below one shoulder of the great mountain, tucked securely into a meadow between thick stands of mountain hemlock and alpine fir.

In the early fall of 1976, while working as a seasonal ranger for the United States Forest Service, I drew the task of burning the White Pass shelter. After all those years, the shelter roof had collapsed like a broken bird wing under the weight of winter snow, and the time was right for fire and replanting. It was part of a Forest Service plan to remove all human-made objects from wilderness areas, a plan of which I heartily approved. So I backpacked eleven miles to the pass and set up camp, and for five days, while a bitter early storm sent snow driving horizontally out of the north, I dismantled the shelter and burned the old logs, piling and burning and piling and burning until nothing remained. The antique, hand-forged spikes that had held the shelter together I put into gunnysacks and cached to be packed out later by mule. I spaded up the earth, beaten hard for nearly a century by boot and hoof, and transplanted plugs of vegetation from hidden spots on the nearby ridge.

At the end of those five days not a trace of the shelter remained, and I felt good, very smug in fact, about returning the White Pass meadow to its "original" state. As I packed up my camp, the snowstorm had subsided to a few flurries and a chill that felt bone deep with the promise of winter. My season was almost over, and as I started the steep hike down to the trailhead my mind was on the cold months I would be spending in sunny Arizona.

A half mile from the pass I saw the two old women. At first they were dark, hunched forms far down on the last long switchback up the snowy ridge. But as we drew closer to one another I began to feel a growing amazement that, by the time we were face-to-face, had become awe. Almost swallowed up in their baggy wool pants, heavy sweaters, and parkas, silver braids hanging below thick wool caps, they seemed ancient, each weighted with at least seventy years as well as a small backpack. They paused every few steps to lean on their staffs and look out over the North Fork drainage below, a deep, heavily forested river valley that rose on the far side to the glaciers and saw-toothed black granite of the Monte Cristo Range. And they smiled hugely upon seeing me, clearly surprised and delighted to find another person in the mountains at such a time.

We stood and chatted for a moment, and as I did with all backpackers, I reluctantly asked them where they were going. The snow quickened a little, obscuring the view, as they told me that they were going to White Pass.

"Our father built a little house up here," one of them said, "when he worked for the Forest Service like you. Way back before we was born."

"We been coming up here each year since we was little," the other added. "Except last year when Sarah was not well enough."

"A long time ago, this was all our land," the one called Sarah said. "All Indi'n land everywhere you can see. Our people had houses up in the mountains, for gathering berries every year."

As they took turns speaking, the smiles never leaving their faces, I wanted to excuse myself, to edge around these elders and flee to the trailhead and my car, drive back to the district station, and keep going south. I wanted to say,

"I'm Indian, too. Choctaw from Mississippi; Cherokee from Oklahoma"—
as if mixed blood could pardon me for what I had done. Instead, I said, "The
shelter is gone." Cravenly I added, "It was crushed by snow, so I was sent up
to burn it. It's gone now."

I expected outrage, anger, sadness, but instead the sisters continued to
smile at me, their smiles changing only slightly. They had a plastic tarp and
would stay dry, they said, because a person always had to be prepared in the
mountains. They would put up their tarp inside the hemlock grove above the
meadow, and the scaly hemlock branches would turn back the snow. They
forgave me without saying it—my ignorance and my part in the long pattern
of loss that they knew so well.

Hiking out those eleven miles, as the snow of the high country became
a drumming rain in the forests below, I had long hours to ponder my encounter with the sisters. Gradually, almost painfully, I began to understand
that what I called "wilderness" was an absurdity, nothing more than a fig-
ment of the European imagination. An "absolute fake." Before the European
invasion, there was no wilderness in North America; there was only the fertile continent, where people lived in a hard-learned balance with the natural
world. In embracing a philosophy that saw the White Pass shelter—and all
traces of humanity—as a shameful stain upon the "pure" wilderness, I had
succumbed to a five-hundred-year-old pattern of deadly thinking that sepa-
rates us from the natural world. This is not to say that what we call wilderness
today does not need careful safeguarding. I believe that White Pass really is
better off now that the shelter does not serve as a magnet to backpackers and
horsepackers who compact the soil, disturb and kill the wildlife, cut down
centuries-old trees for firewood, and leave their litter strewn about. And I believe the man who built the shelter would agree. But despite this unfortunate
reality, the global environmental crisis that sends species into extinction daily
and threatens to destroy all life surely has its roots in the Western pattern of
thought that sees humanity and "wilderness" as mutually exclusive.

In old-growth forests in the North Cascades, deep inside an official
wilderness area, I have come upon faint traces of log shelters built by Suiattle
and Upper Skagit people for berry harvesting a century or more ago—just as
the sisters said. Those human-made structures were as natural a part of the
Cascade ecosystem as the burrows of marmots in the steep scree slopes. Our

native ancestors all over this continent lived within a complex web of relations with the natural world, and in doing so they assumed a responsibility for their world that contemporary Americans cannot even imagine. Unless Americans, and all human beings, can learn to imagine themselves as intimately and inextricably related to every aspect of the world they inhabit, with the extraordinary responsibilities such relationship entails—unless they can learn what the indigenous peoples of the Americas knew and often still know—the earth simply will not survive. A few square miles of something called wilderness will become the sign of failure everywhere.

AT THE END OF RIDGE ROAD

from a nature journal

Joseph Bruchac

Two Owls
September 10, 2000

It is late on a warm September night. The small house that we now call The Camp was built forty-five years ago on one of those ridges of land that sworl on relief maps like great waves of earth at the edge of the range of ancient mountains labeled on those same maps as the Adirondacks. The fifteen acres of property around this house, a few miles south of the blue line that marks the Adirondack Park, are protected by the conservation easement my wife and I donated to the Saratoga Land Conservancy. Although we purchased The Camp as a getaway from our other home, a house on a busy rural corner where my grandparents ran a general store and I was raised, we are not newcomers to this ridge. A mile away from here, on top of Cole Hill, is the homestead where my Abenaki grandfather and his twelve brothers and sisters were born. A hundred-year-old sugar maple in front of that house was planted by my grandfather and his younger brother Jack. Even closer to us are the unmarked burial places of Abenakis and Mohawks and Mohicans who came to the high places to bury their dead, giving their spirits a head start on their journey along "the Great Road" of stars in the sky. The work I've done to protect those burial places from developers is one of the reasons we ended up here on the southeastern side of Glass Factory Mountain in the Kaydeross Range.

Away from the sounds of roads and the glare of carbon-arc streetlights, it is quiet here. Some would say it is peaceful, but that is not the right word. This land throbs with life in every season and at every hour. And the quiet itself is not truly quiet. In the absence of the noise of jets and air conditioners, internal combustion engines and recorded music that blanket our perceptions in most of the human environments of America, ten thousand subtler voices may be heard.

As if in answer to my thought, a great horned owl calls from the pine tree just outside. The tree stands at the edge of the slope behind our camp that leads down to a pond where my grandfather fished when he was five decades younger than I am now. *Hoo, hoo-oooo, hoo, hoo, hoo,* a deep call that resonates.

Across the pond, perhaps a quarter mile to the west, another owl answers, its *Hoo, hoo-hoo-hoo, hoo-ooo, hooo-ooo* a bit higher; the sound of a female. Again the male owl repeats his call, but he doesn't just leave it at that call so well-described in the weather-beaten *Peterson Field Guide to Birds* that sits on the window ledge near my desk. As he continues to call and she answers, the two of them add sounds that are a little like those of a barred owl, a *huuurrrluuuul,* then almost a warble, then a bark, a growl, and finally a sound best expressed in some other language much older on this land than English. In Abenaki traditions, some owls, such as the screech owl, are called the village guardians. Roosting in trees near our wigwams, they would call out in alarm when strangers approached through the forest at night. The great horned owl was also seen as the greatest of the hunters. Abenaki men would wear a cap with two ears on it like the tufts of feathers on the horned owl's head, disguising their silhouette so that they could creep close to deer.

Whenever I hear the great horned owl call from so close in the night, a part of me that is related to the small furred or feathered creatures hunted by those owls gives an involuntary shiver. I see, for a moment in my mind's eye, the scatter of crow feathers I found two moons ago at the base of the old beech tree with a long-ago-healed arrow-shaped scar upon its trunk that says it was once a marker tree. Something deep in my blood remembers that I, too, may be the hunted, that a human being is neither above nor apart, that the land will swallow me as surely as it has the young crow that stirred from its roosting place in the night to be astonished at a sudden, brief burst of starlight as the owl's wide-open talons struck and then darkness swallowed its vision. And from that moment of mortal awareness I find what may seem to some a strange reassurance. To be a native part of the land means accepting it in all of its incarnations. To flow forever with the land, to continue with its cycles means being aware of death, to know that it has many voices and that the owl's call may be one of them.

Owls. Kokohas is one of the names the owl gave itself in the Abenaki language spoken by some of my ancestors. In so many of our native languages, the animals say their own names, and we repeat them as best we can. Today, when we do so, it is usually as haltingly as a tourist trying to ask directions in a foreign land by using a phrase book. But a few of us have listened well enough not only to speak to the animals, but to be answered by them.

The Europeans who came to the northeast were often amazed at the way the Abenaki could "mimic" the birds and animals, calling a moose with a horn made from a roll of birch bark, bringing a fox by making the squealing cry of a rabbit in distress, talking a wary turkey into making itself seen. Vocalizations. So I heard it described when I was a student of wildlife conservation at Cornell University, where none of my professors lectured about animals or birds actually speaking. Bird and animal calls (or cries, or, more poetically, songs) weren't true language. Or, if they did speak recognizable human words—as captive crows and starlings have often done—then those dumb creatures were only mimicking real speech, just as the Abenaki—who, of course, were closer on the evolutionary ladder to beasts than were Europeans—did so well at vocal mimicry of the lower orders. Perhaps you will smile as I do when I remind you that in the early days of the European migrations, there were learned men who believed that American Indians were neither fully human nor truly capable of speech. The ringing grace of native oratory was said to be like bird song, beautiful utterance devoid of meaning. When there were no Europeans around to hear them, Indians were said to growl and mumble at each other in the manner of wolves and bears. It is very much an understatement to say that we were not respected. Few Europeans learned our languages. Like tamed crows, we were expected to speak in their tongues.

The old relationship that my Abenaki people appear to have had with this land, with all that lived upon, within, and above it, was and remains for some of us a dialogue—not a simple one, but one as complex as all life. Today, American Indians have been elevated (or reduced) to the status of environmental icons, as much in balance with nature as the spider is with its instinctively spun web. We have been thrust into a perilous balance. We become noble savages, whether we like it or not. Then, if we (and all our ancestors and all our descendants) do not live up to it, if white researchers can shove enough data onto the page to prove that Indians didn't really act like environmentalists all the time in every situation, we are taken to the other extreme. Such researchers say that rather than respecting the buffalo, the Plains Indians wiped out entire herds indiscriminately—thus using research like a scalpel to cut the cord that bound the human beings to the buffalo people like an umbilical. They conclude that our First Nations didn't wipe out all the buffalo herds simply because our populations were too small, dropping Indians back down to the status that we shared at times in colonial America with the wolf, the mountain lion—dangerous predators with bounties on our scalps. In American culture, iconization is only one step away from exposure and vilification. In American Indian culture, people are not icons and we humans are never more than one step away from every other part of creation.

It is a dialogue still: speaking with, engaging in a deep relationship, marrying the land. So many of our traditions bear witness to such intimacy. As I listen to the owls speaking to each other, moving through the forest, engaging in a slow dance over the next three hours that takes them in a great circle around the pond, up slope and down, from the birches to the pines on the high slope, I remember one of our stories. It tells how Great Horned Owl fell in love with a young Penobscot woman who said she would marry only the greatest hunter. He disguised himself as a human, placing a hood over his head. Then he came into the village carrying a deer he'd killed over his shoulder. Everyone thought he would make a perfect husband, except for the young woman, who was suspicious of this young man who always kept his head covered. She urged him to sit with her by the fire, moving him closer to it until the heat was so great that he had to take off his hood. As soon as he did so his tufted ears stood up high above his head. "This one is not a human being," the young woman cried out as Great Horned Owl assumed his own shape and flew off. "I cannot marry him."

But Great Horned Owl was persistent, trying again and again to win the young woman. Finally, close to despair, Great Horned Owl stopped trying to imitate a human being. He sat in a tree at the edge of the village and began to play a song on his flute, a song so hauntingly beautiful that the young woman could not help but be moved by it.

She left her lodge and walked into the forest. "I will marry you," she said. Then Great Horned Owl flew down and carried her away.

Turkeys
September 11, 2000

The leaves of the blueberry bushes—more than fifty of them planted forty years ago by the people who lived here before, selling us what was their much-loved summer camp—are starting to turn red. This wet spring and summer have made the blueberry crop abundant. We've picked all that we can eat or freeze and given just as many berries away. Such abundance is meant to be shared—as the cedar waxwings and chickadees and blue jays who flutter around my head as I pick are well aware. Though I prune out the dead wood, weed and mulch, the birds know these berries are theirs. In fact, last summer, when the harvest was much less than this one, most of the berries were picked by them.

Before I can write another sentence Carol comes into the room. "Come quick," she says. "The wild turkeys are in the blueberries."

We've put in a new double-glazed picture window, and our view of the berry bushes and the cut through the trees below them is spectacular some mornings. On those days we can see thirty miles southeast—across the hills where the Hudson River winds, invisible most days save for a winding snake of rising mist past Easton, New York, and on to the lower edge of Vermont's Green Mountains. Today, though, the clouds have settled around the hill.

Though we can see our yard, the world beyond it turns into ghostly mist beyond the tall elegance of the white birches.

In the rain-shadowed bushes where I stood barefoot only half an hour ago to pick a pint of berries for our breakfast, one large turkey is barely visible, standing still, head up and listening. Then he bobs his head, making the beard on his chest swing back and forth as he walks deeper in among the bushes. Two more are in the driveway, their feathers bronze, iridescent, glittering as if they carry light with them. We often hear them in the woods around us, the scratching of their feet as they forage for insects, seeds, and berries, their voices repeating the flock call to each other. *Kee-yow, kee-yow.* "You still there?" *Kee-yow, kee-yow.* "I'm still here, where are you?"

Here in the northeast, as the forests have been allowed to reclaim the land that was once cleared, the old ecosystems have begun to reassert themselves. At the turn of the twentieth century, white-tailed deer had become so rare that people came from miles around when one was killed and hung up in front of the country store in Greenfield Center. On this very ridge, there were almost no trees, no deer, no turkeys, only herds of sheep grazing the rock-strewn pastures. But now there are deer everywhere, at times a little arrogantly. I kept finding the same perfect hoof mark, remade almost every morning at the edge of the garden where our canna lilies and hosta were grazed down to the level of mowed grass by a buck who finally moved on to our neighbor's garden for the more interesting salad course of pole beans and sunflowers. Two years ago, the people in the house closest to ours had to rescue their dog when it found itself under the hooves of a doe who resented the fact that the dog had gotten too close to her fawn—which, while Mama danced the *macarena* on Rover, stood next to their driveway with one of those innocent "What is this all about?" looks on its face that children sometimes wear when they've gotten someone else into trouble. The dog was on its back, the doe pounding it so determinedly with her hooves that for a while the deer ignored the fact that our neighbor was hitting her with a broom. (Not a truly wise thing to do, for deer have been known to stand on their hind legs and strike out at people with the sharp hooves.) Even after they rescued the only slightly injured dog and retreated with it into their house, that doe, her ears lowered back against her head, still kept walking back and forth in their driveway, making a chuffing sound like a horse and looking to finish off the job she'd started.

The more you know an animal, someone once said, the more human it seems. So it is that researchers in Africa are always anthropomorphizing the chimps or lions or gorillas that they study, giving them human names. But in the old days, among our people, it was the opposite. The more our native ancestors saw and heard of the natural world around us, the more they realized that we humans were part of it. What European cultures call "wilderness," carefully separating it from "civilization," remained an intimate part of human nature in indigenous cultures. Rather than pasting human masks over the faces of the animals, we recognized the animals as people with nations of their own. Though we often hunted them, we gave them respect. Not only did they provide us with food and material goods, they were always teaching us.

The turkey's loud ululating call was a signal among our people. Sometimes the warriors used it in those days when we tried to protect the land from the inexorable European tide rolling west and north. Turkey, an Iroquois story says, was a great, brave warrior. Long ago there were giants made of stone. They were cannibals who ate the people and broke down the forests beneath the feet. One day, Turkey and Moose decided to make war on those monsters. Moose was another one of the old ones in our Abenaki stories. Like those material objects that bore Abenaki names, the toboggan, the moccasin, the tomahawk, the name by which Moose is known is the one by which we called him, "Mos." The one who grazes under the waters of the pond.

Turkey and Moose found the deep tracks of the Stone Giants. Even without those footprints, which sank at places into the stone itself, it was easy to follow those monsters, for they left a path of devastation behind them like that made by the whirlwind. Turkey and Moose crept up to the place where the Stone Giants were gathered at the edge of a cliff. Turkey gave his loud war cry and flew at them, pecking at their eyes. Moose lowered his horns and charged at them. Surprised by Turkey's cry, struck by Moose's horns, the Stone Giants stumbled backward, fell over the cliff, and were killed. Moose's horns were flattened from striking the Stone Giants. Turkey's throat was stained red by their blood. Then Moose and Turkey each cut the hair from the top of the dead Stone Giants. To this day Turkey wears that hair on his chest and Moose wears it on his chin as a badge of courage.

Despite their courage, the turkeys—like the moose—were wiped out from this land. Yet they are back again now. And not only the turkeys. Over the last few decades the moose populations of Maine, where a remnant population of those great ungulates survived into the twentieth century (though elk and caribou became extinct), have risen. As forests have reclaimed the farmlands, sumac and cherry followed by locust and ash and maple, wandering young bulls and cows have moved back into their old ranges in New Hampshire, in Vermont, and here in the Adirondacks. Just beyond the blueberry orchard, among the young pines, we have found moose scat—white cowflop-shaped piles—as well as the tracks of a bull, a cow, and a calf.

Our old words keep returning to the land.

Turtles
September 12, 2000

We've made a narrow walkway of old planks across the end of Bucket Pond, where its shallow waters give way to hummocks of vegetation, ferns rising up on masses of roots to make small islands colonized by pitcher plants and saplings. This morning, as we crossed, I saw a painted turtle just as it saw us. It turned, its feet churning the dark rotted vegetation that forms the bed of the pond—perfect for African violets, said the man who was disappointed when his offer to buy the pond and dredge it out for greenhouse soil was refused.

As that turtle paddled toward the deeper water of the pond where it could dive down out of sight, I moved without thinking—the fastest way to move through the swamp or the forest. I don't recall leaping off the boardwalk, my feet touching one hummock and then another. I only know that somehow I ended up on my stomach, leaning out over the water as my hand grasped the smooth, strong shell of the turtle. Its long claws pushed back hard against my thumb and fingers. Long claws characterize the male painted turtle. *Chrysemys picta*. I lifted it gently. Its carapace was just a little larger than my palm. The males are smaller than the females. It extended its neck, trying to push free, the yellow stripes from its mouth back along its wet neck glowing almost as if lit from within.

One of our old stories tells how Turtle, long ago, decided to make war on human beings because they were hunting the animals without mercy. Then Turtle painted yellow lines upon his face to show that he was serious about taking the path to war. Great as his plans were, Turtle met failure and barely escaped alive, his shell cracked as a result. But, like this small reluctant warrior I held in my hand, even though every painted turtle since then still wears those martial colors, today turtles flee from the sight of a human being. It is easy to plan war, they've learned, but fighting is a hard thing to do. Perhaps this little one would reinforce that ancient lesson, telling the other turtles in the pond about its narrow escape after I released it.

There are many lessons to be learned from the turtles. On the back of every turtle are thirteen large plates, twenty-eight smaller ones around the edge. Not just the painted turtle, but other turtles around the world share that physical trait. In the late 1960s, I did a three-year stint as a volunteer teacher in West Africa. Near dawn, one day, as I drove the newly completed Tema Motorway, its ten-mile length then the only stretch of four-lane paved highway in Ghana, I saw a familiar rounded shape in the middle of the road. I pulled over to dodge the traffic, brightly painted lorries with such mottoes on their sides as SEA NEVER DRY and NO TELEPHONE TO HEAVEN, to rescue an African land tortoise, shocked into immobility by the unexpected roar of trucks in the middle of an ancient migration path. Its movable fortress might discourage a leopard or a baboon but would offer little protection from the Michelins of a ten-ton lorry. As I carried it far off the road edge into the brush I counted the familiar thirteen plates on its carapace and smiled up at the full African moon still visible low above the horizon.

There are thirteen full moons in any given year, roughly twenty-eight days between one full moon and the next. So it is that the native people of the northeast say that the turtle's back is a lunar calendar, its scutes counting off the moons and days. And, just as it holds the moon, the turtle also holds the earth. Not the painted turtle, but its bigger cousin. *Chelydra serpentina.* The snapping turtle. There are snapping turtles in Bucket Pond, too. It's not surprising. The range of the painted turtle and the snapper overlap. Of the reptiles of North America, it seems that only the garter snake has a wider range than does the snapping turtle. A great many people seem to not only dislike snapping turtles but to be phobic about them. Few people are ever bitten by a snapping turtle—unless they've been teasing one they've taken captive—but the image of snapping turtles swimming up beneath you to take a nip out of whatever tender part of the human anatomy is readily available starts the theme for *Jaws* churning in the subconscious of most people who hear that these tough ancient survivors are in some body of water.

But it isn't that way for us. American Indians see the snapper in a much more favorable way—not always to its benefit. I doubt that snapping turtles themselves appreciate how sweet traditional turtle stew tastes and how good turtle shell rattles sound during a social dance. Yet it also means that a pond with snapping turtles in it has always been seen as a valuable resource. More than one native person has told me about doing as I've done in late summer, gathering up just-hatched snapping turtle babies digging their way from the warm sand to carry them down to the safety of a swamp, sparing them the dangerous overland journey where most such hatchlings are carried off by crows and hawks, foxes and raccoons and skunks.

The ridge above the pond where our small camp was built is open to the rays of the morning sun. Just behind the house, the steep, wooded ridge runs down to Bucket Pond. Beneath the tall pines and hemlocks, maples and beech, there in the rich humus on the well-drained, rocky slope, ground pine and partridgeberry twine around the wide basal leaves of pink lady's slippers *(Cypripedium acaule)*, perhaps the largest of the native North American orchids. They grow here in great abundance. This year, between May and July, when their bright, inflated, moccasinlike blossoms bobbed at the end of their leafless stalks, we counted more than a hundred blossoms. Some had even crept into the blueberry orchard. Abundant as they might seem, we've taken care that our trails down to the pond go around them. They vanish quickly—not just when an area is logged, but also when trampled by human feet. Their beauty has also been their undoing in the past when people have dug them up, thinking to transplant them in gardens—where they fail to propagate. Called "moccasin flower" by both the Abenaki and Iroquois, they were respected as medicine plants. Though I know how their root may be used, I neither dig them from the earth nor tell anyone else what sort of medicine can be made from the lady's slipper. The medicinal use of native ginseng *(Panax quinquefolium)*, also to be found in secluded locations in our woods along with its smaller cousin the dwarf ginseng *(Panax trifolium)*, was too well-known by Europeans. Prized in the Orient as an aphrodisiac and blood stimulant, it has become almost completely extirpated from its original habitat here in the southern Adirondacks.

Because the sandy soil around our camp is open to the sun, it grows warm much sooner than anywhere else on our property. The pink moccasin flowers do not venture out onto that baking earth. But others do—the turtles. Every year, usually when a warm spring rain is falling, we look out of the window to see the rain-glossed shell of one or more female painted turtles, front feet gripping the earth as one back leg scoops a hole deeper and deeper until their backside tilts down into it and they can lay their cache of eggs. Each granular-surfaced yellowish white egg is about the size of the last joint of my index finger. Usually, no more than six or eight are laid about six inches deep in a hole about the width of two fingers. When they are done, they cover the hole thoroughly, scraping earth and vegetation over it so meticulously that it is hard to see that the excavation was ever made. It is important that such care is taken, for the skunks and raccoons nose them out at night. More than once I've gone out in the morning to find only a scraped-out hollow—mute evidence of a midnight snack—where a turtle's nest had been. One such rainy day I watched a single painted turtle for more than two hours on our lawn (if you could use that term for the sandy, unseeded half acre that we give over to native grasses and plants) and observed that nest camouflage is not a mother turtle's only way of protecting the next generation. After finishing one hole, which took her a good fifteen minutes to dig, she covered it rather carelessly and crawled on without laying a single egg. She dug two more such decoy nests before her final one, close to a clump of milkweed that would later serve as late-summer food for monarch butterfly caterpillars. That final nest was the one that was most carefully concealed.

This morning, a particularly warm one, I paid close attention to the small raised garden I made this spring, using old six-by-sixes to hold in the composted soil made in lasagna layers from grass clippings and cow manure, shredded wastepaper and kitchen scraps. A few tomato plants, some beans and onions, carrots and a few rows of snapdragons, zinnias, and dinner plate dahlias have done well there this year, though the heavier than usual rains doomed one planting after another of usually prolific marigolds. The deer have spared this garden, but this past spring brought quite another, unexpected, peril to the survival of the small plants. As a result, I'm looking for another crop this morning, one of dragon's teeth soldiers.

On June 22, an overcast morning, the temperature already sixty-two degrees at seven o'clock, I started to walk down to the pond. Two steps past the garden I did a double take. When did someone put that large round stone in among the tomato plants? That large round greenish gray stone . . . with a head? I turned slowly and crouched to approach my invaded garden on my hands and knees so that I would not startle the female snapping turtle who had chosen that spot for her nest. But I needn't have bothered with caution. She was well settled in and not about to move. She raised her shell slightly, gave one long hiss like a leaking inner tube and then, territorial rights established, settled back into excavating the foot-deep hole beneath the rear of her plastron. Even when I cautiously used a yardstick to measure her shell (roughly 10 1/2 inches across and 12 inches long) she paid no further attention to me. Fearsome and feared as snapping turtles may be to the average person, they pose no real danger. The only time people might be bitten by a snapper would be when they teased one that was on land and seeking to defend itself. In the water a snapping turtle will either ignore humans or swim away from them, despite the many myths about mangled dangling swimmers. We present a great deal of danger to them, though. Migrating snappers often end up crushed on our roadways and they are an easy target for men and boys with .22s who shoot turtles for sport, out of fear, or because they view them as unwanted competitors for fish or ducks. Although snapping turtles sometimes climb out onto logs or banks to bask in the sun, as do our painted turtles, more often than not they engage in aquatic basking. Their heads raised up like small floating sticks, they rest for long periods on the surface with most of their carapace above water. Watching them from the hill above the pond with binoculars, I've sometimes seen two or three engaging in this leisurely behavior, and I'm sad to say that they would then make an easy target for anyone with a scoped rifle.

In the past, though no longer so much today, snappers were a favored food item for Native Americans and rural people who knew how good the cooked flesh of a snapping turtle tastes. Though it is not strictly true, I grew up being told by my grandmother that just as chickens have white meat and dark meat, there were at least seven different kinds of meat on a snapping turtle with the tastes of pork, chicken, turkey, beef steak, veal, lamb, and rabbit. Though it has been many years since I've tasted snapping turtle meat, cooked Mohawk style in its own shell, I can state from experience that while the meat has the richness of good beef, it does not have seven flavors. At Akwesasne, the Mohawk reservation at the extreme northern tip of New York, the people no longer eat snapping turtles. It is not that they are gone. Turtles are still found in large numbers in the Saint Lawrence River, which was turned into a seaway, cutting through the heart of not one but two Canadian/United States Mohawk reservations—Akwesasne, which is divided between New York and Québec, and Kanawake, close to Montréal. The problem with the snapping turtles today is that the turtles, who scavenge the river and take in virtually everything in the food chain, have absorbed immense amounts of PCBs and other toxins.

My friend Ward Stone, a wildlife biologist whose sometimes controversial work for New York State has included studying these levels of toxicity, is amazed at how the turtles have survived despite it all, though many of them have cancers on their bodies. Even when cooked, their meat still contains enough heavy metals and PCBs to endanger the health of those who might eat them. Tom Porter, a Mohawk elder who no longer lives at Akwesasne, remembers the day when his family took their fishing nets and laid them on the banks of the Saint Lawrence, leaving them there to return to the earth, for the fish were not safe to eat. The aluminum plants of Reynolds and Kaiser continue to pour their wastes into the air and river to this day, making the Akwesasne Mohawk Reservation—an American Indian superfund site—one of the most chemically poisoned places in North America.

The snapper was also sought by the Iroquois and other nations of the northeast to use its shell in the making of rattles, with the dried outstretched neck used as the handle (braced by two thin ash withes fastened along the back of its neck from the shell to beyond the tip of its nose). Such rattles are made to this day. I have one hanging over our fireplace here at The Camp, its shell dimensions just an inch or two less than that of my garden turtle. It was given to me seven years ago while I was in Wisconsin by Pam Green, an Oneida Indian poet. It was made by her traditionalist husband, who wanted to thank me for doing storytelling for the teachers and students of the Oneida Indian School. Such a gift is a great honor, not only because of the care required to make such a rattle, but because of the place those rattles hold in our northeastern cultures. Not only do they provide the rhythm for social and ceremonial dances, they are made from the body of one of the most revered of all the beings. To the Iroquois, the snapping turtle is a powerful and sacred creature. It is not just a creature of one element, but travels between both the earth and the water—just as one who is a medicine person is able to travel between the human world and that of the spirits.

But to the Iroquois and perhaps a hundred different American Indian tribal nations all across this continent, the turtle also plays another role—the greatest of all the beings that walk and swim. Long ago, the stories say, there was no earth. Everything was covered with water. For some reason, the water beings decided that earth needed to be created. Each native tradition may differ slightly here. Some, like the Iroquois, tell of a woman who fell from the land above the sky. Seeing her fall, the geese flew up to catch her and the water creatures began to make a place for her to stand. One thing is common to every version of that story, which is called the "Earth Diver" motif by folklorists. Someone had to dive down below the waters to bring up some mud to make the solid land of Earth. But when it was brought up, where could it be placed? One being volunteered. Floating upon the surface, just as an aquatic basking snapper would to this day, Great Snapping Turtle said that the new earth could be placed upon his back. So the mud was placed there, and as it was smoothed and spread out it grew to be the continent of North America—the land that the majority of contemporary American Indians often refer to as "Turtle Island."

For the next half hour the mother snapping turtle remained splayed in position between my staked tomato plants, slowly laying her eggs. There were more than two dozen of them. Each egg was as white and round as a ping-pong ball, though just a bit smaller. As she laid each egg she squeezed shut her eyes—each pupil like a starburst—and there was moisture at the edge of each eye. Though not as dramatically as a sea turtle might, the mother snapping turtle cried as she laid her eggs. At last, almost carelessly, she pulled the edge of her shell up out of the hole and shoved back enough earth to cover the eggs. Then she levered herself out of the garden, dragging herself with her strong front paws up and over the six-by-six wall—which had been no impediment to her powerful nesting urge (and her ability to do this simple equation: soft earth equals easy digging)—to make her ponderous way back to the pond. Behind her was left a perfect turtle-shaped imprint. Her haste to depart had little to do with the fact that I was watching. Unlike the painted turtle, snappers cover their nests rather carelessly. And even more than the painted turtle, snapping turtle eggs end up on the menu of raccoons and skunks.

I looked at my raised garden a little ruefully. There was now one fewer pepper plant and a few slightly mangled marigolds, but she had done surprisingly little damage. But one turtle was enough. I spent the next hour putting up wire fencing around the garden. It would serve two purposes. Not only would it keep out other mother turtles with a yen for an easy nest site, it would also protect that precious clutch of eggs through July and August until the warmth of the late summer sun has finally done its job and it is September. Hatching time. It's been a cool spring and summer. Research has shown that cooler temperatures, around the mid-fifties Fahrenheit at critical times in the incubation of turtle eggs, result in all the hatchlings being female. Males like it hotter, up in the seventies. New as that finding may be to Western science, I was told over twenty years ago by a Mohawk friend just that same thing. "Cool summer, turtle eggs will be mommas." But that was just Indian folk belief and thus (though as right as a vast number of our "folk beliefs" are) less scientifically reliable.

Once again, though, I miss the hatching. I don't dig down that morning in the place I've marked to find if they're emerging. Not only would it be intruding, but I believe that the little turtles do better when they have to struggle up from the earth on their own. Indeed, when I come back to The Camp that evening I can see that the soft earth has been disturbed. When the hatching begins, most seem to come out within a matter of hours. I look around, but see no sign of any little turtles. It is unlikely that I would, for they head quickly for shelter, hiding under the leaves when they are tired, making their way toward the pond. Not unerringly, I have to say, for I have on occasion found a few disgruntled baby turtles in our garage, which is downslope in the opposite direction of the pond. Finally, I probe carefully with my fingers where the nest had been. All that I unearth are a few small, slightly rubbery collapsed shells, pushed open from within. Another year's hatching of turtles has emerged to help hold the balance upon our Mother Earth.

4

PRAISE

RECLAIMING OURSELVES, RECLAIMING AMERICA

Francisco X. Alarcón

Like many others, I went through life without ever looking at mirrors. I found ways to avoid most cameras. Friends and relatives came to expect this from me, another trait of my peculiar nature. Photographs of me were simply unacceptable: the dark stranger in them just couldn't be me. How could I possibly identify or associate myself with this body of mine when almost everything around me negated me? I was nobody, and nowhere was I to find my reflection, my image, my self. I was an alien at home and everywhere, and more importantly, a stranger to myself.

This sense of alienation and shame is shared by countless persons who are the product of the violent expansion of Europe since the fifteenth century. Whole peoples were forced to perceive themselves as the defective copies of idealized realities. Vast territories of this continent were to be projections of imposed models from the "Old World," first "New Spain," and, later, other European cultural models like the French and British as well as the newer Anglo-American ones.

And yet this image in the mirror is me, and I am a Mestizo.[1] I am the physical proof of the violent transformation suffered by native peoples on this continent in the last five hundred years. My face, my body, my soul are in constant turmoil. They don't seem to fit any European profile. Yes, there are elements in me that come from Europe, the Mediterranean Sea, and Africa, but there are other aspects of me that can only come from this continent. One of the most explosive consequences of the contradictory sociopolitical movement known as the Mexican Revolution that began in 1910 was the long overdue recognition that Mexicans were not faulty copies of Europeans but an original amalgamation of cultures and ethnicities with deep roots in their Mesoamerican past. The Chicano Movement of the past three decades has had a similar effect on Mexican Americans, Chicanos, and Mexicans living in the United States.

Behind the seeming monoliths erected by the "official history," there are some forgotten cracks and gaps that sometimes hold the real story. This is the suppressed and mostly unspoken history of the native peoples of this continent, and of their descendants. In spite of the obsession of Spanish colonial authorities to eradicate any trace of this history, an obsession shared by their spiritual and temporal successors, markers of this time and history endure all around us. Their stories need to be told and retold.

Isla Mujeres: The Belly Button of the Nightmare

In the summer of 1989, I stumbled rather unexpectedly into one of those markers that locate the beginning of an important cycle in human history. On August 13, I found myself walking toward the eastern tip of Isla Mujeres, a five-mile-long by half-mile-wide island set in the turquoise waters of the Caribbean Sea, eight miles across from the fancy Mexican resort mecca of Cancún, on the Yucatán Peninsula. "Allá no hay nada" ("There's nothing over there"), I had been told by a passing taxicab driver dispensing free advice on the dirt road I was tracking. But nothing and no one could dissuade me from visiting the easternmost point of Mexico, where Francisco Hernández de Córdoba had first arrived on March 1, 1517, thus beginning the process of exploration, conquest, and colonization of Mesoamerica.

The Spanish chronicler of the Conquest of Mexico, Bernal Díaz del Castillo, who was a member of this expedition, wrote in his *Historia verdadera de la Conquista de la Nueva España,* "On February 8, 1517, we sailed from Havana . . . twenty-one days after we had left port, we sighted land, which made us happy and for which we gave thanks to God. This land had never been discovered nor was there any knowledge of it till then."[2]

Some hundred yards from a whitewashed stucco lighthouse and next to a cliff where the island meets the Caribbean Sea, I ran into an open wound made of stone and rubble, the half-buried memories of the temple of Ixchel, the Mother Goddess in the Mayan tradition. There was no need for a historic marker or my visitor's guide—which didn't even list the site. Somehow I just knew what I knew. What had once been an erect construction had been blown away by the fury of Hurricane Gilbert a year before, in September 1988. And yet, on that spot, I knew I was in front of an ancient oracle. I felt the ominous presence of Ixchel, Great Mother, Protector. She was there for reasons that might have been forgotten, trampled on, and simply discarded, but for me, she was more real and alive than all the modern reality and life embodied by the flashy new hotels of nearby Cancún. That humble pile of rubble stood for the state of abandonment and denial of a past that keeps haunting us. It was a testament of the fate of Mesoamerica. We have deserted our Mother, and sold out for mere trinkets. Standing on a cliff at the edge of the island, all of a sudden, I was once again looking, for the first time, at the mysterious mountains moving out in the sea, and also squinting my eyes aboard one of the approaching Spanish ships.

In his *Relación de las cosas de Yucatán,* written in 1566, Fray Diego de Landa describes the arrival of the Spaniards:

In the year 1517, during Lent, Francisco Hernández de Córdoba left Cuba with three ships to trade for slaves for the mines, as the population of Cuba was much diminished. Others say he sailed to discover [new] land and that he took Alaminos with him as pilot and that he reached the Isla de las Mujeres, and that it was he who gave it this name because of the idols which he discovered there to the goddesses Ixchel, Ixchebeliax, Ixhunic, Ixhunieta; these were dressed from the waist down and had their breasts uncovered in the Indian manner. The building was of stone, which astonished them, and there they found some objects, which they took away with them.[3]

Antón de Alaminos had been Columbus's pilot on the latter's final voyage in 1502. Alaminos had also sailed with Ponce de León to Florida in 1513, and later was a member of the expeditions of Juan de Grijalva in 1518 and Hernán Cortes in 1519 to Yucatán and the Gulf of Mexico.[4]

Francisco Hernández de Córdoba is the first to continue in Mesoamerica this colonial practice of renaming locations already well-known by the natives with brand-new Spanish toponyms. Even today some of our own names are a prolongation of this practice. Yes, my given name is also Francisco, but my *tonal* (sign) in the Nahuatl tradition is *coatl* (serpent). I am ruled by Chalchiuhcueye, the Goddess of Water. I am also a son of Yemayá in the Yoruba tradition via Cuba.

In order to understand history and be able to exorcise the past, we need to relive this history in flesh and spirit. We need to reenact all the misunderstandings, confrontations, and contradictions, all the suffering and havoc brought about by the so-called discovery of this continent by Europeans. I spent the rest of that day among the ruins of the temple of Ixchel in wonder and an altered state of consciousness. I was also overwhelmed by a sense of inner sadness and voiceless rage, mourning, anger, and despair. I walked back to my hotel in almost total darkness, in anguish. The dead I had invoked were as numerous as the stars in the sky. One day I would like to go back to Isla Mujeres and meet Francisco Hernández de Córdoba eye to eye, as one meets one's murderous father for the first and last time: the synchronic nature of poetry and ritual can certainly make this possible.

This first European contact with the native peoples of Mesoamerica took place less than twenty-five years after the October 12, 1492, "discovery" of another island by one Christopher Columbus. A quarter of a century was enough time for the *encomenderos,* governors, missionaries, and miners to wipe out entire populations of native people from the Caribbean islands. On August 13, 1521, only four years after the first landing of Spaniards at Isla Mujeres, Hernán Cortés took for a prisoner Cuauhtémoc, the last Tlatoani (the Reverend Speaker) of Mexico-Tenochtitlán, who along with his people had valiantly resisted a long and terrible siege. The "Discovery of America," or the more sensitive phrase, the "Encounter of Two Cultures," is a mere euphemism for genocide, ethnocide, and ecocide that were the direct result of the invasion and conquest of the Indies.

America was not "discovered" by Christopher Columbus, nor by Viking seafarers, but by the first people who came to this continent from Asia at least fifty thousand years ago.[5] We would begin to understand the scope of the nightmare and holocaust that the arrival of the Europeans meant to the native peoples of this continent if only we could feel within ourselves the sorrow and despair of a native population of twenty million reduced to less than two million in a hundred years. No account is possible. Words are useless. We are forced to experience this knowledge outside language. We must feel again all the new fatal diseases that decimated our peoples. We need to bring back the deceased in order to continue living. We have to reclaim our suppressed tongues and spirits, our burned homes and fields, our slaughtered mothers and fathers, our enslaved sisters and brothers. By reclaiming ourselves, we will be reclaiming America.

I say "America" not in the chauvinistic tradition of "God bless America," or "America, right or wrong." America is a continent and cannot be monopolized by a single country like the United States. America has no borders. It actually runs from Alaska to Patagonia. "America" and "American" have been terms that for too long have been misused to dominate, exclude, suppress, and eradicate the historical consciousness of the native peoples of this continent. America did not begin five hundred years ago. America has fantastic and very deep cultural roots that go back many thousands of years. "Americans" are all the various peoples that once lived on any given part of this hemisphere. For America to be America, it needs to remember its long and painful past with the same energy and dedication it devotes to its present and its future.

1492: Prelude of the Conquest by Sword, Cross, and Grammar

One can ascertain that plain greed played an important role in Columbus's endeavor. In his famous letters to his patroness Queen Isabella describing his explorations, our navigator wrote the word *gold* eighty times with the insistence of an avid prospector searching for any clue of this excrement-of-the-gods, as some natives called this metal. But other important historical facts have been generally overshadowed by Columbus's deed of October 12, 1492. Columbus's voyage was made possible by the successful military campaign of the Catholic rulers Isabella of Castile and Ferdinand of Aragon, against the last Islamic kingdom of Granada in southern Spain. A new unified Spanish state had emerged, and, in the same year of 1492, it decreed some terribly harsh measures, like the expulsion of the Jews from Spain and the forced conversion to Christianity of those who remained. A policy of religious intolerance and ethnic prejudice replaced the more humane practice of religious coexistence of Muslims, Christians, and Jews under more than seven hundred years of Arab rule in Iberia.

Similar oppressive colonial institutions and practices were later transplanted to the Americas by imperial Spain. Religion was to be used as an expeditious weapon of the state. The spiritual conquest of the Americas was as bloody and ruthless as the military conquest. Fray Bartolomé de las Casas's pleas and denunciations of the Spanish *conquistadores* are an eloquent testimony of a Christian missionary deeply troubled by the terrible excesses and abuses of his Christian countrymen. But the missionaries themselves never really questioned the terrifying human price their own evangelization policies demanded from the natives.

If religious and cultural homogeneity was to be obtained at all costs in the newly unified Spain, this goal also included a policy for linguistic conformity imposed on the Arab-speaking communities claimed by Castile. With that in mind, in that fateful year of 1492, the royal chronicler Antonio de Nebrija completed the very first grammar of any Romance language, Castilian. This grammar was later used very effectively to suppress the ancestral indigenous languages in the territories occupied by Spain in the Americas. If Catholicism provided the cross, the Spanish language supplied the nails for the crucifixion of native culture in Mesoamerica.

But no Christian holy sacrament or Spanish grammar rule could wipe out the deeply rooted ancestral Mesoamerican culture. Maybe there were just too many natives in Mesoamerica to contend with. In reality, the dominant culture was never able to eradicate all pockets of resistance. And the same language, culture, and writing system brought over by the oppressors became, at times, agents for cultural survival and spiritual liberation, as Cuban intellectual Roberto Fernández Retamar eloquently stated in his 1971 essay "Calibán: Notes toward a Discussion of Culture in Our America."[6]

For many of us, our America has been taken away. Our America has been invaded, occupied, whitewashed, gagged, suppressed, sanitized, and, at best, ignored. But against all odds, the cultural tradition of Mesoamerica has survived and is alive, and all around us. It cannot be reduced to just museum artifacts, bones, and stones, but it can be found in the flesh and spirit of many contemporary native and Mestizo peoples. Our mere existence is a testimony of our ancestors' will to live. The realization of this basic fact is both simple and complex. Mesoamerica as a civilization permeates all aspects of our daily lives, from the food we eat and the colors we prefer, to the ways we behave, worship, and even dream. Our nightmares and our visions are anchored in the psychodynamics of a Mesoamerican worldview. The dual nature of *La Virgen de Guadalupe* is a case in point—ancient Mesoamerican goddess worship continues under a Catholic disguise.[7]

Mestizos/as have been actively engaged in a profound cultural revolution during the span of the twentieth century throughout this hemisphere. The universalist notion of La Raza Cósmica, proposed in the 1920s by Mexican philosopher José Vasconcelos as the fulfillment of a Western humanistic utopia in which all human races intermingle to form an all-inclusive cosmic progeny, has now been molded into the "new Mestiza consciousness" being advocated by contemporary Chicana writer Gloria Anzaldúa in her moving *Borderlands/La Frontera: The New Mestiza.*

> The new *mestiza* copes by developing a tolerance for contradictions, a tolerance for ambiguity. She learns to be an Indian in Mexican culture, to be Mexican from an Anglo point of view. She learns to juggle cultures. She has a plural personality, she operates in a pluralistic mode—nothing is thrust out, the good, the bad and the ugly, nothing rejected, nothing abandoned. Not only does she sustain contradictions, she turns the ambivalence into something else.[8]

This new consciousness has been shaped by the present realities that we as Mestizos and Mestizas must face in our daily lives in the United States. It also implies a common struggle against the racism, classism, sexism, homophobia, and other forms of oppression still common in our complex society. But Anzaldúa warns, "Awareness of our situation must come before inner changes, which in turn come before changes in society. Nothing happens in the 'real' world unless it first happens in the images in our heads."[9] One of the most pressing changes that need to happen is our recognition and celebration of a cultural face that has been suppressed and denied for so long: our living Mesoamerican heritage.

For me, this has been a very painful process that started the moment I was taunted as *El Indio* by relatives when I was a five-year-old boy in Wilmington, the Mexican barrio in Los Angeles where my family lived. These relatives, originally from Jalisco, as was my father, held some pernicious racist notions about skin color and Amerindian features. I take after my father and happen to be much darker in complexion than my brothers. It wasn't until a family visit to Guadalajara, Mexico, in my childhood, that I got to meet my grandmother on my father's side, Doña Elvirita, *una prietita,* who immediately took me under her guidance and a protection that has endured even after her death when I was eighteen years old. Time has strengthened my memories of her. She was a shining example of a sound Mestizo way of living in unison with the Mesoamerican worldview. This awareness has become sharper and more defined with years of study and reflection and has helped me to take a really good look at myself. Gone are the shame and fear of before. I have come to see myself as part of a cultural continuum. Lots of things are beginning to make more sense.

Mesticismo

This awareness of our Mesoamerican past should be projected into our present and our future in radically new ways. Not in the nostalgic or romantic modes of Jean-Jacques Rousseau ("the noble savage"), but as the liberating practice of a new Mestizo/a (mixed-blood) consciousness. *Mesticismo* purposefully combines *Mestizo* and *misticismo* (mysticism), in order to differentiate it from *mestizaje. Mesticismo* comes out of the experiences that the dominant cultures have confined to the realm of the "other" and the "marginal," those people and cultures condemned to live dangerously in psychological and cultural borderlands. *El mesticismo le da vuelta a la tortilla* (*Mesticismo* turns things around) and sets out a fluid way of thinking about relation in which any notion of self must include the "others," equally trespassing neat demarcations like subject/object, human/nature, us/them, and other similar dichotomies common in Western thought and mythologies.

Mesoamerican myth and wisdom, religion and science are beginning to be studied and understood within their own systematic worldviews. In the past, they were often dismissed out of ignorance and petulance; most missionaries and modern scholars failed to recognize them as another, valid way of being. As a cultural universe in itself, Mesoamerica has always been a constellation of different peoples, a historic area full of contradictions and riddled by conflict and ambiguities. But until now, its sheer originality has been mostly glanced over by missionaries, archaeologists, anthropologists, and museographers. It's time for contemporary artists, poets, and writers to interpret this reality in their own terms.

America must be able to see, hear, touch, taste, and smell this America. This may well lead us to new ways of seeing, reading, feeling, thinking, creating, and living. Why not envision, for example, a new ecopoetics grounded in a heritage thousands of years old that holds that everything in the universe is sacred? Ancient native beliefs could possibly offer some viable alternatives to modern dilemmas. Old keys could open new doors. But the ultimate irony of today is that five hundred years after the first landing of Columbus, America remains as mysterious as ever, and a huge terra incognita for many who act and live as if they had just jumped ashore from one of the first Spanish ships from afar: La Pinta, La Niña, and La Santa María.

Toward Reclaiming an Ecopoetics

For me, this new liberating Mestizo/Mestiza consciousness not only embraces others as equals but also calls for a new global awareness of the oneness of all living creatures and of nature as a whole. This vision of the oneness of all life is shared by many of the ancient Earth-worshipping religions, the shamanistic spiritual traditions of native peoples in the Americas, Siberia, and other parts of Asia. In the Western cultural tradition, mystics (saints, visionaries, poets, and other outcasts) have left moving testimonies of their own epiphanies and encounters with oneness. Some of them experienced very intimate connections with the divine in the cosmos, achieving ecstasies.

In the Mesoamerican spiritual tradition, we encounter manifestations of this engrained vision of the oneness of all life in which the self is not alienated from the surrounding nature. In Mesoamerican mythologies, humans interact with animals, plants, and the forces of nature in very close and profound ways. One of the best examples of this worldview is the *Popul Vuh,* a genesis book of the Maya Quiché people of Guatemala that has been acknowledged as a Mayan bible. This book was written in 1558 by an indigenous scribe who used the Latin alphabet to transcribe Mayan language. It records the ancient oral tradition that survived the burning of most native codices by zealous Christian missionaries and Spanish colonial authorities. In 1701 a Catholic priest named Francisco Ximinéx found the book in his Santo Tomás parish in Chichicastenango, Guatemala, and translated it into Spanish. In 1854 this manuscript was snatched from the library of the University of San Carlos in Guatemala and taken to Europe by Abbot Brasseur de Bourbourg, who translated it this time to French and subsequently sold the manuscript to another collector, Alfonso Pinart. After Pinart died, his widow sold the manuscript to Edward E. Ayer, who brought it back to America, and placed it in the Newberry Library of Chicago, where it is today.[10]

Another notable example of a surviving account of the Mesoamerican spiritual tradition involving native religion, myths, beliefs, and medicine is the colonial treatise on Nahuatl magic and curing practices titled *Tratado de las supersticiones y costumbres gentílicas que hoy viven entre los naturales desta Nueva España, 1629* (Treatise on the superstitions and heathen customs that today live among the Indians native to this new Spain, 1629)[11] by Hernando Ruiz de Alarcón (1587–1646), a Catholic parish priest born in Mexico who had been commissioned by the Spanish Inquisition to record the Nahuatl magical spells and healing practices a hundred years after the Conquest of Mexico. Hernando Ruiz de Alarcón was a younger brother of the more famous Juan Ruiz de Alarcón (1581–1639), also a native of Mexico, who spent most of his life in the Spanish royal court in Madrid and is considered one of the greatest playwrights of the golden age of Spanish literature. Hernando Ruiz de Alarcón, based in his parish of Atenango, a small town in the present state of Guerrero, spent ten years compiling, translating, and interpreting the Nahuatl spells and invocations collected from fifty different Nahuatl informants living in communities in the states of Guerrero and Morelos, in the central part of Mexico.

In a long interview with me by Kenny Ausbel, later published in his book *Restoring the Earth: Visionary Solutions from the Bioneers*,[12] I explained in detail how, mostly by chance, I came across Ruiz de Alarcón's *Tratado* in the National Museum of Anthropology and History located in Mexico City, and how, after studying Nahuatl and reflecting on the *Tratado* written by another Alarcón, who could be a distant relative of mine, I decided to write a poetic response to his *Tratado*. The end result of this process was *Snake Poems: An Aztec Invocation*, a book of 104 poems published in 1992, also the year of the Columbus Quincentennial.

As part of *Snake Poems* I decided to include thirty Nahuatl invocations and spells from the *Tratado* in their original language alongside my English versions of the same spells. *Snake Poems* is a syncretic poetic text in which ancient Nahuatl spells converge with postmodern verse, with irony functioning at different levels. If Hernando Ruiz de Alarcón's main objective in recording this magical tradition was to suppress and eradicate native beliefs and heathen healing practices based on ancient Mesoamerican spirituality and religion, by writing down in scrutinizing details the Nahuatl spells in their original language and then translating them into Spanish, he ironically ended up preserving for posterity the same magical heathen tradition he wanted to destroy. The ultimate irony is that a Chicano poet also named Alarcón, some four hundred years later, using the colonial Alarcón's writings, learns "to undo what is done" by writing a postmodern *tonalamatl* (spirit book) with a diametrically inverse sense of urgency: reclaiming of an ancient Mesoamerican ecopoetics.

This process of cultural reclamation calls for the retrieval of a hybrid poetic practice that I refer to as a form of ecopoetics in order to stress the deep sense of interconnection linking the poetic self and nature. Ultimately this poetic self dwells in the collective consciousness and/or sense of oneness with the surrounding ecosystems. When doing public readings from *Snake Poems*, I usually start by reciting a short invocation that comes from "Prayer to Fire" and burning some sage and copal (tree resin). Since this ecopoetics is eclectic, I believe it should also appeal to all the senses:

ca niman	right now
aman	it shall be
nomatca nehuatl	I myself
nOxomoco	I, *Oxomoco*
niCipactonal	I, *Cipactonal*
nicmati Huehueh	I, the Old Man's friend
nicmati Ilama	I, the Old Woman's friend
niMictlanmati	I, *Mictlan* traveler
niTopanmati	I, *Topan* traveler
nomatca nehuatl	I myself
nitlamacazqui	I, Spirit in Flesh
niNahualteuctli	I, the Enchanter[13]

Then I ask everybody in the audience to join me in calling the four directions according to the Nahuatl tradition. Since one of the main purposes of this ecopoetics is to reconcile the internal split of many Mestizos which is a direct result of the relentless expansion of the West at the expense of conquering, colonizing, and exploiting indigenous peoples, their cultures, and their lands, I make sure to read—in both Spanish and English—a poem addressed to Hernando Ruiz de Alarcón.

HERNANDO RUIZ DE ALARCÓN
(1587-1646)

eras tú	it was you
al que buscabas	you were looking for
Hernando	Hernando
hurgando	searching
en los rincones	every house
de las casas	corner

semillas	for some
empolvadas	dusty seeds
de ololiuhqui	of *ololiuhqui*
eras tú	it was you
al que engañabas	whom you tricked
y aprehendías	and apprehended
eras tú	it was you
el que preguntaba	who both questioned
y respondía	and responded
dondequiera	everywhere
mirabas moros	you saw Moors
con trinchete	with long knives
y ante	and in front of
tanto dolor	so much sorrow
tanta muerte	so much death
un conquistador	you became
conquistado	a conquered
fuiste	conqueror
sacerdote	priest
soñador	dreamer
cruz parlante	speaking cross
condenando	condemning
te salvaste	you saved yourself
al transcribir	by transcribing
acaso	maybe
sin saber	without knowing
el cielo	the heavens

soy yo	I am
el de tu cepa	from your tree
el de tu sueño	from your dream
este cenzontle	this *cenzontle* bird
del monte:	in the wilderness:
tu mañana	your tomorrow[14]

All the Nahuatl spells in the *Tratado* include a phrase, *nomatca nehu-atl,* in which *nomatca* means "myself" and *nehuatl,* "I." This phrase could be translated into English as "I myself." I believe this phrase establishes the position of the speaker in a shamanistic incantation in which the subject and the universe are one. Nahuatl is a compound language in which new nouns can be formed by bringing together different words. In Nahuatl we could link the word *nehuatl,* meaning "I," with *amatl,* which means "paper, book," to form a new compound noun, *namatl,* which defies the Western logic of English since it would mean "I-am-the-book," but makes perfect sense in Nahuatl. In the spell used for planting corn in the *Tratado,* the shamanistic phrase appears at the beginning of the invocation.

FOR PLANTING CORN

nomatca nehuatl	I myself
nitlamacazqui	Spirit in Flesh:
tla xihualhuian	hear me, *Tonacacihuatl*
nohueltiuh	elder sister
Tonacacihuatl	Lady of Our Flesh
tla xihualhuian	hear me, *Tlalteuctli*
Tlalteuctli	Mother Earth
ye momacpalco	on your open hand
nocontlalia	I'm setting down
nohueltiuh	my elder sister
Tonacacihuatl	*Tonacacihuatl*

ahmo timopinauhtiz	don't shame yourself
ahmo tihuexcapehuaz	don't grumble
ahmo tihuexcatlatlacoz	don't laugh at us

cuix quin moztla	tomorrow
cuix quin huiptla	or the day after
in ixco icpac nitlachiaz	I want to see again
in nohueltiuh	the face of my elder sister
Tonacacihuatl	*Tonacacihuatl*

| *niman iciuhca* | let her stand |
| *in tlalticpac hualquizaz* | on the ground |

in nicmahuizoz	I shall greet
in nictlapaloz	I shall honor
in nohueltiuh	my elder sister
Tonacacihuatl	*Tonacacihuatl*[15]

Chicano poets and artists since the 1960s have been involved in the process of reclaiming a sense of a group identity connecting them with the indigenous cultures of the Americas. Cultural celebrations known as *Floricantos* have been organized from time to time in Chicano communities throughout the United States. *Floricanto* is a Spanish compound noun formed by bringing together *flower* and *song*, a translation of the phrase *in xochitl in cuicatl*, which in Nahuatl means "poetry." The last poem of *Snake Poems* is a celebration of this ancient ecopoetics:

IN XOCHITL IN CUICATL

cada árbol	every tree
un hermano	a brother
cada monte	every hill
una pirámide	a pyramid
un oratorio	a holy spot

cada valle	every valley
un poema	a poem
in xochitl	*in xochitl*
in cuicatl	*in cuicatl*
flor y canto	flower and song
cada nube	every cloud
una plegaria	a prayer
cada gota	every rain
de lluvia	drop
un milagro	a miracle
cada cuerpo	every body
una orilla	a seashore
al mar	a memory
un olvido	at once lost
encontrado	and found
todos juntos:	we all together:
luciérnagas	fireflies
de la noche	in the night
soñando	dreaming up
el cosmos	the cosmos[16]

An important celebration in the Chicano/Latino communities of the United States that brings about heightened awareness of a personal and collective connection with the Mesoamerican tradition takes place around *Los Días de los Muertos* (The Days of the Dead) on the first and second day of November. Some people mistakenly refer to it as the Mexican Halloween. But this is a hybrid celebration that on the surface is a Catholic feast but in reality is a commemoration of Mesoamerican spirituality. Instead of the fear of death and the cover of disguises pretending to trick death, there is a celebration and acceptance of the cycle of life that includes death. It involves all aspects of the human drama, the sublime as well as the humorous. In San

Francisco, since the mid-1970s, this celebration involves a community procession with the participation of thousands of residents and visitors, with colorful paper banners and Aztec dancers. This procession ends in a neighborhood park where community altars honoring the dead are built. For many years I have been involved in this community celebration by calling the four directions at the beginning of the procession and in each of the four focal points during the procession. In 1996 I read, as part of the ritual ending the procession, an invocation I had written dedicated to our friends, family members, acquaintances, and all people who have died of AIDS. This invocation could well summarize the healing purposes of an ecopoetics that reclaims the past in order to forge a better future.

TLAZOLTÉOTL!

Goddess of Love
Goddess of Death
Eater of Filth
Mother of All Seasons:

Mother of the Rivers
cleanse your son
with waters flowing
from the Fountain of Youth

Mother of the hummingbirds
dry off his last tears
kiss each aching bone
dress him in morning flowers

Mother of the Mountains
caress him with murmurs
take him into your bosom
the dream of your deepest canyon

Mother of the Night
weep with us
light his path with the stars
of the Milky Way

Mother of the Sea
embrace his ashes
turn him into bright red coral
amidst schools of laughing fish

Mother of all Seasons
Eater of Filth
Goddess of Death
Goddess of Love

Tlazoltéotl![17]

A TAPESTRY OF BROWNS AND GREENS

Nalini Nadkarni

The tapestry of life's story is woven with
the threads of life's ties, ever joining and breaking.
—*Rabindranath Tagore,* Fireflies

When I look closely at a hanging tapestry, I observe that the pathways of individual threads wend through warp and woof, each one unconnected to
the other. Yet if I stand back and look at the whole tapestry, its intricate
and beautiful patterns emerge. In a roomful of such carpets, I observe that
those with the most compelling patterns are composed of individual threads
that have the highest intensity and most contrasting of colors. When I reflect on the tapestry of my own half-century of life, I see that the threads
that have provided the greatest amount of influence on how I understand
nature and my place in it are those that came from the vividly mixed ethnic
background of my Indian/Hindu and Brooklyn/Jewish parents, threads that
set me somewhat apart from the mainstream culture of white middle-class
America in which I was raised. Being myself composed of different-colored
threads has allowed me to see the complexities of nature, and to communicate them to a wide range of audiences.

It was near midnight at 10105 Dickens Avenue in October of 1966. The sleeping bags of my sixth-grade girlfriends lay like spokes around the central coffee table. Martha Bunn, my best friend since we were seven years old, asked me: Nalini, what does it feel like to look so different from everyone else? I remember opening my eyes wide in the dark room at her question. I had no answer. Until then, I had not realized that I looked different from my white friends in the sleeping bags next to mine. But at that moment, I realized that my mixed heritage apparently did set me apart from others in my suburban Maryland neighborhood—at least from their perspectives. My father was a Hindu who emigrated from India in 1946 for his doctorate in pharmacology. My mother was raised as an Orthodox Jew by parents who had fled the pogroms of Russia in 1916, and who spoke Yiddish in their home in Brooklyn, New York. My parents met in graduate school, married, and moved to Bethesda, Maryland, where my father spent his career doing cancer research at the National Institutes of Health.

The five Nadkarni kids were varying shades of brown. I was the third child, and was the darkest of the five, the most Indian in my facial features and body look. In contrast to other immigrant Indian families in the area, who seemed to assimilate into Western culture as quickly as possible, my parents made our home a "Little India." They gave us all Indian names, which had meanings in Sanskrit: Saroj, lotus flower; Susheela, well-behaved; Nalini, water lily; Vinay, gentleness; Mohan, charmer. Even our dog and cats had Indian names: Tipu, Manya, Nisha. At dinnertime, we sat on the kitchen floor and ate Indian food with our fingers, my mom circling the six of us, doling out curry and vegetable bhaji. We slept on mattresses on the floor, just as my father had done in Thane, the small village of his birth.

Christmas morning brought neither a crèche nor presents from Santa, as it did for all of our school friends. Rather, the family gathered around our fireplace, bereft of Christmas regalia, while my parents read excerpts from writings of Jawaharlal Nehru and Mahatma Gandhi. Each month, we received a letter from my father's bhataji, or family priest, with a dozen Indian stamps pasted in the corner of the odd-sized envelopes. Even unopened, these were redolent of sandalwood paste and prasad, the sweet powder he would distribute to each of us at the small alter of Ganesha, the god of good fortune and remover of obstacles. The little ivory carving of our family deity resided on a bookshelf in the kitchen pantry, where we gathered if a family member was sick, or traveling, to give prayers for their health or safe journeys.

Our family found it very natural that Ganesha sat right next to our Menorah, Haggadah, and Hebrew dictionary, objects that embodied my mother's religion. The image of our elephant-headed god was not at all a strange bedfellow to these three representations of Judaism, a faith that forbids any representation of God. Our two religions lived side by side, just as my sisters and I slept comfortably together on our floor-level mattresses. Although my mother's heritage was not as apparent as the Indian elements, Jewish traditions had a presence in our home. At Passover, we welcomed packages of honey cake and Matzoh from my maternal grandmother, our Bubby. These represented her acceptance of the marriage of her daughter, who had committed the unthinkable action of marrying outside the faith. Out of deference to her own parents, my mother had not told her mother that she was married until after I—the third child—was born, because of the shame it would bring to her family. Civil law at that time also worked against them. My parents were not able to legally marry in Washington D.C.—our nation's capital—because of the miscegenation laws that still ruled seventeen states. These forbade my dark-skinned Indian father—who was classified as a Negro—from marrying my white mother. They had to take a bus to New York and marry there to have their union be legal.

That initial awakening at Martha Bunn's slumber party, reinforced by my family history and the way we lived, made me aware that I was somehow different from others. But those deep cultural differences my family embodied did not create a conflict. Rather, they fostered something enriching, just as different-colored threads created the richness of Tagore's tapestry. It set the stage for the way I have come to view nature—not as consisting of monochromes, but rather as comprising many colors and textures, all necessary to creating a complex and resilient whole.

Nature As Protected and Protector

My early experiences provided me with two seemingly contradictory roles of nature. The natural world both needed protection and provided protection. Although my father was stern and authoritarian, he had a benevolent attitude toward nature. On weekends, he tended our two-acre lot of garden and trees. I remember the care he showed when we transplanted saplings from one part of our yard to another, a near-reverent tenderness that I seldom saw in him. He made sure that the space surrounding each tree's young roots was big enough to absorb the shock of being uprooted. He would unfailingly water it afterward, to welcome it to its new environment. I liked to pat the soil in the handprints that he had lain down. His big handprint surrounded my little one in the dark soil beside the slender brown trunk that upheld the pliant limbs, so like mine, ready to grow. I have wondered if he saw himself in those transplanted trees, a fellow migrant from his small village in India to the culture of suburban America. Those actions gave me a strong ethic of protecting nature.

I learned also that the converse was true—nature protected me. The elm tree that stood outside my childhood home and tapped companionably on my bedroom window kept me company on scary, windy nights, assuring me that my favorite playmates—the trees that lined our driveway—awaited me outside to join them when daytime returned. Tree climbing was a near-daily pleasure for me. When I got home from school, I chose one of the eight maple trees that lined the driveway to climb for the afternoon. Those perches were refuges from the world of homework, chores, fights with siblings, and strict parental directives. I could look out across my home territory, check on the progress of squirrel nest constructions, and feel the strong limbs of the trees holding me up for as long as I wished. In my imagination, those treetop roosts became in turn a place to sequester Anne Frank, a sanctuary for injured birds, a refuge for wounded soldiers, and a rescue vessel in case of drastic emergency neighborhood flooding. It was my Ark, and modeled nature as a place of safety, a place that protected me and those I cared for.

Nature As an Object of Study

As with many children of immigrants, the strongest directive from our parents was to behave properly: to be obedient, respectful, and studious. Education had been the key element for the success of both of my parents, and they believed it would help us find our place in life. In the tradition of India, girls marry and go off to the family of their husbands, which requires large dowries, rendering them more of a burden than a gift. As the third daughter in a family of two cultures that value sons over daughters, I worked hard to gather straight A's, played on three varsity sports teams, joined the Latin Scrabble Club, and implemented my own private After School Shakespeare Reading Project. This emphasis on academics created another thread—the use of the scientific process and the intellect—that I wove into my relationship with nature.

In college, I discovered the world of forest ecology through the lectures of Dr. Jon Waage, who carried out research on damselfly behavior. He posed seemingly narrow questions that later turned out to relate to much broader issues about competition and mutualism, and the evolution of life on Earth. Wrestling through the labyrinth of the scientific literature, I learned to trace citations to their sources and recognize the key players in a scientific discussion. I enjoyed the challenge of untangling the endless puzzles I encountered in nature. I entered graduate school in forest ecology at the University of Washington. I took a graduate level field course in tropical biology in Costa Rica. Whenever we struck out on a rainforest trail, my eyes went upward to the plants and animals that I saw in the treetops, located far from the reach of those who were stuck walking on the dark, damp forest floor. At that time, in 1979, almost no one had studied—or even climbed into—the forest canopy. Many of these tropical trees have unnervingly long straight trunks with no branches for one hundred feet, rendering my childhood tree-climbing skills useless. I learned mountain-climbing techniques to climb trees from Don Perry, an early pioneer of forest canopy access, and was on my way to making a niche for myself in the barely existing—but emerging—field of forest canopy studies.

It took some struggles with my graduate committee to help them understand that climbing trees could be serious science, rather than "Tarzan and Jane stuff," as they called it. Eventually, they helped me carve out a dissertation project, a comparative study of the biomass held within the epiphytes—the plants that grow perched on tree branches and trunks. My fieldwork took place in the spectacular temperate rainforest of the Olympic National Park and the tropical cloud forests of Costa Rica. For four years I identified, marked, and tagged all the trees in study plots at both sites, and collected epiphyte samples to calculate their mass relative to the whole ecosystem.

In the more than twenty-five years that followed, I continued this academic approach to nature, collaborating with students and colleagues to produce scientific papers and scholarly books about canopy ecology. We have learned that treetop versions of traditionally terrestrial invertebrates—beetles, ants, springtails, and even earthworms—are found in this canopy-level soil. We documented that epiphytes intercept and retain considerable amounts of nitrogen from rain and mist. One study involved perching on platforms in trees for six hours each day, revealing the importance of these plants to arboreal animals. Thus, these little-known and structurally small plants that live their lives high above the forest floor are critical threads in the integrity of the complex tapestry of rainforests.

Learning from Many Sources

During my academic appointments at the University of California at Santa Barbara and The Evergreen State College in Olympia, Washington, I immersed myself in the academic approach to understanding nature. I received scientific grants, carried out fieldwork, gave talks at meetings, and published scientific papers, just as my peers did. However, I soon sensed that this world of the ivory towers was incomplete, recognizing that the growing distance between scientists and non-scientists, and the widening gaps between humans and nature were two grave societal problems that most scientists did not seem to address. I found myself compelled to reach out to sources of information outside of academia that seemed equally valid to those inside it—sources that recognized the medical, recreational, aesthetic, and religious values of nature.

In 2000, I set out to understand the multiple values of trees and to link these with public audiences outside of academia. I began by speaking to classes of medical students about the relationships between trees and human health. I presented examples of the many medicinal products that are derived from trees. For example, the bark of the Pacific Yew tree (*Taxus brevifolia*) contains taxol, an enormously effective anticancer compound. Trees also reduce stress in psychological ways. In the early 1990s, Dr. Roger Ulrich published studies showing that patients who had a view of a tree outside their window recovered more quickly and with fewer complications than patients having the same operation whose views were concrete walls. These studies have since been applied to hospital design, and several companies provide artificial tree scenery consisting of backlit panels hung on walls and ceilings of examining rooms. Thus, the many health values of trees can be woven into the tapestry that describes the total significance of trees.

Urban youth is a segment of the population that can be hard to educate about the importance of nature. To connect young people from the inner city with science and natural ecosystems, I engaged a young rapper named C.A.U.T.I.O.N. to interact with field scientists—a marine biologist, a forest ecologist, and an entomologist—along with thirty middle school children from Tacoma, Washington. Each day included field time—with the rapper singing about the trees, clams, and bugs we encountered—and sound studio time—when the students made up their own rap songs about their field experiences. At the end of the week, the children had cut their own CD, which they presented to their families and peers. Their insights also served to open my eyes to the many colors of nature that they saw with fresh eyes in the familiar forest of my own college campus.

The element of formal religion is a powerful force in our society, but one which generally has a low profile in academia. Perhaps communicating how people of different faiths describe trees in their own holy texts and in their own places of worship would inspire its followers to be better stewards of forest ecosystems. To test this, I developed a sermon about trees and spirituality that I offered to deliver in churches, synagogues, and temples. This required that I consider multiple religions without judgment, just as Ganesha and the Menorah sat side by side on my family's home altar. For several months before taking the pulpit, I acquainted myself with the tone and practice of each group by attending their services as a guest. I offered clergy my sermon, not as a scholar of religious studies nor as a particularly religious person myself, but rather as a scientist interested in understanding trees with my intellect, and as a human being who cares about forests.

The twenty-two congregations I addressed ranged from fundamentalist to progressive, and included Episcopalians, Baptists, Unitarians, Zen Buddhists, Jews (Conservative and Reform), Catholics, Methodists, and interfaith organizations. My source materials came from the Bible, the Talmud, the Qu'ran, as well as Hindu and Buddhist scriptures. Congregants listened attentively, participated in discussions after the sermon, suggested texts and hymns that I had overlooked, and passed me on to other churches. On one occasion, I spoke from the *bima* (meaning "high place," the raised platform from which the holy scripture, the Torah, is read) of the Jewish synagogue in Olympia, Washington. Something of my mother's teachings about the holidays, coupled with the memory of those packages from my Bubby, made me feel a connection to the sounds and smells of the synagogue. I spoke to the congregants about links between trees, spirituality, and Judaism, and suggested that the holiday of Tu B'Shvat exemplified the relationship between humans and trees. It began by the Torah's requirement that farmers must give a tenth of all crops grown to the priests of the Holy Temple; Tu B'Shvat marked the date when those taxes were tallied. Gradually, the holiday became a day of celebration of trees, and of Jews' connections to nature. The day is celebrated with tree-planting ceremonies, and through these actions, modern Jews affirm a future filled with fruit, shade, and beauty for their children.

I also spoke about the role of trees in the Hindu religion in the places of worship I visited, drawing from the teachings of my father. The early inhabitants of India perceived a godly element in places of natural beauty, especially in trees. Centuries ago, many villages set apart sacred land for the "tree spirits," or *vanadevatas*. Would-be parents propitiated the spirits by tying toy cradles to the branches of those trees. Damage to the sacred grove, especially the felling of a tree, might invite the wrath of the local deity, causing disease or the failure of crops. Over the centuries, spiritual beliefs have been the prime force that preserved these groves into modern times. In many areas, they are the last remaining threads of native, wild biological diversity in a country of one billion people.

Over the past ten years of this type of outreach to non-traditional audiences, I have learned much more about trees than what came from ecology lectures and the tomes that fill library stacks. Science is a domineering force if you choose to take it on, often leaving little room for the dream works of a Mary Oliver or the quiet prayers of a Buddhist monk. I reflect on the affinity between trees and people, the word affinity from the Latin word *affinis,* which indicates a relation by marriage. Although we are not of the same family, we can consider ourselves as being married into each others' families, with the challenges, responsibilities, and benefits that come with being so linked. I have found that I must do more than simply carry out another experiment, get another grant, and write another scientific paper to complete my relationship with nature.

Trees and My Own Spirituality

Although the opportunities I have been offered have been numerous and positive, there have been times in my adult life when I have encountered dark colors. Some of the murky times may have been a consequence of my mixed background. Did they stem from struggles to prove myself to my parents and the bigger world? Did I need to show myself and others that a small brown woman is as worthy—or more than worthy—of opportunities as a large white person? Whatever the cause, there have been times when I have misplaced my sense of self, when I have not heard my own voice, when I have nearly drowned in a place of no light.

During those times, I found spiritual solace and guidance by looking to trees and other representatives of nature. One of the most basic ways to gain—or regain—my sense of self was through meditation and conscious breathing, and this, I realized, is also linked to trees. The word spirit is derived from the Latin word, *spirare,* to breathe, the same root for spirituality, inspire, and expire. Although trees do not have lungs or gills as animals do, they breathe. Day and night, plants inhale oxygen and exhale carbon dioxide through the process of respiration. By day, through the process of photosynthesis, they harvest energy from sunlight, convert it into sugars, and breathe out oxygen that replenishes our air supply. Because of the complementary way in which these gases are exchanged, every leaf becomes a connector among living things. Knowing this, in those dark times, I could merely look out at the maple tree in our backyard and be reminded that I am connected to other living things.

Many humans have a sense of spirituality, an awareness that we are linked to something larger than ourselves. Cosmologists have conceptualized the *axis mundi,* or the central universal pivot of the entire cosmos, portrayed as the imaginary line that links heaven to Earth. The Tree of Life and the Tree of the Knowledge of Good and Evil are introduced in the very first book of the Old Testament. Buddha achieved enlightenment as he sat under the spreading limbs of the Bodhi tree, breathing in and breathing out in silence, as does a tree. On one Sunday when I was visiting churches on my trees and spirituality project, I arrived a bit late to the Westwood Baptist Church in Olympia, and slipped into the back pew to listen. The pastor was speaking on the need for all of us to find an entity that will protect us, and hold us in his arms to help us feel secure when we are frightened, and safe when there is danger around us, helping us to find calm in our lives. I was amazed and pleased that the pastor would include a description of trees and their spiritual benefit to humans in his sermon. I recalled a line from a William Stafford poem: "I rock high in the oak—secure, big branches—at home while darkness comes." It was only at the end of his sermon that I realized he was talking not about trees at all, but about Jesus. I realized that he and his flock view Jesus the way I view trees, as entities who hold us in their strong limbs and protect us.

Protecting Trees - Redux

This distance between humans and nature is particularly apparent in certain segments of society, and I describe here one project—involving prisons and prisoners—that has addressed the closing of that gap. Prisons epitomize perhaps the most severe endpoint of humans inhabiting built environments without nature. In 2004, I initiated a project to both resolve a pressing environmental issue in the Pacific Northwest—harvesting mosses for the horticulture trade—and bringing together nature with humans who have been denied contact with it. The environmental issue of unsustainable moss-collecting motivated me to begin. The collection of moss from forests in the Pacific Northwest is a growing industry for the horticultural and florist trade. Since 2000, the moss industry has grown rapidly, reaching an economic value of over $260 million in 2005. This has raised concern among ecologists, because canopy-dwelling mosses fill important ecosystem roles, in nutrient capture and in providing resources for wildlife. When moss communities are disturbed or removed, however, they take decades to regrow, so stripping mosses from trees is not sustainable. This prompted me to learn how to "farm" them in non-forest conditions to reduce collecting pressure.

Unfortunately, methods for moss growing in greenhouses had not yet been developed. While considering how such methods might be developed, a time- and energy-consuming project, I was reminded of a study by horticultural therapists which found that gardening can be beneficial for incarcerated persons. As a result, I initiated the Sustainable Prisons Project at Cedar Creek Correctional Center, a local prison, to help solve the problem of the non-sustainability of moss harvesting, working with prisoners as partners in exploring ways to best cultivate moss. We used wild moss collected by my students with permits as "seed material." Our questions were basic: Which species should we use? How much water and nutrients do mosses need? What substrate should we use? We gave each inmate a notebook and pencil to write observations. They quickly learned to identify common moss species, using their scientific names; contrived ways to deliver water with tubing and hardware clamps; and learned how and why to retrieve randomized subsets of mosses for our moss-growth measurements. Prisoners observed and recorded the vigor of moss samples, which we then weighed to quantify growth rates. After eighteen months, the results of the project were dramatic. The corrections center staff were astonished at the energy, interest, and patience the participants exhibited. Several of the inmates found training in the horticulture field after they were released. As an outgrowth, I launched an in-prison lecture series called "Sustainable Living—Sustainable Lives," in which visiting lecturers from regional universities delivered talks on sustainability and natural history to inmates and prison staff. Participating researchers gained a sense of satisfaction and accomplishment in communicating to an audience that proved to be attentive. This experience reinforced the concept that all voices, all approaches, and all types of people can contribute to keeping the great tapestry of nature intact.

Reflections

In my childhood, I saw trees as my protectors, my refuge from the periodically confusing and chaotic atmosphere of our family. Following my parents' expectations and my own proclivity to participate in the intellectual world, I jumped into academia and became part of that tribe; approaching the mysteries of nature as puzzles to decipher with experiments and statistics.

Frustrated at not being able to disseminate what I had learned from nature to non-scientists, I explored partnerships that would link my values of trees and nature to the values of others. I moved into the worlds of spirituality and realized that, at times, understanding comes from being open to things I cannot measure. Finally, and in a continuing way, I have moved toward forest conservation, becoming a protector of trees and nature.

What has fueled this journey, which has taken me from the ivory towers of academia to the watchtowers of prison yards? Having a hybrid background allowed me to "see" nature and my connections to it in complex ways, a gift and consequence of my brown skin and my mixed upbringing. It has compelled me to look outside my own discipline to fully understand what I am curious about. The strong colors of the Indian culture of my father and the vibrant hues of the urban Jewish culture of my mother mixed but did not merge. They coexisted, retaining their own purity, and complemented rather than conflicted with each other. This allowed me to see multiplicity in everything around me: the subtle differences between species niches in forest canopies; the multiple values that trees provide humans; and the many valid ways that people come to understand nature and the world. I now see nature as a precious and multicolored tapestry, which has made me mindful about protecting its intricate patterns from raveling, fading, vanishing.

PORPHYRIN RINGS

Jennifer Oladipo

Atomically, there is little difference between hemoglobin—blood—and chlorophyll. The two are one microscopic atom away from each other, sharing another 136 atoms in common. That discovery made me think of how the smell of fresh-cut grass, so pungent, arrests the nostrils and imprints the mind, sharp as a needle pressing against the skin. Then, oddly, I thought of what seems to be an ever recurring news story, a refugee's account of fleeing a massacre scene, how she described the persistent odor of blood, the smell, I imagine, of bodies turned inside-out.

Although the mere sight of it can be alarming, even those of us in safer parts of the world are constantly aware of our own blood. We, the warm-blooded snowbirds, cold-blooded killers, blue-blooded Americans, can scarcely live a day without some reminder of the fluid flowing through us. Blood pressure for centuries has been our first measure of health, while blood sugar rapidly becomes our biggest concern. It's as if we are born with the understanding that we are nothing without our blood, little more than containers for a liquid that somehow thins and coagulates, makes and remakes itself as it runs through every one of our most obscured recesses. Blood draws the lines by which we trace our ancestries, and so will always know us a little better than we know ourselves. Yet with the change of a single atom, it could be something else entirely. Or maybe not so entirely.

There is a longing that digs at us. It's evident in everything from our inclination to complement and coax houseplants, to our fascination with literary worlds made real with the sights and sounds of flora that seem to live with just as much purpose as human characters. It's in the foods we love. My cupboard houses a bottle of honey I bought in Nigeria. Flavored with the nectar of West African wildflowers and flowering trees, it's much less subtle than the North American varieties I know, dark and strong as a cup of fresh coffee, with all the gustatory nuances of a well-aged shiraz. Sometimes it reminds me of smoke. I imagine the plants whose essences create that singular flavor to be richly colored, with thick stems and strong taproots reaching deep into the earth for moisture during the dry *harmatan* season, or roots that spread far just beneath the surface, ready for abundant rainy season waters. I'm not as familiar with the plants as I am the people, whose traditional dress, all vivid color, reveals not one ounce of cultural shame about showing off. Family and religious ties, whether Christian, Muslim, or traditional, run deep, upholding society. Like the root systems of the plants I imagine when I taste the honey, Nigerians can be found far, far from home, spread out in networks all over the globe. Those African flowers create nectar that likes high temperatures, I've found, and so I use it for baking bread. It makes a good, strong bread.

Plants from elsewhere are called *alien,* and are often *invasive.* So are people. When I was about seven years old, rifling through my mother's purse in search of grown-up things, I discovered a laminated plastic card showing her picture and other information. It said ALIEN across the top. It was green. Her image had been stretched laterally to fit the space, giving my mother too-thin eyes and an overly wide, creeping mouth that did in fact make her look like something from another planet, vaguely humanoid. I mulled over the word and all my Hollywood-generated connotations of it, and tried to reconcile them with anything I knew about my mother. The murmur of prayers coming from her room in a foreign tongue was notable, but not much more exotic than the incantations I heard every week at Catholic Mass. She cooked different food from other parents, but the worst of what she made I liked a thousand times better than the ubiquitous peas and instant side dishes I encountered in other homes. Besides that, Mom had cranked up Michael Jackson records on the stereo just as loud as anyone else, and knew the dances, proof that she was no alien. I decided the card and the word had little if anything to do with my mother.

Among naturalists, however, aliens are not so easily dismissed. Invasives especially are anathema. It turns out a type of xenophobia can be expressed toward plants as easily and frequently as toward people. For me, proof that we recognize on some level the sameness, the blood-bond between plants and people comes from listening to some naturalists explain native, alien, and invasive plant species. As discussion continues, the difference between alien and invasive can become unclear, if it doesn't disappear altogether. Not only are invasives out of place, but the name implies that they are maliciously so. Left unchecked, they encroach, climb, stealthily choke other plants above and below ground. They stay obnoxiously green through the coldest winters while native vegetation stands bare and moribund. Away from natural predators, invasives can thrive with reckless abandon, in teeming masses you might say, heedless of anything but the opportunity to thrive, and of some people's desire to see them disappear.

Yet what many people consider native—of this place, right, acceptable— sometimes is not. Countless wildflowers and medicinally valuable plants living within our borders aren't endemic to this part of the world, but somehow have gotten a pass. The majority of plants that hitchhiked with European settlers—found a niche and fed us, became part of the familiar landscape, slowly developed their own characteristics while remaining clearly related to their European ancestors—those are just fine. They're the subjects of song and folklore. We love them the way we love family members simply because they've always been around, so closely resembling what we already know. So we rarely acknowledge that the dandelion is a Eurasian import. Even a Peterson Field Guide, the bible for naming the natural world, calls dandelion a "familiar weed" where others plants are labeled "perennial" or "annual." Similarly, the farthest abstraction most people will take with a clover is to link it to Ireland, though its roots actually lie in Eastern Mediterranean and Asian soil. Then there's the apple, whose proliferation relied on human intervention and favoritism, and which probably originated in a southern Asian mountain range. Nevertheless, nothing is more American than apple pie.

And so the fruit-toting Johnny Appleseed enjoys a place of esteem never to be reached by the seditious landscapers who brought newer arrivals like kudzu or Japanese honeysuckle. These plants make foreign our familiar scenery, crowd out our pine and box elder saplings, thrive despite all of our best efforts to cut and kill. Some plants are even loathsome. I learned this from Bob. He was the guide on a group hike I took through a state park a few years ago. The man had remarkably in-depth knowledge and concern for the local plants, and absolute antipathy toward invasives. At one point, he delicately held the droopy head of jewelweed flower, remarking on its brilliant orange and yellow sunset-like hues, almost smiling at its red freckles, applauding its medicinal properties. Ten feet later, Bob was an angry man.

"Now this is winter creeper," he said. "As you can see, the stuff is everywhere."

He bent down and ripped a chunk of vine out of the ground as he described the tedium and drudgery of trying to eradicate it. Bob spat a little, I think.

"See? You just can't get rid of the darn stuff. It's horrible." He sighed heavily. "Just terrible. As you can see."

He didn't wait for acknowledgment from the group before he began clawing the vine away from the gnarly bark of an ash tree with both hands until he became winded. Then he held the just-yanked vines away from his body like a bag of wet diapers. Autumn was long gone, and the wintercreeper was one of the few plants that still held tight to shiny green leaves. That deep green foliage with contrasting yellow veins might have been the final insult to Bob. Not only did this plant find and overtake the area, but it managed to keep looking lovely the entire time. No wonder he spat. To follow Bob through the woods while he extolled one plant and derided another was to watch the superb human intellect at work. It seems we are quite capable and willing to extrapolate "us and them" biases across species. I wonder if anyone in the group that day was aware of the uncanny similarity between Bob's violent, grasping hands and the aggressive nature of the very plants he was trying to grab.

One hundred thirty-seven, give or take one iron or magnesium atom. We've got the iron, plants, the magnesium. The other 136 are arranged in identical structures called porphyrin rings that include exactly the same ratios and atomic arrangements of carbon, hydrogen, oxygen, and nitrogen—the stuff of life. It's amusing, then, to think of the bloodlust of thousands of paid and volunteer plant lovers, their 136 atoms rising red to throbbing temples whenever they encounter invasive plants that then find their own 136 spilled green as they're dutifully ripped, cut, or even poisoned. It's the kind of impassioned violence we normally reserve for our own kind.

Yes, invasives can do awful things to their new homes. Driving through parts of the southeast, I've been struck by how kudzu is dominating the landscape. It climbs up shrubs and trees, taking them down slowly so that driving by a large patch of it is like watching the scenery melt before your eyes. The loss is astounding. Still, as something of the earth, its ignominy is unsettling. Kudzu has long been used in traditional Chinese medicine for ailments from headaches to skin rashes. It can be used to remediate our agricultural lands after we abused them. But nobody ever mentions that.

Our disdain for some plants stems from the same branch as the symbiotic relationships we have with others. Enslaved Africans brought plant seeds tied into their braids. They knew instinctively that however harsh, the future could somehow be tolerable with familiar plant life in tow. Before them, European immigrants had the same notion, ferrying potatoes, oregano, and tomatoes, now omnipresent. People historically moved with plants because they had no other choice. And now, even as we distance ourselves from wild plant life, even as the world's ecological forecast grows grim, we crowd the greenest places available every spring and summer, and keep florists and garden shops in business year-round with our desire for vegetative presence. History and the future will hold that where plants grow, people go, and vice versa, even if the present doesn't acknowledge this truth.

Something more than habit is at play on spring nights when the earth begins to warm, winter-thin air becomes richer with the moist exhalations of new leaves, and I lie awake with every window open, every inch of my skin seemingly charged. It's funny to be robbed of sleep by the incessant impulse to throw off the sheets and run outside to greet the new growth like a friend come to visit, only to discover that my neighbors, too, have found themselves inexplicably out on their porches. I suspect this phenomenon stems from something more urgent than a simple appreciation for fair weather, more uncanny than spring fever. It's an unquenchable need for green that is, like porphyrin rings, quite simply, in our blood.

In fact, there is a place where that connection between people becomes sensual reality, and the oxygen that plants exhale finds its way throughout our bodies. It is inside our own beating hearts where silently, elegantly, we fully accept what plants give and begin to incorporate it into every part of us, as newly oxygenated blood flows to every limb. If we who have cultivated protective and even rhapsodic relationships with native plants can try to understand, from the inside out, our deep connection to all vegetative life, then perhaps that understanding could also encompass our connections to other people, however "alien" they might seem. We constantly take in so much of our environment, which includes an atmosphere of divisive cultural discourse that affects attitudes even across species. But surely an opposing process is possible. Surely our intrinsic sameness should lead us to embrace and value people with the same fervor that we do plants, and to let go of fictions of social and biological stasis in favor of a more inclusive and more accurate view. We know the truth just as well as we know that, no matter how much we fear spreading clumps of winter creeper, we can't yank them out without damaging part of the world around it. With so many lives so intricately enmeshed in the same soil, it is not only the deepest roots that matter in nature. More often than not, what matters most is some connection we can't immediately see, but that makes all the difference—or maybe that shows us all of the sameness—once we do.

BECOMING MÉTIS

Melissa Nelson

Growing up in America, most of us are challenged with integrating different parts of our lives, as most of us represent a mix of cultures, backgrounds,
traditions, and worldviews. My particular challenge has been to find my au-
thentic voice as a mixed-blood person who has both Native American and
European ancestry. I am Métis, or *"Michef,"* as they call us at my home reservation at the Turtle Mountain Chippewa community in North Dakota. I
am blessed with inheriting one of the rich, land-based cultural traditions of
North America. I have also inherited blood of my Nordic and French ancestors who, two centuries ago, fled from the injustices of their homelands to
seek a better life in a new land. Through the Saint Lawrence River, travelers,
voyageurs, and fur traders entered the Great Lakes region. On the forested
shorelines, they found beaver and birch bark and met the Anishinaabe
dreamers in their woodland homes. Greeting each other in their respective
tongues—"bonjour," *"boohzhoo"*—some of the French and Ojibwe united,
coevolved, became Métis.

The reservation where my mother was born and raised is called the Turtle
Mountain Band of Chippewa Indians. The word "Chippewa" is a French

interpretation of the name my ancestors called themselves, "Ojibwe," which refers to the type of moccasin they wore. But there are other interpretations of this word. The older, original name for my people, "Anishinaabe," describes a larger group of Native Americans in the Great Lakes region. This name goes back to the creation stories and is usually interpreted to mean "original or spontaneous being."

Today I am concerned with learning how to honor all parts of myself: the spiritual traditions of my Ojibwe ancestors as well as the traditional knowledge of my European ancestors. I keep asking, how do I simultaneously honor the past and transcend the past in order to live in the present? I am also looking for that place in myself, independent of my heritage, that is completely new and different each moment, the part that is constantly revealing itself.

Not having grown up on the land my indigenous ancestors called home and being the most recent offspring from a long line of "half-breeds" on my mother's side, I was not raised within my Anishinaabe tradition. My mother remembered some of her Anishinabemowin, her native tongue, but even that was mixed with Cree and Canadian French. When she was sent away to Catholic boarding school she was forbidden to speak this strange "Michef" language. My father remembered some Norwegian, but his parents discouraged him from speaking it. Emerging from the fifties, both my parents were swayed by the dominant culture to "become Americans—drop that past nonsense." For my mom this "choice" was reinforced by the implementation of federal relocation and assimilation policies. After she returned to her reservation and completed high school, she was selected to be a part of the relocation program that sent reservation Indians into major urban centers around the country. My mother was given a one-way train ticket to California and ended up in downtown Oakland, close to where I was later born.

Neither of my parents fully took in the strict Catholic and Lutheran religions they were immersed in as children, nor did they put any pressure on me or my brother to conform to the rigors of those religions. My imagination was free to wander through the many possible explanations and descriptions of the eternal mysteries. Not feeling connected enough to my indigenous heritage to claim an Indian identity and spiritual path, I wandered, like so many other young people, through the books and lectures and ashrams of the many branches of Buddhism, Taoism, Christian mysticism, and the meditations of classic and contemporary nature writers and philosophers such as Robinson Jeffers, Arne Naess, Gary Snyder, Carolyn Merchant, and Theodore Roszak.

The deep ecology perspective offered me some very satisfying ideas about the connection between humans and the natural world. It explicitly emphasized the intrinsic value of nonhuman nature and the peace found in "wilderness." Part of my interest in deep ecology also stemmed from the fact that it was articulated by an old Norwegian man, Arne Naess, who closely resembled my father and his uncles. There was something in the slate-blue eyes, those charming eye folds that evolved to protect us from the glaring snow, the high, brooding forehead, and the adamant sense that being "outside" in the open air was so much better than being indoors. I was joyfully surprised to discover such an environmentally sensitive philosophy coming from Norway.

But where was my Native American family in the deep ecology philosophy? Haven't these ideas been a part of traditional cultures for thousands of years? Yes and no. Within the deep ecology movement people often make a distinction between an anthropocentric worldview and a "biocentric" one. This distinction can support a "people versus nature" type of thinking that has very little meaning for indigenous peoples. A friend, native restoration ecologist Dennis Martinez, has said, "We need to move beyond the anthropocentric-biocentric dichotomy and see that we are really kin-centric," meaning we must recognize the reality of our extended family—the rock people, the plant people, the bird people, the water people—and human beings' humble place in this web of kin.

I learned, too, that even in the deep ecology movement there are those who share the racist and colonial assumptions implicit in a lot of mainstream environmentalism. Many deep ecologists adhere to a myth of pristine wilderness and consider Indians anti-environmental because they want to "use" the "untouched" wildlands. Yet more and more people are finally realizing that the precontact North American landscape was well cared for and highly managed by its original inhabitants. Many conservationists I've talked with still believe the stereotype of the "lazy, dirty Indian" and consequently, do not consider local Native Americans valuable contributors to discussions about how to manage resources. The more I got involved with traditional native ceremonies and indigenous resource-management practices, the less interested I became in deep ecology.

To indigenous peoples, the basic tenets of deep ecology are just a reinvention of very ancient principles that they have been living by for millennia before their ways were disrupted, and in many cases destroyed, by colonial forces. To learn who I am today, on this land I live on, I've had to recover that heritage and realize a multicultural self.

In exploring what a multicultural self is, I found myself swimming through a sea of racial beliefs—pure, full-blood Indian, pure, full-blood European; tainted mixed-blood, diluted soul. This internal division parallels other prevalent dichotomies—mind and body, civilized and savage, rational and impulsive, science and folklore. It is difficult not to fall into the "either-or" pattern and to integrate all of these differences.

By studying the process others have gone through to embrace the cultural richness of diverse backgrounds, I have come to understand the importance of decolonizing my mind.

Decolonizing the mind is not disregarding rationality or European heritage. It is transcending the self-centered, ethnocentric, and exploitive patterns of Western hegemony. It is explicitly questioning the so-called objectivity and universal character of the Western scientific paradigm. Decolonizing the mind allows other more diverse and mysterious ways of knowing the world to enter the field of perception. For example, intuition and imagination are part of the creativity necessary to decolonize the mind. To facilitate my own creativity, I write poetry and have started to play the *selje flute,* a Norwegian folk instrument. I was fascinated to discover that *selje flutes* are often made out of birch bark, the same subarctic tree so sacred to the Ojibwe. Birch trees and their bark have become a living symbol of my heritage.

Another powerful way I have found to decolonize my mind is by simply questioning my certainty about things and asking, Where do my thoughts and ideas come from? Because colonization is based on the belief in Manifest Destiny, that is, the spreading of so-called universal truths, I also began to ask, Are there really any universal truths? On the other end of the spectrum is the perspective of cultural relativism, which assumes that any cultural differences, be it genital mutilation or human sacrifice, are justified in the name of culture. How far can cultural relativism be taken? Where do ethics step in? Whose ethics?

Such questions helped me to see that, contrary to the popular opinion of wannabes, there are no special spiritual "goodies" in being part Native American. Traditional knowledge is really a deeper knowledge of the self within a wider ecocultural context. It comes with patience, hard work, and sacrifice. As I have learned from many elders and teachers, if someone is interested in Native American spirituality, they must also learn about the colonial history of North America and be aware of contemporary Indian issues such as treaty rights and land claims, poverty and health problems, and efforts to gain federal recognition and revitalize tribal sovereignty. They must learn to honor the local, the distinctive, in the place where they live.

For example, because I live in central coastal California, which is primarily Ohlone territory, I support and work together with some Ohlone people and other California Indians who are working to protect the diversity and quality of all life in this region: endangered species, languages, habitats, songs, stories, and the free flow of rivers. Managing a native nonprofit organization dedicated to these native land protection goals, I have spent many nights and weekends faxing letters to Congress, writing letters of support for tribes and communities, grant writing, compiling and sending out educational and technical information packets, and responding to various requests. This activism has been a part of my commitment to my own native heritage. I am learning to take care of our Mother by honoring the traditional way local native people have lived on and loved their homelands, be it harvesting certain plants and using fire at particular times, or conducting world renewal ceremonies. Giving something back to the earth, through ceremony, is one of the most important parts of Ojibwe and other native spiritual traditions. Ceremony is a unique blend of tradition and innovation. Ultimately, ceremony is creativity, where our own imaginations unfold and become part of the divine creative force of life. Vine Deloria Jr. has written, "The underlying theme of ceremony is one of gratitude expressed by human beings on behalf of all forms of life, and they complete the largest possible cycle of life, ultimately representing the cosmos in its specific realizations, becoming thankfully aware of itself."

We all have earth-based spiritual traditions in our past and we should work to uncover our heritage. But we also have our own individual creativity, imagination, and distinct relationship with what we call the sacred. Our own heart-minds in this very moment of life can show us how to pray, praise, worship, give thanks and blessings. I have been deeply inspired by the teachings of the East Indian educator and philosopher Jiddu Krishnamurti, who has written, "To sing we must have a song in our heart, but having lost our song, we pursue, instead, the singer." We often sacrifice our own song, our individual connection to the sacred source within, by seeking wisdom outside of ourselves. But we don't need an endorsement from any priest, guru, or medicine person. In fact, these teachers' greatest gift to us is to show us that we have our own unique relationship to life and that no one but ourselves can facilitate that connection to the source of creation.

I am sitting outside with an Ojibwe elder and some other people, mixed-bloods like myself (urban Métis and Mestizo), a few Lakota visiting from South Dakota, some nonnative Berkeley students, a Sami woman from Norway, a Yurok California Indian man. We are facing what the Bay Miwok call "the mountain where the little animals play." Before entering the lodge, we get oriented, literally and metaphorically. We find our place in the cosmos. First we pray to the four sacred directions. Some tobacco is given to each orientation. We then honor the sky above, the earth below, our Mother. Then the final orientation is acknowledged, within ourselves, the inner origin. In silence, under the valley oaks and sycamore, individually and as a group, we embrace the mystery of which we are a part.

IN THE VALLEY OF ITS SAYING

Debra Kang Dean

Too expensive. Don't waste. These were words that my parents, generous as they were, used like mantras when I was growing up, and their apparent linking of cost and waste created in me the reactive desire for conspicuous consumption, which meant not only buying things, but also feeling that I could *afford* to throw things away. Before it became fashionable, my parents were already recycling, keeping any- and everything that might be reused—glass bottles, empty cans, milk cartons, plastic bags, aluminum foil, Styrofoam or plastic deli containers, newspapers, phone books, fabric scraps—though they did throw out Chinese takeout containers.

Needless to say, my parents were also power savers, continually telling us to turn off lights and clustering errands to save on fuel. Living in Hawai'i, climate control meant opening and closing windows, so that, at least, wasn't an issue. We went to work or school or to visit family, but mostly we stayed home. We lived on the slopes of Punchbowl Crater and had, until I was about twelve, a daily glimpse of the sun setting into the ocean. In our yard were three mango trees, two plumeria trees, a lychee tree, an avocado tree my grandmother had planted from a seed, and a tangerine tree. I had outside chores, mostly raking and cleaning up after the dogs and picking up fallen fruit. When I was in elementary school, my sister, a few neighbors, and I might "camp" under a big piece of canvas slung on the frame of an old swing set in the yard during the summer. When I was in high school, I took great pleasure in simply sitting in the yard after track practice and listening to the clatter of leaves, my arm draped on my dog. There had been summers at the beach and summers on one of the outer islands with relatives, but mostly when I was growing up, this yard was Nature as I knew it: a touch, a sound, a scent not always pleasant.

In my adult life, I have recycled for many years, though in recent years not absolutely religiously; I have two jobs and live a disordered and disorderly life, not one I'd imagined. So I confess to a certain uneasiness with the way, for example, one is encouraged to recycle water bottles to help save Nature or Mother Earth. Well, yes, I know it helps. But sometimes I feel like the vegetarian I saw picking pieces of pepperoni off a slice of pizza and throwing them away. And though I have eaten and served them, I'm still not sure what I think about veggie *burgers*. But to return to bottled water: I sometimes still hear the faint echoes of my parents' voices saying, "Why waste your money on water?"—and I ask myself if perhaps I've bought into a lifestyle, simply traded one thing for another; whether this act is a kind of tithing, as it were, or a way of editing rather than doing the difficult work of revising my life.

My family seldom had hamburgers at home because it meant a special kind of shopping. It meant my father crumpling newspaper and splintering off bits of kindling to light the charcoal in the hibachi—hardly worth the waste or trouble for a few burgers. So when the first McDonald's opened in Honolulu, it gave us easy access to food that, in our daily lives, was comparatively exotic. Back then I thought it pretty amazing that everything was sized uniformly and portioned out individually, no assembly required. Here was food one had to unwrap. It was almost like Christmas. And it made me feel very American, and being very American seemed other than what I was.

My late husband Brad, part of a military family, came to identify strongly with the American West although both of his parents are from Michigan. During the early years of our marriage we lived first with, then later near, his parents in the state of Washington. A few weeks after we were married, the family went on a camping trip out near Flathead Lake; though as a child, I had done some beach camping through Honolulu's Parks and Recreation Department, I had not experienced anything quite like this adventure. Having come from "the provinces," this seemed to me a thoroughly American world. And I loved it. Back at Fairchild Air Force Base, starter fluid made grilling—my family always called it barbeque, which meant teriyaki, usually beef—quick and easy. With the burgers came no-fuss canned beans, homemade or store-bought potato salad, chips, all the condiments, and soft drinks; and with paper plates and napkins and plastic cups, cleanup was "quick and dirty"—all of it a mirror of the meals we'd had camping out.

Since Brad's death in early 2006 and having lived in the Midwest for nearly three years, I've been thinking about mountains. Watching Ang Lee's *Brokeback Mountain,* I immediately recognized the lure of the West that had acted so powerfully on Brad's imagination—I'd already had glimpses of it: in the story Brad told many times of the unforgettable trip during which he, as an eight-year-old, had accompanied his father and a couple of other men to Colorado to hunt deer; or on a motorcycle trip we made to that same area a few years after we were married; or in my joining him for part of what would turn out to be his last motorcycle trip out West in the mid-1990s. The town of Silverton, Colorado, was a kind of touchstone place for someone who had been born on what is now known as Clark Air Base in the Philippines and had attended thirty-seven schools by the time he graduated from high school.

Apparently, on that last motorcycle trip, he'd had several days of perfect riding weather—clear but not too hot—and he was looking forward to more of the same; however, the afternoon I landed in Denver, the sky had begun to turn cloudy, and it continued to rain intermittently while we were on the road. Over and over he expressed his disappointment in the weather; on that trip, we would end up having to ride in the rain at night to meet up with friends. Possibly hypothermic, I had stopped shivering uncontrollably by the time we reached the motel. It was awful, but wonderful, too; an in-the-elements kind of quickening experience that memories are made on—though it wasn't exactly the kind of memory Brad had wanted for me. He had, I think, wanted the world to answer to his experience of it so that I might see, too, the indescribable thisness of his West that no photograph could capture. More than a glimpse of it, on this trip I'd had a literally bone-chilling feel of it.

I have come to believe that Brad's trips out West were partly "animated by the need to establish an enlightened relationship with a grand alpine wilderness" after we ended up on the eastern part of the continent.[1] One might view such need, like the road trip that embodied it, as quintessentially American—Think big, we say; supersize it—and therefore dismiss it, but I can no more do so than I, the grandchild of immigrants, could divorce myself from Brad. Moreover, I believe that the movement and speed, the heightened awareness of the body and what is required to merge with the road's contours and textures were part of what he craved; it is experience requiring response, not thought. On the road, life was simple: we stopped to eat or get gas, began looking for a place to pull off the road around late afternoon, and, on trips we took when we were younger, slept under a lean-to God-knows-where. But because the landscape was, for me, largely unstoried, what remains are only fragmentary images, and with them the scents and sensation of travel; I have very little to anchor them in place. All that was required of me as a passenger was faith in the driver; then it was simply a matter of holding on.

In a well-known passage from *The Maine Woods,* published posthumously, Henry David Thoreau uses the language of the sublime to recreate the experience of his ascent of Mount Katahdin in August of 1846:

> I stand in awe of my body, this matter to which I am bound has become so strange to me. I fear not spirits, ghosts, of which I am one,—*that* my body might—but I fear bodies, I tremble to meet them. What is this Titan that has possession of me? Talk of mysteries!—Think of our life in nature,—daily to be shown matter, to come into contact with it,—rocks, trees, wind on our cheeks! the *solid* earth! the *actual* world! the *common sense! Contact! Contact! Who* are we? *where* are we?[2]

The passage draws from that experience an age-old lesson that to find oneself one must first lose oneself, must let go of everything one thinks one knows. This, I believe, is not an American experience, but a human one; it is therefore not surprising that in many cultures, mountains are regarded as sacred places. They challenge us, knock us out of our normal cognitive bounds—what we think of as the "real" world—and return us to the fact of our bodies, the part of the "actual" world we inhabit that is mortal, that is part of Nature.

I have a photograph of my son when he was just a few months old, staring intently at his hand during that moment when children begin to make a connection between themselves and that hand, that body. The experience Thoreau describes seems to me like this. And I would further describe it in the life of an adult as the strong tonic that may be required to see the body anew in a sexualized, youth-oriented, no-pain-no-gain culture where we often attend more to how the body looks than how and what it feels. What Thoreau describes so beautifully, it seems to me, is the astonishment we feel in realizing that we live in two worlds.

I have come the long way around to address what I most wish to speak about: the body. Near at hand, it is the locus of the senses, the medium through which we are connected to the world. It seems to me, therefore, a good place to begin to think about Nature. And for this I must turn to *taiji*. Etched in my memory is a question that for me echoes Chuang Tzu's "Can you afford to be careless?"[3] The late Jou Tsung-hwa uttered it to the group during the last workshop he conducted in North Carolina in April of 1998: "How can you control the world when you can't even control your own body?"[4]

In August of 1857, Thoreau made a final excursion to Mount Katahdin. That November, he wrote a letter to H. G. O. Blake of Worcester, Massachusetts, whom Thoreau had judged not "strong enough" to make this trip and so had not invited him along:

> It is after we get home that we really go over the mountain, if ever. What did the mountain say? What did the mountain do?
>
> I keep a mountain anchored off eastward a little way, which I ascend in my dreams both awake and asleep. Its broad base spreads over a village or two, which do not know it; neither does it know them, nor do I when I ascend it. . . . I keep this mountain to ride instead of a horse.[5]

"Nor do I [know] when I ascend it," Thoreau wrote, and I feel sympathy with those sentiments precisely because my mountain experiences had offered me a perspective on "the village." But single now and older, I find that it is *taiji* practice that gives me access to the kind of experience Thoreau describes in the Katahdin passage, but, of course, on a different scale; there are moments, though rare and fleeting, when I apprehend the self as spirit; like Thoreau, I *know* it not while, but only after the experience. Inside the moment, I am like my son staring at his hand.

In his introduction to *Mountain Home: The Wilderness Poetry of Ancient China,* David Hinton discusses the rivers-and-mountains tradition and within it the fields-and-gardens tradition. T'ao Ch'ien stands at the head of this tradition of "wilderness poetry" but is most closely identified with the latter tradition. Of his work, Hinton writes:

> T'ao Ch'ien's domestic fields-and-gardens feel more a reflection of his profound contentment than some fundamental difference in his poetic world: unlike Hsieh Ling-yün, whose poems are animated by the need to establish an enlightened relationship with a grand alpine wilderness, T'ao effortlessly lived everyday life on a mountain farm as an utterly sufficient experience of dwelling, his poems initiating that intimate sense of belonging to natural process that shapes the Chinese poetic sensibility.[6]

T'ao Ch'ien has been compared to Thoreau, the Thoreau at home rather than on an excursion, and to those familiar with *Walden,* Hinton's description of T'ao's work makes the connection evident. Here is a poem by T'ao, part five of "Drinking Wine," that will reveal a more direct connection:

I live here in a village house without
all that racket horses and carts stir up,

and you wonder how that could ever be.
Wherever the mind dwells apart is itself

a distant place. Picking chrysanthemums
at my east fence, I see South Mountain

far off: air lovely at dusk, birds in flight
returning home. All this means something,

something absolute: whenever I start
to explain it, I forget words altogether.[7]

There's a consonance of ideas and feelings in the opening lines of this poem and the excerpt from Thoreau's letter; both, it seems to me, are prosaic but no less profound versions of the sublime articulated in the Katahdin passage.

I rent a house on the corner of a busy intersection, where it is not uncommon for my window panes to rattle when loud music blares from cars stopped there or loud engines roar on a speedy takeoff. There are three large oak trees on the property. When news of Hurricane Katrina reached us, I remember wondering whether the wind that had knocked branches off the trees was connected with the system that did so much damage elsewhere. Here in Bloomington, Indiana, there is no view of mountains, and yet, gazing out over the side yard in the wake of my husband's death, I witnessed sunsets so vibrant my heart ached, and I could not say why my vision had changed except that to be touched by death, to touch it, is to be stricken by grief, yes, but also to be vivified; at least for a short while, to be awakened and alert beyond words. Soon enough, though, the racket of twenty-first century carts, those private bubbles that are emblematic of our increasingly rootless lives, turned me back inward as I moved from climate-controlled room to car to office. Pressing back against it, my mind seeks the "distant place" that is sensed more than known.

It is difficult to express how unnerving I found the fact that I could manage corresponding via e-mail even though it was a rare occasion when I was not in tears during a phone conversation in the wake of Brad's death. In "Song and Story," Ellen Bryant Voigt writes, "Pain has no music, / Pain is a story."[8] Grief had broken my voice, but how did/could the brain manage to circumvent the heart to get to the hands? And yet, also during this period, I couldn't practice *taiji,* which is both imaginative act and rhythmic movement. Pain has no music. However, in the simple tasks of caring for a yard and the contact with nature such tasks afford—raking leaves, trimming hedges, mowing, hauling branches—I found solace in the work itself and in the way such work, despite our differences, connected me with my neighbors. And through them and the care they extended out beyond the limits of their own yards, I was learning something about larger circles of connection. In this way, Nature made its way back into my life; it was not larger than life but life itself, a steady contact with nature that allowed me the greatest freedom to work and to grieve. And I believe that it was precisely in the sweat and chill, the scents and odors of the world without a screen to seal off all senses but sight—and in the release from language—that nature could do its work. I was returning to a place I knew by feel.

I had practiced *taiji* alone for several years until I decided last summer to seek out a school and found instead the T'ai Chi Club at Indiana University. My return to a small community of *taiji* practitioners has also provided me with something unexpected, a further lesson in connection, for part of the practice of *taiji* is push hands, two-person work that requires that participants touch others and allow them into their space. Well-supervised, it is perhaps one of very few situations where people can touch each other in non-sexualized ways. Through this contact, one may hope to develop the skill to "read" the other, but it cannot be done effectively until one learns how to quiet the self. This, I believe, is what Jou meant when he suggested that change might begin with the effort to control one's own body. One of the governing principles in *taiji* movement is differentiating the substantial from the insubstantial; it strikes me as a wonderful metaphor. I began studying *taiji* in earnest in 1996, and I don't know that I will ever be able to master this principle.

I still find it astonishing, even after nine months, that someone can, by holding my wrist, get to my collarbone or down to the soles of my feet—and equally astonishing when I can read someone else's body that way. Through this practice I have had an inkling of the way we are different but the same, an understanding that comes not through conceptual knowledge but the immediacy of touch. Though few can use *taijiquan* as a martial art, it is important to acknowledge that it was developed as one. It is said that Zhang Sanfeng was inspired to develop this art by watching a serpent eluding the attack of a magpie.[9] It is my understanding that, at heart, *taiji* is an art that seeks to deflect an attack rather than to meet it with a counter-attack; that it is an art acknowledging that the cost of direct conflict, whether warranted or not, is always too high and thus seeks to avoid conflict. Because that is not always possible, however, it is also an art in which one trains to develop the skills that will enable one to engage in a way that expends the least amount of force/energy. These aims, it would seem, mirror my parents' imperatives about conservation: Too expensive. Don't waste.

When my aunts visited, they and my mother might sit at the kitchen table talking story, gossiping, really, and I liked to listen; through their talk, the women were making implicit moral judgments. I don't recall any stories that helped me to make sense of their concerns for cost and waste; they may have thought the whole business was self-evident. In our concerns for the larger, fragile world, if we must talk, rather than imperatives or facts, perhaps what we could use more of is the storying of the landscapes in which we find ourselves, a process that might bridge the conceptual gap between a plastic bottle and Nature and show us how to care. "Poetry makes nothing happen," Auden wrote, I know. But he goes on to say:

> . . . it survives
> In the valley of its saying where executives
> Would never want to tamper; it flows south
> From ranches of isolation and the busy griefs,
> Raw towns that we believe and die in; it survives
> A way of happening, a mouth.[10]

It is in the saying of it that we may hope to move and be moved beyond dollars and the recycle bin to slow down enough to save what we love.

TARSENNA'S DEFIANCE GARDEN IN WHICH I LOVE TO SPIT

Thylias Moss

Spit out some fiction, and some fact can grow; I have seen a tongue uncurl and expose (what I took to be) some little pumpkin seeds as white as little flowering lies can be, a vine later that season hyped and pumped toward readiness to try out for the beanstalk and a shot at a golden goose, a sky-high American dream, though it couldn't get off the ground where it was studded with squash-lobed invitations to trick or treat—Tarsenna's garden trampled by witches and Hershey-fisted ghosts. Halloween spirits loved stomping there, their first few steps down the road beyond the garden pumpkin-gut streaked.

But every year pumpkins grew, tomatoes
that could be squished to rid the world of flimsy horrible hearts.
The tulips came back. Wildflowers she didn't even plant
sprouted. What wanted to grow, what could (find a way to) thrive
in that environment did, even as it changed, replacing

more fragile grasses that couldn't fight for themselves,
defying poor soil quality, lack of fertilizer
other than what died there, a natural diet complemented
with variable sun and rain, snow, ice,
temperature dips and spikes, cold and hot spells,
always some form of orchid.
Always signs of mutants, displacements,
from time to time: evidence of elegant distortions.

One tricky thing about lies, assumptions, and fictions is that once they come into being (once conceived, once launched, once planted), they're part of reality, and sometimes as threatening to certain preferred cultivations as weeds—which often become known as weeds because they interfere with agendas. Specific agendas are not universal; each is a function of and collaborator with conditions in a particular location, on some scale, for some duration of time, so there are not the same weeds in all situations since a designation of *weed* tends to be agenda-specific. Anything is, has been, or can become a candidate for *weed* (on some scale, in some location, for some duration of time) in the agendas of accelerated and variable growth patterns that result from humanity's current position as drivers of environmental changes good and bad, chauffeurs of evolutions, mutation breeders and developers, as some mix up the gene pool and blur the races and/or blur thinking while others resist.

An advantage of diversity of the genes has a corollary, false or not, in diversity of thinking: any point of view can cast itself as a *best* cognitive crop, and can recommend (if not demand) that the field be purged of rival cognitive species. Intolerance requires conditions that support its growth if it is to attain, then sustain, perennial status. A healthy crop of intolerance is not a likely outcome of the harvesting of chance alone. Tough decisions become necessary. For the beauty of the garden, and the form and purpose of garden desired, some plants must go—to an appropriate setting, a garden meant for them, sometimes a killing field or field of minor-league obscurity, an agricultural pesticide-ridden or penal death row. Preference is often related to something practical; an engineered (genetic or acquired) preference for what sustains and is or becomes accessible. Belief can be beautiful as it blossoms and can also be toxic, some systems adjusting over time, adapting to a tolerance of the toxin, mutating to a dependence on the toxin that for others proves lethal. This is part of existence's slow—at least on a human scale (often the only scale perceived as relevant by some humans)—enchantment, the magic of what we do (including what we think), what we become able to do; how what is possible and what becomes possible happens—and only that; never what is impossible. So the cumulative impact of movements and changes initially perceived as slow or subtle can be compounded; they can (seem to) become profound as they become more noticeable, to some degree in response to the notice which is also some of the change contributing to the increase in the rate, amount, and distribution of change.

Unfortunately, some terrestrial life is adapted so well to a narrow band of cooler success that it can't succeed as the lowest-level hotties. It made sense for evolving, emerging, and stabilizing ecosystems to gamble on the stability of a local temperature range that was many thousands of years old, stability older than human religions, trustworthy even for giant sequoia and Galápagos giant tortoise lifetimes in local environments to which many ecosystems are confined, now that continents have drifted and acquired regional and subregional identities that are entangled with climate systems whose definitions have been incredibly reliable: savannah, tundra, permafrost, coral reef, chaparral, jungle, taiga, littoral zone, polar. But the rules are changing, and some life can't shift the vital temperature range in which it can survive to match the accelerated rise (despite how slow it is on some scales) to a higher average world temperature—we're giving the world fever in the morning, and fever all through the warmer polar nights. But for birds with the wing power, avian range expansion so far is proving a necessary option; some species flying further to find suitable conditions, for as long as those conditions exist to be found. Flowers are much more rooted to an existing home base, requiring intervention for major relocation.

My nose was rewarded anytime it stuck itself in Tarsenna's garden. I loved being pulled in by perfumes, invisible nets that became part of my body, the fragrances entering my nose, molecules of aroma binding with receptors in the nostrils, the nasal hairs increasing binding opportunities, resulting in a pleasant session with some sweet-loaded esters. This was a shared attraction

as there were other mammalian, avian, and entomological fools addicted
to her garden, all of us behaving normally in those circumstances of what
seemed (to me) like unremitting growth, defiance against struggle, suffering, misery (portions of it in Tarsenna's own lap). For the gladiolas and the
orchids, though, that misery was of no consequence; tears shed there didn't
hurt them. It was chromatic audacity, the flowering occurring in the midst
of personal and national crises and crimes, the flowers there to attract insects,
each petal a welcome mat; no locks on perfumed botanical doors. Their seductive beauty assured pursuers and willing vehicles for seeds—an excellent
economy of motion and home-based lifetime, nomadic dispersal of generations handled with finesse; my lips, for instance, blowing dandelion tassels
into Tarsenna's garden, into sidewalk cracks, into lawns that some days were
an uninterrupted yellow kingdom.

Tarsenna wasn't without witchery herself; her face aged into, with that
profound narrowing of chin, a replica of the orchids she loved and filled
her garden with, including some models, artificial reality plants with plastic
stems, rubberized colorful heads that defied any season, any assault except
the most malicious uprootings, discouraged by her attempts for a little fiend-
ish Mendelianism: the crossbreeding of orchids and padlocks between which
she assumed kinship of metaphor because of resemblance. She couldn't have
chosen a better flower family for botanical daughters, a range that though
clustered in the tropics extends to the Arctic Circle: the coralroot orchid, common and lesser twayblade, white frog, and to Macquarie Island's corybas orchid in the diaspora of Orchidaceae. This prolific family includes vanilla,
once exclusively extracted from seed pods of *Vanilla planifola,* an orchid once
distinctly Mexican, like Tarsenna's husband whose diminishing accent was
a flavoring of everything he said to her, especially what he whispered to her
as he died in her arms, rumor has it at her own hands so she could have that
kind of romantic finish of desires that may have taken him elsewhere just following the petaled skirts of Tarsenna's orchid brood around the world. Fact:
Tarsenna lives alone (currently the sole occupant of her grave—fact: an assumption; I have not looked into her plot in the graveyard though that too
is a garden). Her spice racks (three, tiered on the wall like a small staircase)
full of finger-length (fact: depending on the fingers) bottles of vanilla extract
(fact) double as arsenal. I don't think she knew the story (that is my favorite)

of vanilla's origin though the rumor of her husband's death, the only admit-
ted Mexican on the block at that time, fits well with the story, extends it,
because there isn't an ending to anything yet that is really an ending, with
no continuation in any form to interact (form networks) with other things
and extend the contributions of residue. Vanilla happened when forbidden
love took to the jungle (how Edenic) and was caught, the lovers decapitated,
and the vines of (love-sweetened) blood twisted into vines of vanilla-bearing
orchid. The beauty of death and sacrifice, the ability of vanilla to sweeten
the bitter and darker chocolate that may have a legitimate reason for bitterness. I didn't ask Tarsenna when I had a chance, and she's dead now; I don't
try to contact her through reading smoke formations from the burning of
vanilla incense. Maybe I do spit in the incense from time to time, but to ex-
tinguish it, not to insult her memory, and spit's a good thing, as I'm going
to talk about soon. And maybe she was curbing with a flagrant fragrant orchid to mask her own libidinous tendencies, the word *orchid* derived from
what's Greek for *testis,* another way of saying testicular *padlocks* in the language of Tarsenna's subconscious, so pleasure is appropriately complex, with
biochemical components. There is science involved in feeling good; and in
allergic reactions to certain reproductive pollens and other pleasure dusts.

Orchids' enduring links to human grief and lust are fortified with some
complicity of their own, as *their* scent, *their* appearance encourages these
links to human grief and lust, also linked at times; orchids known as *hand
of the dead virgin* seem to have earned the name that they seem to request.
There is recognition. There are vampire orchids, orchids of human sacrifice
(Mesoamerican human sacrifice most often emphasized in history of orchid
texts) and genocide of those chosen for the privilege of sacrifice, the orchid
named for an essential maleness in the rape of a priestess that a general orchid structure resembles—metaphor is a wonder vehicle. With it, it becomes
possible to travel meaningfully and quickly anywhere. Then again, flowering
plants are associated with sex or would not flower, would not emit seductive
aromas. They have their own form of survival agenda.

As I was saying: *The beauty of death and sacrifice, the ability of vanilla to
sweeten the bitter and darker chocolate that may have a legitimate reason for
bitterness*; fact, true enough, but vanilla is from a black bean itself, and when
the whole seed is used, when the vanilla-laden product boasts itself to be

all natural, there's going to be black specks that are visible to the unaided human eye, maybe even some tactile grit. The Aztecs even called the vanilla beans black flowers. Okay, so maybe I'm also spitting up a little bit in thinking about pedigrees, about the necessity, for instance, of the presence of fungus, right at the roots, in order for orchid seeds to germinate. But some forms of humanity were just outright foreign to the neighborhood; something about the composition didn't attract some populations, and probably couldn't have supported some populations even if, generalized as much as possible, it's possible to say that any population wants what it considers best for itself, its own secular and spiritual salvations. Some *bests* just aren't compatible, which might indicate a problem with having to identify the best (as if what is at a perceptual or manufactured hierarchical peak is necessarily an indicator of any but a perceived or manufactured, limited notion of perfection), because those bests successfully identified have nowhere to go, especially when it comes to growing and harvesting meanings which, despite all the best efforts at purification, are likely still going to be black-flecked.

There was power in Tarsenna's garden, insistence on growth wherever it could happen, in defiance of what seemed to be against that form of growth in that location at that time. People in a war planting foodstuff, to be sure, but also flowers whose human purpose is a beauty to defy and compete with the also-present but not necessarily prevailing agendas of deprivation and destruction; a profound willingness to risk death for some remnants of Eden. In Tarsenna's garden there were tall flowers I could be lost in as if in a jungle till I was seven years old, and grateful that even now I can recall dodging bees that were eccentric asteroids in a shrunken universe. At home in tangible atoms, charged atmospheres. Belonging to that space without having to claim it; it remained *Tarsenna's garden,* but while there, I treated it as if it were my welcomed responsibility, as if it was a privilege, which it was. I thought I had nothing to fear from any Triffid, that time spent in Tarsenna's garden endowed me with an ability to tame Triffids, to convince them to be still and act pretty despite the viciousness with which they'd been bred, which they could learn, with my help, to overcome. Noticing mergers of butterfly wings and petals, flying flowers, the scales (small petals) that could be rubbed off the wings leaving a powderlike pollen on my fingers—unintentional damage of the wings in my adoration of the species. I caught them by the upraised wing-set, painted the whorls of my fingerprints with organic glitter. Was this a black thing to do? A mixed-race interaction with other parts of nature? Must have been, since I did them without need of racial approval or denial. I had not excluded myself from informal or formal nature studies, and could be perceived as excluded when framing systems were used that excluded me, but not all framing systems, especially my own, accomplished the same exclusions and inclusions, as *constructed perceptual systems* they were (re)configurable, not fixed. I feared wasps in case I was allergic to the chemical cocktail of the sting, the stinger oscillation sort of like a pendulum to target just the right moment to inject, but I loved the libraries they built, paper hexagons about survival that my own father destroyed around our garage and yard. I came as physically close to them as I dared, feeling bolder anyhow in Tarsenna's garden, and coming even closer in imagination influenced by *The Wasp Woman* and the Outer Limits episode *Zzzzz* where insects were not only greatly magnified to human scale, but also became women. The Queen Bee wants to mate with a man to conquer a world already interested in their honey and royal jelly, but he doesn't fall for protocols of the hive as an insider, he's just an outsider, just a scientist.

I loved such mergers, that they could happen where they did, on film, on *The Planet of the Apes,* in imagined locations, and not literally in Tarsenna's garden—within what was possible, allowing that the possible is configurable. Allowing that imagination (and just about anything else) is incapable of exceeding what is possible within protocols prevailing on some scale in some location for some duration of time, within limits of possibility within which whatever those mechanisms are that maintain existence, maintain it, making it possible to assume that whatever has been, whatever is, whatever emerges not only can emerge, but is, has, or becomes part of a system that maintains the broadest possible existence in some form, modifications galore, but holding steady with changes that don't make some form of existence impossible. So if we annihilate ourselves, exhaust tolerance, compassion, exhaust fresh water, exhaust planetary resources, including breathable air, before we can evolve into forms with mutated respiratory function, some form of existence, perhaps without us, may emerge from the debris of human accomplishment.

Physical, social, economic, and mental environments are both exceedingly punishing and forgiving in that; accepting somehow anything done in and to them but also fully allowing consequences of actions and interactions to unfold. As if something feeds on change, gobbling the tiny energies produced by even subtle shifts, small discrepancies as little strings of white lies enter the atmosphere of verbal exchanges. Something is always happening to the world. And sometimes spitting, sometimes trying to hold things together with spit is all you can do while you feel sunken in a hopelessness that fortunately tends not to last, sometimes just in defiance of situations that seem to prevail. Tarsenna's coping roots. A library of them. I loved libraries. The fossil record as library. Geologic strata as libraries. Cemeteries as libraries. Each attached and fallen leaf. Each story. Borges's *Library* (or *universe*) of Babel, an infinite library system or infinite subsystems or galleries, my being thus steered to make two small films in 2008 about libraries of realities: *Wannabe Hoochie Mama GALLERY OF REALITIES Red Dress Code* and *Hypnosis at the Bird Factory*. Whatever we do marks existence in some detectable or, as yet, undetectable way, writes chapters that in some form or some scale may outlive, outlast, may survive us. The script is dynamic.

TALKING SPIT (a little bit—as promised)

Now spit itself is fascinating, and very much part of nature, part of many chapters. I am of a mind that tells me that everything is part of nature; sometimes I claim to not understand how something can exist outside of nature—human beings are part of the planet's wildlife, and what human beings make is made out of materials that exist and that can be used to bring derivatives, hybrids, facsimiles, and copies into existence. So the scent of the rose, the essence, and sweet synthetic esters, can be dabbed on my throat so that I don't have to go into a garden and rub my body with petals and pollen, not that I wouldn't enjoy that, especially if on the occasion of the rubbing I once again find those tiny frogs the size of fingernails that filled our yard and Tarsenna's garden when I was a size and age that encouraged me to perceive things as being full. Those frogs were often muddy; at first I thought that they were black, each one like one of King Kong's eyes or one of his strange tears; but rinsing the frogs with the hose (after first spitting on them, and rubbing off some of the dirt with my fingers, eager to see more of what spit-cleaned areas were exposing, so hosing them) revealed spots and freckles, leopard-backs. I suppose that I was polishing the frogs, although they probably didn't need polishing. And I wasn't thinking at all about some possible reaction between enzymes in my saliva and enzymes in the goo apparently exuding from the frogs' somewhat bumpy (along a couple of ridges) skin, but those shrunken-coin-size spit-cleared patches of frog back were beautiful. So I spit some more, all over Tarsenna's garden, as if inspired by a crazed, maybe race-based (who knows? depends on who's configuring and why) appropriation of Johnny Chapman Appleseed's fruit tree conquest, that includes dedication to conservation and generosity.

After generously spitting, I watched ants march through saliva pools. I loved to watch them so undeterred by being spit on. It's hard for people to take that though that's often the mildest form of protest against groups attempting to exercise what they've configured as right. The ants certainly didn't solicit saliva baths, or disrespect, but once it descended on them, they handled it; they didn't freeze up or suddenly become something other than the ants they were.

Spit pools resembled egg masses of frogs, both of which are like colonies of bubbles and maybe a kind of model for how realities might be arranged in clusters, super clusters of various geometries, varying densities and opacities. The idea that tadpoles might emerge from my spit pleased me. Made me feel like a goddess of Tarsenna, something that I evidently needed to feel, could feel—in defiance of what some might have felt was appropriate for me. So I behaved accordingly. And a mass of wriggling tadpoles reminded me of active devil tongues, something I also evidently needed to construct. Could. I didn't want to be without a healthy assortment of devil-tongue communities since I tried to develop some all over Tarsenna.

Saliva is a culture medium in various lab experiments, capable of growing and sustaining various bacterial colonies, useful to store teeth that have been accidentally or erroneously forcibly extracted (though studies have shown milk to be better at this if the teeth are to be replanted). Human tears are also a culture medium in various lab experiments.

Okay, now if the spit is really the host of soon-to-hatch tadpoles, then being spit on is to have eggs thrown, not that that's better, but an ability to connect things extends a form of symmetry, a kaleidoscopic form of symmetry that has the ability to connect everything, any thing able to be at the center, to function as a hub of kaleidoscopic extension.

Start anywhere, and it's possible to consider everywhere from the (variable) context of that start: Tarsenna and the world. Tarsenna and the world and the universe. Libraries that when indexed contain paths, networks that between them all, access all that is accessible (at the time that that *all* is *all*)—in defiance of insurmountable difference, indeterminable relevance and value of any particular thing.

KE AU LONO I KAHO'OLAWE, HO'I

(The Era of Lono at Kaho'olawe, Returned)

Pualani Kanaka'ole Kanahele

I recall our beginnings when we held workshops, did our research to prepare for Makahiki, a celebration for the god Lono. We read the books by [Samuel] Kamakau and [David] Malo, talked to many *kumu hula* and *kūpuna* on the subject of traditional rites; however, for all of us involved with Kaho'olawe, we had not practiced our Hawai'ian culture to the extent of understanding it fully. We wanted to be involved with ritual and ceremony to learn to acknowledge and thank Lono for our 'āina and to ask Lono for assistance in the revegetation of Kaho'olawe. This was our primary goal for the reinstitution of the Makahiki, not to stop the bombing or to return the island from the U.S. Military. The intention for the rituals was that life would once again abound and grow on this little *moku*, or island. After all, this is our greatest gift. This land that sustains us is above all else our foundation.[1]

—*Ka'iana Haili, from a December 1992 interview*

The following words are mainly for those of us with Hawai'ian ancestry. We have the gift of ancestral memory, and we must choose how to use it.

294

If we disregard it, or feel fear, that is our decision. Some of us find this gift worthless and old-fashioned, eventually tossing it aside, while others are determined to use this gift as an intellectual exercise. Others of us see that this is all we have; it is our foundation. This gift offers us many lifetimes of experiences: love, pain, belief, understanding, and wisdom. We must take our time unwrapping it, take the time to enjoy and understand each layer before going on. Remember, this gift took many lifetimes to wrap. We must not be in a hurry to unwrap it, and become frustrated in doing so. It will unfold precept upon precept, and each has a code to inspire or prompt us on to the next layer.

The pivotal refocusing on the elemental gods of our ancestors began in January 1976. The time had come to fight and win back the true spirit and culture of the Native Hawaiʻian. This struggle cannot be evaluated yet, as a modern recovery of native gods has yet to be achieved in the Pacific, and we have nothing to compare this struggle to. Many people contributed their time, talents, money—and in some cases, their lives—to the return of the island of Kahoʻolawe.

The struggle for Kahoʻolawe included court battles, educating the general public about its rights to challenge the political system, reinvestigating the sacredness of the island, convincing Hawaiʻians of the rich cultural connection of this island to the Polynesian Islands south of us, and developing the leadership among the *kumu hula* (*hula* teachers) and *kūpuna* (elders) who would help support this effort. The fact we all had to emphasize was that this ancestral land was worth saving.

This was the time to unite and become reacquainted with traditional practices. This was the land of our ancestors. Therefore, the struggle would have to include the spirits of our ancestors who were familiar with this *moku* (island) of Kahoʻolawe and its stories. And so, as the political battles ensued, the care of the island was placed under the god Lono, the spiritual manifestation of the island, who would aid in the revegetation of the land.

The last Lono ceremony prior to 1982 was held one hundred sixty three years before, prior to the religious battle fought in 1819. The victors of that battle did away with the old religious system, which included the worship of Lono and the Makahiki, and the worship of Kū, which took place at *luakini* temples. This change had a tremendous impact, because the care and use of the land were regulated by the old belief system. During the time of Lono and the Makahiki, which the organization Protect Kaho'olawe 'Ohana was trying to revive, the cycle of life—meaning the use of land and ocean, but also the time to do battle—was regulated by the season and the god of that season.

The newly introduced religious system did not concern itself with the cycle of earthly life, but only with people. The new religions stressed the salvation of people and taught that man was superior to other living creatures. There was no longer a respect for equality among the ocean animals, the large trees, the fresh water, and the newly created earth.

After we were indoctrinated for 163 years in the new religion, our morals and values concerning the interrelationship of all earthly creatures and elements were critically altered. The belief in man's superiority eroded the sense of *aloha 'āina* (love of the land), which is not limited to just the land, but includes the creatures and vegetation of the land, the creatures of the ocean and the ocean itself, and the air and the space above us.

The credo of the newly introduced religion emphasized that human superiority permits the devastation of the forest and the destruction of fishponds and taro ponds, which are covered over and built upon whenever there is economic justification. But even the elimination of, and barring from, beaches due to the construction of large hotels, and the elimination of fishponds, taro fields, and forests, do not compare to the atrocity of the bombing of Kanaloa.

When the first young people went to Kaho'olawe, they were overwhelmed and devastated by the destruction they saw. Indeed, their feelings, which were a reflection of the instinctive values of our ancestors, ignited the movement to take care of the land and, eventually, to stop the bombing of the only island in Hawai'i that bears the name of a god.

The initial contact one has with the world of the unseen is simply a sense of "feeling," which prompts further investigation. In the days of our ancestors, feelings warned of something to come, so one paid attention and reacted accordingly. Through their instinctual feelings, Native Hawai'ians were able to reach out from the physical world to the world of the invisible and to their ancestors, who might reach back in return. The contact did not always have a visual manifestation, and many times the feelings through which contact was made might be described as inspiration, insight, prompting, or an instantaneous quickening. Many of our ancestors were aware of this interrelationship between the physical and the invisible worlds, and so in the past the movement between the two worlds seemed easier. Today, if we acknowledge the validity of the physical and nonphysical worlds—just as the *kūpuna* of old did through their *ʻaumākua* (guardian spirits)—then as Native Hawaiʻians, we can accept that those Hawaiʻians who made the first landing on Kahoʻolawe in 1976 were urged to return there by the *ʻaumākua* of the island.

The fact that many people involved with the Kahoʻolawe movement did not recognize the 1976 landing there as a cultural or spiritual manifestation of *mana* (power) transfer is evidence of the success of Christianity and other foreign religions in modifying our spiritual thought and behavior patterns. Nevertheless, the land and environment still retain those guardian spirits from the days of our ancestors. The ability of our *ʻaumākua* to affect us still remains, whether or not it is recognized. The need that we feel now to address and recognize the elemental gods indicates that their spiritual guidance and insights are still available to us. This tenet—that we could reach out to the *ʻaumākua* and be assured of reciprocation—was a basic principle of our culture's spirituality.

The American Indian Freedom of Religion Act became law in 1978 and, whether by political or spiritual design, encouraged Native Hawaiʻians to insist that the spiritual significance of Kahoʻolawe be recognized. The reestablishment of traditional ceremonies at Hakioawa on Kahoʻolawe had already begun in February 1976. Kahuna Sam Lona and Aunty Emma DeFries prepared and made offerings to the *ʻāina* of Kanaloa, thus establishing a model to be followed by younger Hawaiʻians. In 1979 the life on Kanaloa was recognized and celebrated by John Anuenue Kaʻimikaua and his *hālau hula* (*hula* dance troupe). They literally gave back to the earth by burying certain significant food articles in the ground, symbolizing thanksgiving for the earth's bounty. The *hula kahiko* (ancient-style *hula*) they performed reflected this celebration of life. Papa Paul Elia offered a prayer for strength, organization, and further protection of the land. Aunty Emma DeFries, because of her concern for the island's spiritual neglect by Hawaiʻians and its devastation, then did a *hoʻouē'uē* (lament) for the *ʻāina*.

All of these spiritual and cultural acts of giving back to the earth demonstrated the basic Native Hawaiʻian belief in *lōkahi* (primal unity). The belief in the concept of being one again with the earth and the sea is the life-generating force needed by Kanaloa/Kahoʻolawe to begin to manifest its earth and ocean life cycles for this era.

The Makahiki of 1982 began with the recognition of and expression of gratitude to some of the older *kūpuna* who had lived long enough to lend their support to the Kahoʻolawe movement. These *kūpuna* were Sam Lono, Aunty Emma DeFries, Aunty Edith Kanakaʻole, Auntie ʻIolani Luahine, Uncle Sam Hart, Aunty Luka Naluai, Uncle Henry Lindsey, and Aunty Gardie Perkins. They believed in the young warriors committed to the fight for Kahoʻolawe, and encouraged instead of criticized them. These *kūpuna* committed their *mana* and efforts to the reinstitution of respect for the Native Hawaiʻian ancestral spirits and Native Hawaiʻian elemental gods.

Indeed, the movement to emphasize the importance of the elemental gods was expanding. The 1982 Makahiki began with Kumu Hula Nālani Kanakaʻole providing instruction in how the chants for Lono were to be recited and used in the ceremony. The chant that was to bring everyone to attention and to begin each formal assembly, whether for ritual or social purpose, was "E Hō Mai Ka ʻIke," composed by Edith Kanakaʻole.

E HŌ MAI KA ʻIKE

E hō mai ka ʻike
Mai luna mai, ē
I nā mea huna noʻeau
O nā mele, ē
E hō mai, e hō mai, e hō mai, ē.

GRANT ME THE UNDERSTANDING

Grant me the understanding
From above
This wisdom hidden
In the chants
Transfer this to me, grant this to me,
Give this to me.

Hawaiʻians who had not chanted before were now beginning to try. Unfortunately, many of their parents, grandparents, or great-grandparents had not acknowledged their ancestral spirits for many generations, denying their progeny this hunger for cultural insights, and so they had much to learn.

The ceremony opened with the *hiʻu wai,* a ritualistic cleansing done in saltwater or freshwater. Through immersion, one washes off all of the old problems, takes on a new soul through a changed perspective on people and the environment, and focuses on *pono* (good thoughts, energy, and balance). Then there was a procession to the *hoʻokupu imu* (gift-giving oven), and all the *hoʻokupu—niu hiwa, lama, ʻawa o Lono, puaʻa hiwa, kalo o Lono, ʻulu, ʻuala, maiʻa, iʻa, kūmū* or *ʻāweoweo,* and *ipu o Lono* (calabash of fresh water)—were placed inside the *imu.*

A *waʻa ʻauhau* (gift-bearing canoe) was constructed to deliver the *hoʻokupu* to Kahiki and Lono via Kealaikahiki. The first *akua loa* (staff with the image of Lono) since the abolishment of the old religious system was made for this occasion.

The *akua loa* was the focal point of the ceremonies. This *akua loa,* the repetition of the ceremonies, and the show of respect to the *ʻāina* were the parts of the ceremony intended to encourage rain clouds to gather and the rain to fall on Kahoʻolawe.

One of the lessons taught and learned involved the gathering of the *hoʻokupu.* The ultimate goal was to be able to grow or gather one's own *hoʻokupu,* which would ensure the perpetuation of *hoʻokupu* each year and would intensify the commitment and responsibility of the individual to the ritual.

The Hale o Papa (temple of Papa) found at Hakioawa and used in antiquity was renovated for use during the Makahiki. The Hale o Papa represented Haumea, or Earth Mother, the female energy needed for the revegetation of Kahoʻolawe. The use of the Hale o Papa reemphasized the importance of the female roles of mother, creator, and procreative force on earth. The Hale Mua (male temple) was where the male life force was celebrated and offerings made.

Four major Lono ceremonies were planned: two at Hakioawa, one at Moaʻulanui, and the last at Kealaikahiki. The first was at Hale o Papa and the second at Hale Mua. Both of these Lono ceremonies were performed in one day, before sunset. The ancillary ceremonies—the *hiʻu wai,* the *hoʻokupu imu,* and the *pāʻani* (games)—were also held on this day. The next day, the *akua loa* was taken to Moaʻulanui, where a noon ceremony took place, followed by a long walk to Ka Lae o Kealaikahiki, the location of the final ceremony: the sending off of the *wa'a 'auhau* before sunset. The final event of the Makahiki was the *pā'ina* (feast).

These ceremonies—along with the responsibility of collecting *ho'okupu,* training the new participants, preparing the *imu,* memorizing the chants, memorizing the protocol of the ceremonies, and instilling in everyone the belief that this was not playacting—were an ambitious undertaking. When we consider the great lapse in time between the last Makahiki and this modern-day one, this ambitiousness is reinforced.

Nālani Kanaka'ole chose nine men as *kahu* (caretakers) of the Lono ceremonies. These men were responsible for obtaining the right *ho'okupu,* for starting the ceremonies at the proper time, for seeing that the protocol of the ceremonies was followed effectively and efficiently, and for ensuring that the chants or prayers were recited correctly. The number nine symbolized the first nine people who landed on Kaho'olawe in 1976. It was decided that this group would bear the name of *mo'o Lono* (descendants of Lono). The name was chosen to focus on the need for revegetation of the island. The first nine *mo'o Lono* were Keali'i Ioane, Palikapu Dedman, John Spencer, Kaliko Kanaele, Moke Day, Ka'iana Haili, Kanē Buster Padilla, Emment Aluli, and Burelle Duvachelle.

For the Protect Kaho'olawe 'Ohana, the Makahiki season begins with the rising of the Makali'i (Pleiades) at sunset, usually in late October or early November. The closing of the Makahiki is celebrated in January or early February. Traditionally, Makahiki was a time of peace, cleansing, athletic games, dancing, prayers, and, most importantly, the recognition of the god Lono.

The following is the Lono prayer used by the *mo'o Lono* and composed by Nālani Kanaka'ole.

KĪHĀPAI O LONO

E ke akua
E ke akua ao loa—e ke akua ao poko
E ke akua i ka wai ola a Kāne
I ke kai ola a Kanaloa

I ke ao ʻekaʻeka o Lono
Kūkulu ka ipu ʻekaʻeka o Lono
Hō mai ka ipu lau makani o Lono
Iā hiki mai ka ua o Lono
Hoʻoulu ke ea—hoʻoulu ke kupu
Hoʻoulu ka wai nape i ke kama o Hoʻohōkūkalani
Iā hiki mai ke ala a Makaliʻi i kahikina
Eia ka ʻawa i lani—ʻawa i Kū—ʻawa i Hina
Eia ke kupu puaʻa
Eia he kalo o Lono
Eia ke kupu ʻāweoweo
Eia ke kupu kino lau
Ko hānai ʻia ke akua mai ka lani nui a Wākea
Ko hānai ʻia nā akua o kono hanauna hope
Hoʻoulu mai ke kupu o ka ʻāina
A ua noa—ua noa—a ua noa.

THE RELIGIOUS DUTIES OF LONO

O God
God of the long cloud—God of the short cloud
God of the living waters of Kāne
Of the living sea of Kanaloa
Of the dark clouds of Lono
The dark container of Lono grows
The container of the numerous winds of Lono goes forth
Upon the arrival of the rain of Lono
Life is encouraged—the budding shoots creep upward
The undulating water induces growth for the child of Hoʻohōkūkalani
Upon the appearance of the Makaliʻi in the east
Here is the sacred *ʻawa*—the consecrated *ʻawa* of Kū of Hina
Here is the pig, body form of Lono
Here is the taro of Lono
Here is the *ʻāweoweo* body form
Here are the many manifestations of Lono

The god of the great expanse of Wākea was fed
The gods of his generations after were fed
The fruits of the land shall grow
The taboo is lifted—the taboo is lifted—the taboo is lifted.

This Lono chant concentrates on the *kino lau* (physical manifestations) of Lono that encourage growth. The prayer uses a formula found in many traditional chants: a recognition and invocation of the great gods of the elements; an account of the gods' creations; an enumeration of offerings; a statement of the physical shapes the deities take; and the reason for the prayer. The reason in this case is the need to ensure vegetation and growth on the island. The last line of the chant releases the formal communication with the god. This was the first prayer chant composed for a formal modern-day Makahiki ceremony.

Another traditional chant was added to the Makahiki ceremony. This chant, recorded by David Malo in *Hawaiian Antiquities,* featured Lono, his many physical manifestations, and the fertility of life. Rain was the focus of this prayer chant.

PULE HO'OULUULU 'AI

E Lono, alana mai Kahiki
He pule kū kēia iā 'oe, e Lono.
E Lono lau 'ai nui,
E ua mai ka lani pili
Ka ua ho'oulu 'ai
Ka ua ho'oulu kapa
Popo kapa wai lehua
A Lono i ka lani
E Lono ē, ku'ua mai kōkō ai, kōkō ua.
'Ulua mai
Ho'oulu, 'ia mai ka 'ai, e Lono
Ho'oulu, 'ia mai ka i'a, e Lono
Ka mo'omo'o, Kīhe'ahe'apala'ā, e Lono!
'Āmama. Ua noa!

PRAYER FOR GROWTH AND INCREASE

O Lono, rising for Kahiki
This is a prayer direct to you, O Lono
Lono of the broad leaf
Let the low-hanging cloud pour out its rain
The rain that makes the crops flourish
The rain that makes the *tapa* plant flourish
Wring out the dark rain clouds
Of Lono in the heavens
Lono, shake out a net of food, a net of rain
Gather them together for us
Inspire growth
Food is propagated by Lono
Fish is propagated by Lono
The *wauke,* the dyeing plants also
The prayer is said. The taboo is lifted!

In 1989 another chant was incorporated into the Makahiki ceremony. This chant and the ceremony accompanying it were taught by Edward Kanahele. The chant is traditional and was also taken from David Malo's *Hawaiian Antiquities.* The chant complements "Pule Hoʻouluulu ʻAi," and the two of them complete the net ceremonies for Lono. In this chant, growth is emphasized not only on Kahoʻolawe, but also in the greater communities of Hawaiʻi.

KA PULE KŌKŌ

KAHU: E uliuli kai, e Uli ke akua ē!
E uli kai hākōkō
Kōkō lani o Uli
Uli lau ka ʻai a ke akua
Piha lani kōkō; e lū!
NĀ POʻE: E lū ka ʻai a ke akua
E lū ka lani
He kau ʻai kēia

E lū ka honua
He kau 'ai kēia
Ola ka 'āina
Ola iā Kāne
Kāne ke akua ola
Ola iā Kanaloa
Ke akua kupe 'eu
Ola nā kānaka
Kāne-i-ka-wai-ola, e ola!
Ola ke ali'i Makahiki!
'Āmama; ua noa!
KAHU: Noa iā wai?
NA PO'E: Noa iā Kāne
Ua noa, ua noa, ua noa!

THE NET PRAYER

KAHU: To the deep blue sea, god Uli
The rocking blue sea
Heavenly net of Uli
The leaves of the food of the gods are green
The heavenly net is full, scatter it!
NĀ PO'E: Scatter the food of the god
The heaven shakes
This is a season of plenty
The earth scatters its yield
This is a season of plenty
The land lives
Life from Kāne
Kāne is the god of life
Life from Kanaloa
The mischievous god
Life to the people
To Kāne of the living waters, life!
Life to the chief of the Makahiki!

The prayer is said. The taboo is lifted!

KAHU: Free from whom?

NĀ POʻE: Free from Kane

The taboo is lifted, the taboo is lifted, the taboo is lifted!

In this prayer, Uli, the female deity of the dark blue areas of the earth (such as the sea and the sky) is invoked. The male deities of the dark blue areas are also involved: Kanaloa of the deep blue sea and Kāne of the deep blue sea. The chant complements "Pule Hoʻouluulu ʻAi"—which includes the forms of Lono that transport the life-giving force, freshwater—by adding the male and female counterparts of sky and sea, thus encouraging procreation and abundant crop production for the Makahiki season.

The first step necessary for Kanaloa/Kahoʻolawe was to heal the land. Lono was a familiar deity who symbolized peace and life. Lono is also synonymous with the seasonal rains, which are needed for healing the land. Therefore, these significant qualities of Lono were part of the initial ceremonial focus, making it the rebirth of Lono-i-ka-Makahiki.

In December 1992 the *moʻo Lono* gathered on the island of Hawaiʻi to learn an *ʻawa* ceremony that was to be added to the ceremonial rebirth of Lono. I composed an *ʻawa* chant to accompany the ceremony.

MO ʻO LONO, PULE ʻAWA

E Kāne i ka wai ola

E Kanaloa i ke kai neʻe

E Kū i ka wao nahele

E Lono holo i ke ao panopano

E hoʻomalu ka lani, e hoʻomalu ka honua

Ke ola nei nā pulapula

E kono ʻia ana ʻo Mauli Ola

E inu i ka wai a Kāne

A awaikū ʻawa i Kū

ʻAwa na nā Akua i ka lani, ka lani

ʻAwa na nā Akua i ka honua, ka honua

ʻAwa na Kāne a Lono, a Lono

Na nā Mo'o Lono, O
'Eli'eli kapu, 'eli'eli noa
Lele ke kapu, noa ke kānoa
Ola ka honua, ola nā Mo'o Lono
'Āmama, ua noa.

DESCENDANTS OF LONO, PRAYER FOR 'AWA

O Kāne of the living waters
O Kanaloa of the moving sea
O Kū among the dark forest
O Lono who travels in the dark clouds
Protect the space above and the earth below
The buds are rejuvenating
Breath of Life is being invited
To drink of the water of Kāne
And to the benevolent spirits of Kāne,
The ceremonial *'awa* is presented
'Awa for the guardians of the atmosphere, the atmosphere
'Awa for the guardians of the earth, the earth
'Awa for the men of Lono, of Lono
The descendants of Lono, yes!
A profound *kapu,* a profound freedom
The *kapu* flies, the bowl is free
The earth lives, the descendants of Lono survive
The prayer is said, the taboo is lifted.

Healing was not only for the island but also for those who visited Kaho'olawe during the Makahiki. During the closing Makahiki season of 1986 Kū Kahakalau was inspired to write this *mele:*

KAHO'OLAWE I KA MĀLIE

Ma Hakioawa i lohe 'ia ai ka pū
Aia nā ho'okupu ma ka Hale O Papa me ka Hale Mua
Ma Moa'ula i lohe 'ia ai ka pū

Aia nā hoʻokupu ma ke lele luna
Ma Keanakeiki i lohe ʻia ai ka pū
Aia nā hoʻokupu ma ka waʻa
Holo ka waʻa i Kealaikahiki
E hiki mai hou ana ke akua me Makaliʻi
ʻIke maka ʻia nā hōʻailona
Ke hoʻoulu nei ʻo Lonoikamakahiki i ka ʻāina
ʻĀina aloha ʻia e kākou
ʻĀina hana ʻino e nā koa
E haʻalele e ka poʻe hana ʻino
E mālama, e aloha i ka ʻāina
ʻĀina punahele o kākou
ʻO Kahoʻolawe i ka mālie.

KAHOʻOLAWE IN THE CALM

At Hakioawa the conch shell is heard
There are the offerings at Hale O Papa and Hale Mua
At Moaʻula the conch shell is heard
There are the offerings at the high altar.
At Keanakeiki the conch shell is heard
There are the offerings in the canoe.
The canoe sails on the path to Tahiti
The god will return again with Makaliʻi
The omens are visible
Lonoikamakahiki is greening the land
The land that is loved by all of us
The land that is destroyed by the soldiers
Go away, people of destruction
Protect and love the land
Our favorite land
Peaceful Kahoʻolawe.

The intention for the rituals was that life would once again abound and grow on this little *moku*. . . . The god will return again with Makaliʻi. . . . The omens are visible. . . .

These words and the *mele* above express the sentiments of those who have been to Kaho'olawe and shared the hurt of Kanaloa/Kaho'olawe—experiences that have enhanced the innate passion of young Native Hawai'ians to continue on the pathway of their ancestors.

Editor's note*: The most inspiring story of the Hawai'ian movement for cultural recovery is that of Kaho'olawe, the smallest of the major Hawai'ian islands, and one richly marked with a history of ritual and legend. For many decades it was stripped to the bone by sheep and goats. In 1941 the United States government claimed the island for bombing practice and continued to shell it until as recently as the 1980s. After many grim years of activism and court actions against the Navy (and the martyred lives of two young men attempting to occupy the island in protest), the military occupation was stopped, and in 1994 the island was re-dedicated as the symbolic homeland of Hawai'ian sovereignty.*

BELONGING TO THE LAND

David Mas Masumoto

The land belongs to those who own it, work it, or use it. Or no one?

In the Sixth Grade

In 1966, while in the sixth grade at Del Rey Elementary School, I sat next to Jessie Alvarado. We had what, I later learned, was a symbiotic relationship. We'd cheat on tests together—he'd open a book so I could read the needed information, and then he copied my response. I provided the answers, he took the risks.

But that was before they told me he was Mexican and I was Japanese. Our cultures were different, they said: he ate tortillas at home and I ate rice. We each had "our own thing" and belonged in different worlds, despite both living in this small farm community just south of Fresno, California.

That was before they told me that my family was the farmers, and his family was the farmworkers. We owned the land; they came to work for us. Nature rewarded us differently. While we talked about profits, Jessie's family spoke of hard-earned wages. We worked in all four seasons in our fields, they came to labor seasonally. My family would pass on the land to the next generation. His family's dream was for the next generation to get out of the fields. We were supposed to be on opposite sides, even though we both sweated and itched the same each summer as we picked peaches in one-hundred-degree heat.

That was before they told me he was poor and I was rich. It made me feel guilty yet confused as a kid growing up. I guess his brother's Chevy Impala wasn't as good as my brother's '58 Ford with a V-8 engine. During lunch, I learned that no one wanted my peanut butter and jelly sandwiches when lots of the other kids had fat burritos kept warm by wrapping them in aluminum foil. We all wore hand-me-downs from our older brothers, and I remember once when a very poor boy in the second grade had to wear a blouse from his older sister. Jessie and the other kids were cruel and viciously teased him until he ran home crying.

That was before an early spring frost hit our vineyards in late March and we lost over half our grape crop. I remember Jessie's father coming by to check on us the next morning, slowly walking out into the fields with my father. They both stood and silently watched the sun rise over the fragile shoots, now frozen and blackened by the frigid temperatures. Jessie's father pawed the ground with his feet, knowing he'd have to look for other work. Dad shook his head, figuring he'd still have to work to keep the vines thriving, knowing there'd be no pay for his labor, and he'd have to work for free the rest of the year. We seemed a whole lot poorer at that moment.

Was I supposed to feel sorry for Jessie? Wasn't nature supposed to be fair and democratic? I wonder what they have told Jessie since the sixth grade when we cheated together, and what stories we have left behind.

White Ashes

At a Buddhist funeral, we chant a passage about white ashes. We may live a full life, yet no matter what, in the morning we have radiant health, and in the evening we are nothing more than white ashes.

I'm a third-generation Japanese American farmer, but am quite sure my lineage in agriculture dates back centuries. The Masumotos are from a solid peasant stock, rice farmers without even a hint of samurai blood. I'm proud of that fact.

My grandparents journeyed from Japan to farm in California. They spoke Japanese instead of English or Spanish or German. They were Buddhists instead of Protestants, Catholics, or Jews. They came in 1898 and 1917 instead of the late 1700s or early 1800s. They sailed east instead of west, yet their voyage was similar to those of hundreds of thousands of other immigrants who crossed an ocean to the land of opportunity. They hoped to farm. They wanted land.

On the west coast of North America, Asian immigrants found the beginning of a new continent, not the end. Traditions had yet to become firmly entrenched, and, if anything, the West had a tradition of conquest and change. Ownership of land became the first step in carving a place in this landscape, controlling nature an essential step in controlling one's destiny.

My grandfathers left little behind in Japan; both second sons of peasant farmers, they had no claim to family rice plots. Yet in California they discovered Alien Land laws of 1913 and 1920 that prevented "Orientals" from land purchases, singling out the immigrants from Asia and condemning a generation to life as laborers. But they stayed, working the fields for strangers. Some Japanese Americans saved and purchased land by forming an American company or waiting until they had children and buying the land in the name of the second generation, the nisei—Americans by birth. Most, though, waited until their nisei children were grown and working so they could pool their labor and buy a place together as family. They sacrificed so the next generation could have opportunity.

Dad explained the advantages of land ownership. "It's American!" he claimed. "You keep all the profits." But I knew him better. He also meant you had a place of your own, a place the family could plant roots. A piece of the earth with time—he'd work one season, gradually improving the soils, replanting grape vines or peach trees, with the intention of returning the next year and the year after that. Owning your own farm meant you had "next years."

My family were quiet folk, preferring to communicate through their actions rather than their words. I was born in the fifties, and only learned of their lives through the occasional story.

Once, during a dreadfully hot day in a summer with daytime readings of 105 degrees and low temperatures that never dropped below 70 degrees, Dad told me a story of our family during the Great Depression. "We knew nature very well," he said, "almost too well." He explained that the family were farmworkers, laboring in the fields, living in shacks, constantly exposed to the elements, feeling each minute change in weather. In the heat of summer the family would sleep outside on a low wooden platform my grandfather built, staring up at the stars. "You could hear a breeze rustle the grape leaves," Dad told me. "The sound makes you feel cool." Life was hard but they knew their lands and how to work and live with nature.

Dad then revealed to me another side of nature, this time human nature. For the first few years of his education, he jumped from school to school, the family moving from field to field, working and leasing different pieces of land. Profits were thin for everyone in the 1930s. Japanese Americans had it rougher. He explained: "Had to rent on a 50/50 percent agreement with owners. Others got at least a 60/40 split, the ones working the land got the bigger share like it should be. But Japanese didn't have an option, they couldn't own land. We were still good farmers though, took care of places. Not a whole lot of choices."

The Masumotos eventually found a place to rent on Manning Avenue, just outside a small town called Selma (about ten miles southeast of Fresno, California). The fields were productive, with grapes that were dried into raisins. Despite the meager earnings, they leased the same place for years. They could "stay put for a while," although Dad said they still hoped for their own place. "If it was ours, we'd do a lot better 'cause we could plow back the profits into the land, like adding manure after harvest, build up the soil for better crops. For the future, years down the road," Dad said.

The Masumotos were optimistic by 1940. My uncle George, the oldest son, had finished high school and was working full-time in the fields. Dad, the second son, would finish soon, and there were two other younger boys old enough to help during the summer harvest season. Together, as a family, they started saving money despite half their income going for rent. They began to pull together and pool resources, until they could afford a place they could call their own. And then, all plans changed in the fall of 1941.

Uncle George was drafted into the army; the oldest son left to serve his country. The family kept farming, still planning for a future on the land, until December 7, when Japan bombed Pearl Harbor. Overnight, everything changed and was turned upside down. My family was suddenly considered the enemy. Dreams of the land—forging a relationship with nature, working with her bounty—were shattered and lost. By the late summer of 1942, the United States government had commanded all persons of Japanese ancestry to be evacuated from the West Coast and imprisoned in relocation camps located in desolated areas of the country. The Masumotos were exiled to Gila River Relocation Center, in the high deserts south of Phoenix. But the farm we were renting stayed behind; so did the harvest of 1942.

They were given weeks to pack up and leave. Even on rented land, they had gradually accumulated various household goods, which had to be sold, given away, or left behind. Desperate emergency sales were held, buyers knowing well the sellers had to part with their processions. Uncle George had just purchased a new car. Gone, sold for half the price. Clothes, kitchen goods, farm tools—pennies were exchanged for them.

But the biggest concern was the grape crop of 1942. Military orders decreed that by mid-August, all Japanese Americans were to be herded on trains to depart for unknown destinations. No one knew when or if they'd return. But grapes would need to be picked in September and dried into raisins. A year's worth of labor harvested in a month, a year's worth of hope and work bundled into a single moment each year. It was the calendar of farming, part of the rhythm of working with nature.

My grandfather and grandmother had immigrated from Japan and never learned English. As the August deadline neared, Jiichan/Grandpa Masumoto grew nervous about the vines he had pruned, irrigated, and fertilized. He and Baachan/Grandma Masumoto had "made" the crop. Only harvest was needed, the most rewarding time of the year.

The Caucasian widow who owned the land was worried too. Not over the departing "Japs" but rather who would pick the grapes and manage them as they dried in the sun into raisins? She was scared. With thousands of Japanese Americans leaving, a cheap source of labor would be lost: vineyards could lay unpicked, harvests lost. The Fresno County Farm Bureau had issued a resolution calling on the government to delay evacuation at least until the grapes were picked. Then the Japanese aliens could be hauled off, the crop safely in.

So Dad had to do the negotiating. He'd talk with the widow. She didn't say much. He'd try to explain the situation with his folks, already traumatized by the sudden orders to leave. "How can this happen in America?" Jiichan whispered.

Without warning, Dad was informed that the widow had found a tenant. An "Okie" would take over the ranch and harvest the grapes. Stories circulated in the farming community: because of the war and the potential opportunity for food demands, the price of raisins could double from a year before. In 1940 raisins sold for fifty-six dollars a ton. They'd be worth over a hundred in 1942. The depression was ending for farmers and landowners.

(Raisins prices indeed soared during the war, boosted by government support and the reduction of imports, especially of sugar and sweeteners. From the decade of the thirties, when prices hovered between $39 and $60 a ton, prices per ton rocketed to $109 in 1942, $157 in 1943, $194 in 1944, $195 in 1945, and a high of $309 in 1946, the year Japanese Americans began to trickle back to the San Joaquin Valley, released from their wartime prisons.)

The "Okie" had a demand though—he wanted a place to live with his family. So the landlord "kicked us out," Dad said. "Hell, we'd be leaving in two weeks—maybe forever. But the owner told us to get out now." Dad managed to negotiate a settlement; for the year's worth of work the Masumotos would receive twenty-five dollars per acre or about twelve dollars a ton for the crop. The owner and the new renter would split the profits from that bitter harvest. "No wonder the 'Okie' wanted to move in so fast. All he had to do was pick the damn grapes and count his profits for a month of work," Dad fumed.

My grandparents were hurt. This was the landlord they had been with for years. Dad grew angry. He felt that at least nature—bad weather, spring frosts, hail storms, rain on the raisins—was democratic. It didn't matter the color of your skin or your religion or where your family came from. But human nature was worse, it left scars that would not heal.

My family was homeless. A sixty-year-old immigrant and his fifty-year-old wife were once again aliens in a land they had called home for thirty years. A number-one son caught in the United States Army, Uncle George wrote: "After Pearl Harbor, they didn't know what to do with us. Finished basic training but they wouldn't issue us guns to keep training. No one knew what to do with us."

On a neighboring farm across the street, the Nakayamas, another

Japanese-American family, prepared for departure. But their landlord was a good man. He had heard of my family's situation and felt awkward; he allowed the Masumotos to stay in his barn for those final two weeks. He even gave a ride to the Masumotos to the train station where they were to report. He was a good neighbor.

So to this barn the family dragged their few suitcases and packed boxes, all tagged "No. 40551." What couldn't fit or be carried, they would have to leave behind.

But Dad would not go quietly. He was not the reserved father whom I came to know later—the man who could silently watch a rainstorm devastate a crop or slowly shake his head as he felt a wicked summer wind topple peach trees and batter nectarines a few days from harvest. This humble man who fought with nature, knowing well who would ultimately win, responding the next day by walking his fields with a passion to start work over again. Dad didn't leave quietly.

As he vacated the house, he smashed every dish and cup they owned rather than leave them. He broke every piece of furniture they had bought or Jiichan had made, including the family's "summer platform" and tossed them into a pile. Then he burned them. The flames danced into the evening sky and glowed in the night's darkness. They would be used by no one. All he'd leave behind was white ashes.

Bitter Melon

"Let's eat," Francis said.

Marcy, my wife, and I weren't expecting supper. We had dropped in to chat with Francis, a Nisei woman in her sixties, recently widowed. Even though their farm was miles from ours, we still considered them neighbors. Her late husband, who had died in the early 1990s, and Dad had known each other for decades—together they had learned to farm through good times and mostly bad. More than once I heard the silence they shared after a rainstorm or freeze, two farmers standing next to each other staring into empty fields. Our families became friends for generations and now Marcy and I were paying a visit to see how she was coping alone.

We sat around a polished cherry-wood dining table the couple must have used daily. The finish had faded in two spots at the corner of the table; the natural, lighter grain matched where elbows and place settings must have rested. I believed I was seated where her late husband had sat.

Parts of the room were immaculate, free from clutter and dust. In other areas—a bookshelf near the phone, the counter beneath the china cabinet—sat piles of papers, stray envelopes, old magazines, and Japanese newspapers. I was surprised by the clutter because whenever I drove into their yard, their vegetable garden was pristine. Cucumbers were neatly tied up a lattice, tomatoes were staked and grew upright, squash plants flourished with huge leaves that dominated one corner. Clusters of bright flowers grew, rows of bulbs along one edge, even wildflowers scattered along the fencerow. The soil was damp but not muddy. Weeds grew only in a few places and didn't compete for nutrients—they looked as if they too had been planted. I was reminded of a joke the late husband had once told me. "Work ethic," he said. "My folks worried so much about me growing up the right way, I swear they planted weeds to make sure I always had enough work to keep me busy."

From the kitchen, Marcy carried three glasses filled with ice water and small bunches of dark purple currant grapes floating in them.

"What's this?" I asked.

Through a small window that connected the kitchen to the dining room, Francis poked her head and answered, "We've had them for years but even after retiring and selling the place, he still took care of that one outside row, right next to the garden." She pulled her head back into the kitchen and continued. We leaned forward and turned our ears toward the kitchen. "I once saw in a gourmet food magazine, a place setting with crystal glasses and sparkling water filled with currants—they called them 'Black Corinths' but you know they were just fresh currants floating in the water. Well I always wanted to try something fancy like that! I don't think Herb would have minded. He actually smiled when I talked about the idea."

Herb was a quiet man and very hardworking. He had a grin, even when I passed by in my truck and he was at the end of a row, leaning on his shovel, using the excuse of a neighborly wave with a dip of the head to take a brief break from his work.

But he'd smile, wave, and dip his head. In my rearview mirror I could see his gray work shirt was soaked with sweat, a deep stain across his chest and along the spine. Maybe the gesture made him feel a little cooler, help to tolerate the heat and accept the daily tests of nature.

At the table, Francis opened three of the serving dishes and we watched steam escape out of them. Two were filled with zucchini, one appeared to be fried in butter and the other steamed. The third bowl was filled with hot corn on the cob.

She smiled and announced, "From his garden." Francis spooned out the zucchini and a huge gob plopped onto my plate. "Personally I like mine microwaved, keeps it as natural as possible." she whispered. "Help yourself to the corn, picked it this morning."

"How you doing with the garden?" I asked.

"Two hours in the morning, two in the evening," she answered. "It's a lot more work when you're by yourself. Much more than I thought. I never realized how much we did together. I'm exhausted."

She smiled gently, her lips tight but grinning and showing no teeth. I poked at a cob and set it on my plate.

Francis said, "Go ahead, taste it. Tell me how sweet it is. Really how sweet."

I bit into it, knowing I'd agree with her. But I was surprised. I couldn't help but raise my eyebrows. It was sweet, very sweet. The natural taste exploded in my mouth.

Marcy's bite seemed just as pleasantly surprising. "My god, you can eat this for dessert," Marcy mumbled with her mouth full. Francis glowed.

"The hardest part is the watering. I tried keeping all these little notes taped on clocks and doors, telling me when to start or shut off a hose. He had so many different furrows and raised plots. No one knew how he kept it all on schedule."

Marcy and I devoured the food and looked up for more. Francis smiled and brought out a chilled platter with thin slices of some type of yellow melon. We eagerly grabbed for the fruit with our hands and bit into the flesh. My left eye squeezed closed, and my lips puckered. Francis giggled out loud.

"He used to trick us too." Her voice dropped as low as it could, mimicking Herb's soft voice. "It's not all sweet like candy."

"What is this?" Marcy asked.

"I think it's a type of Chinese melon. He was trying to breed them for years but no one knows if this was what he sought. I think he just wanted to leave behind a taste, a different flavor."

I sucked on my tongue and swallowed.

"Wait a while," Francis advised. "It'll start tasting better, sort of bittersweet."

AFTERWORD

Alison's Hopes:

A news item has popped up on my screen: "In a Generation, Minorities May Be the U.S. Majority." The census calculates, reports the *New York Times,* "that by 2042 Americans who identify themselves as Hispanic, black, Asian, American Indian, Native Hawai'ian and Pacific Islander will together outnumber non-Hispanic whites." What complicates this process is the language we use to describe ourselves, but that language will surely change as the demographics do. The article recalls that in earlier eras "the Irish, the Italians and Eastern European Jews were not universally considered as whites. As recently as the 1960s, Hispanic people were not counted separately by the census and Asian Indians were classified as white." With more and more individuals counting themselves as "multiracial"—a term which itself raises hackles as the very notion of "race" has been revealed to be a fiction—how will our grandchildren and great-grandchildren refer to their cultural identity? Will the word "American" come to mean quite literally "of mixed ancestry"? Will the hostile borders of inclusion and exclusion finally settle into peace, because it will become impossible even to demark and define "the other"?

My hope in this project was to be educated not just with the facts of our social/environmental predicament and woe, but to have my emotions educated, my empathy cultivated, my activism spurred by new stories. My larger hope is that this work will spur the same emotions in others. This anthology—so richly elaborated since it was first conceived of—tells me that we are on the right track.

Lauret's Hopes:

I came to know many child-forms of despair as a brown-skinned little girl in 1968 America. Only years later, at age fourteen, did I begin to fathom the reasons for such dis-ease. We had read Aldo Leopold's *A Sand County Almanac* for a ninth-grade assignment. That the book was hailed as "landmark," or in Wallace Stegner's words, "a famous, almost holy book in conservation circles," I knew nothing about. In his last essay, "The Land Ethic," Leopold wrote that "obligations have no meaning without conscience, and the problem we face is the extension of the social conscience from people to land." But what social conscience was evident? Taught history offered Manifest Destiny, slavery, "Indian wars" and removals as justified, necessary pieces of an innocent and impelled chronology of American *progress.* Only estrangement seemed within my teenage reach, as if every "we" or "us" excluded me and other people with ancestral roots in Africa, Asia, or Native America. Why was it that in the United States I knew at age fourteen human relations could be so cruel?

Self-protective silence and denial have kept too many Americans from knowing who "we the people" really are, and have kept a language of possibility impoverished. The hard thing to cultivate is a capacity to ask significant questions about our lives in a larger world, and about lives not our own. My hope is that this collection helps bring into dialogue what has been ignored or silenced, what has been disconnected or dismembered. As Nalini Nadkarni has noted elsewhere, to be truthful—full of *troth,* the Old English word for tree—we must recognize the hidden parts, the roots and soil of ourselves in relation. By reimagining and enlarging our language and frames, the writings here invite creative interaction with many audiences, a calling back and forth, an exchange. Through the multiplicity of true voices, and their real stories, we might limn larger stories that all of these are part of. Then perhaps we might be able to begin dismantling the patterns of living in this country that fragment, exclude, and allow one to believe you don't *have* to think about or care about some . . . "Other."

NOTES

Notes to "Widening the Frame"

1. Reputable information sources on current environmental justice issues and activism include the Environmental Justice Resource Network (www.ejrc.cau.edu/) and the Deep South Center for Environmental Justice (www.dscej.org/).

Notes to "Working in a Region of Lost Names"

1. "Vollman's Market" is the invented name of an actual market I've written about in fictional terms. The invented name holds such a powerful place in my memory I write it once again in this essay.

2. My thoughts on the bloodline are shaped by Ernest J. Gaines's *Mozart and Leadbelly: Stories and Essays* (New York: Knopf, 2005). I'm especially moved by his eloquent thoughts on the migration and exile of fathers, when he writes, "I wanted to see on paper the true reason why those black fathers left home—not because they were trifling or shiftless, but because they were tired of putting up with certain conditions" (9–10).

My adolescence might be characterized as a series of events filled with silences and transitions. Through these events I learned to silence one language, Spanish, in order to learn, work, and live with another, English. That language taught me that memory is a fiction (and this is a particular lesson that becomes clearer every time I try to write memories that I cannot hear or see just in English, and the force of this lesson is all the more brutal every time I try to address my father's silences). The fiction of my memory is most evident in this fact: every time I write "my father," it seems as if I'm committing a lie to paper. Chago, what I called and still call my father, the diminutive of Santiago, moreover, is a name lost to me for many years, a name I never thought to understand, and thus a name I've only recently begun to search for in a region of lost names.

Notes to "70117"

1. In my cultural experience, there is a standing and highly significant take on the question "who is we?" "We" is used both inclusively and exclusively, and the task for the listener, or the speaker, or the powerful, or the excluded—is to decide whether or not they themselves are included in this "we." In general, the powerful always expects to be included, as they also expect to speak (and often do). I write "we" in this piece to incorporate the requirement to question. Of course, from a position of power, the people who say "we" always include themselves, and many times exclude the "we" I am a part of. This essay is meant to waver on that score.

Notes to "Dark Waters"

1. Geoffrey C. Ward, *The West: An Illustrated History* (Boston: Little Brown, 1996), 30.

2. Yusef Komunyakaa, "Looking for Choctaw," in *Magic City* (Middletown, Conn.: Wesleyan University Press, 1992), 25.

3. Komunyakaa, "The Millpond," in *Magic City,* 17.

4. Komunyakaa, "Poetics of Paperwood," in *Magic City,* 50.

5. Sophie Cabot Black, "Nature, Who Misunderstands," in *The Misunderstanding of Nature* (St. Paul: Graywolf Press, 1994), 54.

6. P. H. Chase Jr., "On Paradise," in *St. John of Damascus: Writings, Translation* (New York: Fathers of the Church, 1958), 230.

7. Don Byron, introductory notes for Don Byron, *Tuskegee Experiments,* WEA/Atlantic/Nonesuch, 1992, compact disc.

8. William Finnegan, "The Poison Keeper," *New Yorker* (January 15, 2001): 62.

9. Chet Raymo, *Skeptics and True Believers* (New York: Walker, 1998), 173–74.

10. Raymo, *Skeptics and True Believers,* 177–78.

11. Washington Office of Environmental Justice, "Principles of Environmental Justice" (Washington, D.C., October 1991).

12. "Principles of Environmental Justice."

13. Komunyakaa, "Fog Galleon," in *Neon Vernacular* (Middletown, Conn.: Wesleyan University Press, 1993), 3.

14. Bogalusa Heart Study, *American Journal of Medical Sciences* (Supplements), (December 1995): 310.

15. Jim Motavalli, "Toxic Targets," *E: The Environmental Magazine,* 9, no.4 (July-August 1998).

16. Motavalli, "Toxic Targets."

17. Antonio Machado, "He andado muchos caminos," in *Times Alone: Selected Poems of Antonio Machado,* trans. Robert Bly (Middletown, Conn.: Wesleyan University Press, 1983), 16–17.

18. Shirley Ayers, *Dispatch* 7, no. 1 (spring 1996).

19. Emily Dickinson, "A Bird came down the Walk—," in *The Complete Poems of Emily Dickinson,* ed. Thomas H. Johnson (Boston: Little, Brown, 1960), 156.

Notes to "Mujeres de Maíz"

For further reading:

On the movement in defense of maize farmers' and consumers' rights: http://www.organicconsumers.org/corn/index.cfm

On evaluating the controversies and activist responses connected to GE foods: See numerous academic publications by sociologist Abby J. Kinchy and Daniel Lee Kleinman, Abby J. Kinchy and Jo Handelsman, eds., *Controversies in Science and Technology, Volume One: From Maize to Menopause* (Madison: The University of Wisconsin Press, 2005).

On local maize cultivation practices in Mexico: Roberto J. Gonzalez, *Zapotec Science: Farming and Food in the Northern Sierra of Oaxaca* (Austin: University of Texas Press, 2001).

On children emigrating atop Mexican trains: Sonia Nazario, *Enrique's Journey* (New York: Random House, 2007).

To make "written contributions" to the FTAA discussion: http://www.ftaa-alca.org/Alca_e.asp

Notes to "Silent Parrot Blues"

1. Reverend Ben Chavis Jr., former executive director of the NAACP, coined the term "environmental racism." He is a founding leader of the environmental justice movement.

Notes to "Reclaiming Ourselves, Reclaiming America"

1. *Mestizo* is a Spanish word that identifies a person of mixed racial/ethnic background. It does not have the negative connotations of its English equivalents, "half-breed" or "half-caste," and it has been increasingly accepted as a self-identity term by Latinos both in Latin America and in the United States.

2. Henry Wagner, *The Discovery of Yucatán by Francisco Hernández de Córdoba* (Berkeley, Calif.: Cortes Society, 1942), 59.

3. A. R. Pagden, ed. and trans., *The Maya: Diego de Landa's Account of the Affairs of Yucatán* (Chicago: J. Phillip O'Hara, 1975), 33–34.

4. Pagden, *The Maya,* 168.

5. The date of arrival of the first "Americans" keeps moving farther back in time. Many scholars hold that there is evidence that people arrived at the American continent at least 50,000 years ago, like Dr. Albert C. Goodyear, Director of Southeastern Paleoemerican Survey, who has carried out an archaeological investigation of South Carolina's Topper Site with a radiocarbon dating report indicating that artifacts excavated from the Pleistocene terrace in May 2004 were recovered from soil dating some 50,000 years. This date implies an even earlier arrival for humans in this hemisphere than previously believed, well before the last ice age. Dr. Albert C. Goodyear, "Update on Research at Topper," in *Legacy,* Vol. 13, No.1, March 2009.

6. Roberto Fernández Retamar, "Calibán: Notes toward a Discussion of Culture in Our America," in *Caliban and Other Essays,* trans. Edward Baker (Minneapolis: University of Minnesota Press, 1989).

7. According to tradition the *Virgen de Guadalupe* appeared and spoke in Nahuatl to Indian Juan Diego in Tepeyac, a hill on the outskirts of Mexico City, where Tonantzin, "Our Mother Goddess," was worshipped. Her image has been espoused to several social movements and causes both in Mexico and the United States Southwest. For example, she was on the first Mexican flag of Father Miguel Hidalgo's Indian army fighting for independence from Spain in 1810, on the banner

of the Mestizo popular armies of Emiliano Zapata in the Mexican Revolution of 1910, and also appeared in California along picket signs in the 1965 Delano grape strike organized by Chicano union leader César Chávez.

8. Gloria Anzaldúa, *Borderlands/La Frontera: The New Mestiza* (San Francisco: Aunt Lute Books, 1999), 101.

9. Anzaldúa, *Borderlands/La Frontera,* 109.

10. Victor Montejo (illustrated by Luis Garay), *Popul Vuh: libro sagrado de las mayas* (Mexico City: Artes de México, 1999), 7–8.

11. The most complete and scholarly edition of Ruiz de Alarcón's *Tratado,* which includes the original spells in Nahuatl and their English translations, as well as versions in English of Ruiz de Alarcón's introductions and commentary written in Spanish, was edited by J. Richard Andrews and Ross Hassig as *Treatise on the Heathen Superstitions That Today Live among the Indians Native to This New Spain* (Norman: University of Oklahoma Press, 1984).

12. Kenny Ausbel, "The Riches of Human Experience" in *Restoring the Earth: Visionary Solutions from the Bioneers* (Tiburon, Calif.: H. J. Kramer, 1997), 65–84.

13. Francisco X. Alarcón, "Prayer to Fire," in *Snake Poems: An Aztec Invocation* (San Francisco: Chronicle Books, 1992), 103.

14. Alarcón, "Hernando Ruiz de Alarcón," in *Snake Poems,* 8–9.

15. Alarcón, "For Planting Corn," in *Snake Poems,* 74.

16. Alarcón, "In Xochitl In Cuicatl," in *Snake Poems,* 150.

17. Alarcón, "Tlazoltéotl!" in *Goddess of the Americas/La Diosa de Las Américas: Writings on the Virgen of Guadalupe,* ed. Ana Castillo (New York: Riverhead Books, 1996), 309.

Notes to "In the Valley of Its Saying"

1. David Hinton, "T'ao Ch'ien," *Mountain Home: The Wilderness Poetry of Ancient China* (New York: Counterpoint, 2002), 7.

2. Henry David Thoreau, "Ktaadn," *The Maine Woods,* ed. Joseph J. Moldenhauer (Princeton: Princeton University Press, 1972), 71.

3. Chuang Tzu, "In the World of Men," *Basic Writings,* trans. Burton Watson (New York: Columbia UP, 1964), 57.

4. Jou Tsung-hwa, *The Tao of Tai-Chi Chuan: Way to Rejuvenation* (Warwick, NY: Tai Chi Foundation, 1991).

5. Henry David Thoreau, *Letters to a Spiritual Seeker,* ed. Bradley P. Dean (New York: Norton, 2004), 152, 159.

6. Hinton, *Mountain Home,* 7.

7. T'ao Ch'ien, "Drinking Wine," *Mountain Home,* ed. and trans. David Hinton, 13.

8. Ellen Bryant Voigt, "Song and Story," *Messenger: New and Selected Poems, 1976–2006* (New York: Norton, 2007), 111.

9. Jou, *The Tao of Tai-Chi Chuan,* 6.

10. W. H. Auden, *Selected Poems,* ed. Edward Mendelson New ed. (New York: Vintage, 1989), 82.

Notes to "*Ke Au Lono i Kahoʻolawe, Hoʻi;* (The Era of Lono at Kahoʻolawe, Returned)"

1. This essay originally appeared in *Manoa: A Pacific Journal of International Writing,* and it is reprinted here with gratitude and in memorium to Mahealani Dudoit.

2. The information on the various firsts of the 1982 Makahiki ceremonies was obtained in a December 1992 interview in Hilo, Hawaiʻi, with Makanani, Lopaka ʻAiwohi, Craig Neff, Keoni Fairbanks, Kaʻiana Haili, Nālani Kanakaʻole, Edward Kanahele, Kala Mossman, and Ahiʻena Kanahele.

ELMAZ ABINADER is an Arab American writer from Oakland, California, who has won the *San Francisco Bay Guardian's* Goldie Award in Literature, the Josephine Miles PEN Oakland Award for poetry, and an Arts Council Silicon Valley Grant for Fiction. Her publications include *In the Country of My Dreams,* a collection of poetry, and *Children of the Roojme: A Family's Journey from Lebanon,* a memoir. Her performance plays have toured eleven countries, and *Country of Origin,* a three-act work, won two Drammies from the Portland Drama Critics Circle. She is a cofounder of VONA, a foundation that holds summer writing workshops for writers of color.

FAITH ADIELE is the author of a memoir set in Thailand, *Meeting Faith,* winner of the PEN Beyond Margins Award for Best Biography/Memoir; writer/subject/narrator of *My Journey Home,* a documentary film based on her travels to Nigeria and Finland to find family; and coeditor of *Coming of Age Around the World: A Multicultural Anthology.* The recipient of fifteen residencies in five countries, she is the Distinguished Visiting Writer at Mills College in Oakland, California.

FRANCISCO X. ALARCÓN, award winning Chicano poet and educator, is author of twelve volumes of poetry, including *From the Other Side of Night: Selected and New Poems,* and *Snake Poems: An Aztec Invocation.* His latest book is *Ce•Uno•One: Poems for the New Sun.* His book of bilingual poetry for children, *Animal Poems of the Iguazú,* was selected as a Notable Book for a Global Society by the International Reading Association. His previous bilingual book titled *Poems to Dream Together* was awarded the 2006 Jane Addams Honor Book Award. Alarcón has been nominated for Poet Laureate of California on two occasions and teaches at the University of California, Davis.

FRED ARROYO, assistant professor of English at Drake University, is the author of *The Region of Lost Names: A Novel*. A recipient of an Individual Artist Grant from the Indiana Arts Commission, he has published fiction, poetry, and essays in various literary journals. Also a faculty mentor in the University of Nebraska MFA Writing Program, Arroyo is working on new fictions and completing a book of essays, *Close as Pages in a Book,* in which he explores his interest in literacy and a writing life, while returning to memories of childhood, migration, and work.

KIMBERLY M. BLAESER, a professor at the University of Wisconsin–Milwaukee, teaches creative writing, Native American literature, and American nature writing. Her publications include three books of poetry: *Trailing You,* winner of the first book award from the Native Writers' Circle of the Americas; *Absentee Indians and Other Poems*; and *Apprenticed to Justice.* Her scholarly study, *Gerald Vizenor: Writing in the Oral Tradition,* was the first Native-authored book-length study of an Indigenous author. Of Anishinaabe ancestry and an enrolled member of the Minnesota Chippewa Tribe who grew up on the White Earth Reservation, Blaeser is also the editor of *Stories Migrating Home: A Collection of Anishinaabe Prose* and *Traces in Blood, Bone, and Stone: Contemporary Ojibwe Poetry.*

JOSEPH BRUCHAC spent three years at Cornell University, majoring in wildlife conservation, before transferring to creative writing. Internationally known as a storyteller and writer for children, his work often draws on his American Indian (Abenaki) ancestry, and he is the author of more than seventy books. His honors include a Rockefeller Humanities fellowship, a National Endowment for the Arts Writing Fellowship for Poetry, the Cherokee Nation Prose Award, the Knickerbocker Award, the Hope S. Dean Award for Notable Achievement in Children's Literature, the Lifetime Achievement Award from the Native Writers' Circle of the Americas, and both the Writer of the Year Award and the Storyteller of the Year Award from the Wordcraft Circle of Native Writers and Storytellers.

ROBERT D. BULLARD is the Edmund Asa Ware Distinguished Professor of Sociology and director of the Environmental Justice Resource Center at

Clark Atlanta University. He is the author of several books on sustainable development, environmental racism, urban land use, industrial facility siting, community reinvestment, housing, transportation, climate justice, emergency response, smart growth, and regional equity. His recent books include *The Black Metropolis in the Twenty-First Century: Race, Power, and the Politics of Place* and *Growing Smarter: Achieving Livable Communities, Environmental Justice, and Regional Equity.*

DEBRA KANG DEAN is the author of three collections of poetry, including *Precipitates,* which was nominated for the William Carlos Williams Award. Her work has been published in many journals and anthologies, including *Best American Poetry, The New American Poets,* and *America! What's My Name?* She currently lives in Bloomington, Indiana, and is a contributing editor for *Tar River Poetry.* She teaches in Spalding University's brief-residency MFA in Writing Program.

CAMILLE T. DUNGY is the author of three books: *Smith Blue, Suck on the Marrow,* and *What to Eat, What to Drink, What to Leave for Poison.* She has received fellowships from the National Endowment for the Arts, The Virginia Commission for the Arts, and Bread Loaf. Dungy is associate professor of creative writing at San Francisco State University. Editor of *Black Nature: Four Centuries of African American Nature Poetry,* she is also co-editor of *From the Fishouse: An Anthology of Poems that Sing, Rhyme, Resound, Syncopate, Alliterate, and Just Plain Sound Great,* and assistant editor of Cave Canem's *Gathering Ground.*

NIKKY FINNEY was born by the sea in South Carolina. Her books include *On Wings Made of Gauze, Rice,* and *The World Is Round.* A volume of short stories, *Heartwood,* was written to assist adult literacy students. She also edited *The Ringing Ear,* a collection of one hundred poetic black voices. Finney is professor of creative writing at the University of Kentucky, and also has been the Grace Hazard Conkling Writer-in-Residence at Smith College.

RAY GONZALEZ is the author of *Consideration of the Guitar: New and Selected Poems; The Religion of Hands: Prose Poems and Short Fictions; Turtle*

Pictures, which received the 2001 Minnesota Book Award for poetry; and several other books of poetry, short stories, and short-short fiction. He has written two works of nonfiction, *The Underground Heart: Essays from Hidden Landscapes* and *Memory Fever,* and he is the editor of several anthologies. Born in El Paso, Texas, Gonzalez is currently a professor in the MFA creative writing program at the University of Minnesota in Minneapolis. His awards include the PEN-Oakland Josephine Miles Book Award for Excellence in Literature, and the American Book Award for Editing (The Before Columbus Foundation).

KIMIKO HAHN is the author several books of poems, including: *Earshot,* which was awarded the Theodore Roethke Memorial Poetry Prize and an Association of Asian American Studies Literature Award; *The Unbearable Heart,* which received an American Book Award; *The Narrow Road to the Interior;* and *Toxic Flora.* She has also written for film and was commissioned to write text for *Everywhere At Once,* which was narrated by Jeanne Moreau and premiered at the 2008 Tribeca Film Festival. Hahn is a recipient of fellowships and awards, including a Guggenheim Fellowship, The PEN/Voelcker Award, The Shelley Memorial Prize. She is a distinguished professor in the MFA program at Queens College, The City University of New York.

bell hooks is distinguished professor in residence at Berea College, not far from where she grew up in Kentucky. Among her books are *Salvation: Black People and Love*; *All about Love: New Visions*; *Killing Rage: Ending Racism*; *Ain't I a Woman: Black Women and Feminism*; *Bone Black: Memories of Girlhood*; and *Remembered Rapture: The Writer at Work.*

JEANNE WAKATSUKI HOUSTON coauthored *Farewell to Manzanar,* the story of her family's experience during and after World War II internment. In print since 1973, it has become a standard work in schools and colleges across the country. Houston's writings have earned numerous honors, including a United States–Japan Cultural Exchange Fellowship and a Rockefeller Foundation Residency at Bellagio, Italy. Her novel *The Legend of Fire Horse Woman* explores the lives of three generations of Japanese American women.

PUALANI KANAKA'OLE KANAHELE is a Native Hawai'ian who grew up in Hilo, Hawai'i, and whose life has revolved around *hula 'olapa* and *oli,* which she calls the "spiritual foundation" of her "cultural growth and understanding." Taught these arts by her mother and maternal grandmother, she is—along with her sister Nālani Kanaka'ole—the *kumu hula* of Halau o Kekahi. She also teaches Hawai'ian studies at Hawai'i Community College and has written books and articles on, and appeared in video productions about, cultural values and practices. Her honors include the Regents' Medal for Excellence in Teaching, the National Governors Association Award for Distinguished Service, the Governor's Award for Distinguished Achievement in the Arts, and the National Endowment for the Arts' National Heritage Fellowship Award.

ROBIN WALL KIMMERER is a mother, plant ecologist, writer, and professor at the State University of New York College of Environmental Science and Forestry in Syracuse, New York, where she is also the director of the Center for Native Peoples and the Environment. She is an enrolled member of the Citizen Band Potawatomi. Kimmerer's research interests include the ecology of mosses and the role of traditional ecological knowledge in ecological restoration. Her first book, *Gathering Moss: A Natural and Cultural History of Mosses,* draws on both scientific and indigenous ways of knowing and received the John Burroughs Medal for outstanding nature writing.

JAMAICA KINCAID, former staff writer for the *New Yorker,* was born in Saint John's, Antigua. She is the author of several books of fiction: *At the Bottom of the River*; *Annie John*; *Lucy*; and *Mr. Potter,* as well as several books of nonfiction, including *A Small Place*; *The Autobiography of My Mother*; *My Brother: A Memoir*; *My Garden*; and *Among Flowers: A Walk in the Himalaya.* She has taught creative writing at Bennington College and Harvard University.

YUSEF KOMUNYAKAA won the Pulitzer Prize in 1994 for *Neon Vernacular: New and Selected Poems.* His most recent works include *The Wishbone Trilogy, Part 1*; *Pleasure Dome: New and Collected Poems*; and *Talking Dirty to the Gods.* He coedited with Sascha Feinstein *The Jazz Poetry Anthology* and *The Second Set: The Jazz Poetry Anthology,* volume two. Komunyakaa's lyrics have been featured on several CDs, including Pamela Knowles's *Thirteen Kinds of Desire*. He was awarded the Bronze Star for service in Vietnam. Elected a chancellor of The Academy of American Poets in 1999, Komunyakaa is Global Distinguished Professor of English and Distinguished Senior Poet at New York University.

J. DREW LANHAM is a native of Edgefield, South Carolina, and the dwindling remnants of "wild" piedmont that persist amidst development in the mid-western reaches of the state. A lifelong birder and naturalist, he is currently a Professor of Wildlife Ecology at Clemson University. Lanham's writing interests center on the interspersions between nature, culture, and place. Of particular interest are the relationships between African Americans and the natural world, especially in his native South. His forthcoming collection of essays is *The Home Place: Memoirs of a Colored Man's Love Affair with Nature*.

DAVID MAS MASUMOTO grows certified organic peaches, nectarines, grapes, and raisins on his family farm in Del Rey, California. He is the author of *Heirlooms: Letters from a Peach Farmer*; *Letters to the Valley*; *A Harvest of Memories*; *Four Seasons in Five Senses*; *Things Worth Savoring*; *Harvest Son*; and *Epitaph for a Peach*, among other works. Masumoto won the University of California–Davis "Award of Distinction" from the College of Agricultural and Environmental Sciences in 2003. He was a founding member of California Association of Family Farmers.

MARIA MELENDEZ publishes *Pilgrimage* in Pueblo, Colorado, a literary magazine serving a far-flung community of writers, artists, naturalists, contemplatives, activists, seekers, and other adventurers in and beyond the Greater Southwest. Melendez has published two poetry collections: *How Long She'll Last in This World*, and *Flexible Bones*, and her essays appear in *Sojourns Magazine: Natural & Cultural History of the Colorado Plateau* and *Isotope: A Journal of Literary Nature and Science Writing*. She serves as contributing editor for *Latino Poetry Review* and aquisitions editor for Momotombo Press, a chapbook publisher featuring prose and poetry by emerging Latino writers.

THYLIAS MOSS, winner of many literary prizes, also makes video, sound, and three-dimensional *poams* (products of acts of making). Her work has appeared in print and online journals, film festivals, art galleries, the forkergirl you tube channel, and Limited Fork podcasts. She teaches and learns Limited Fork Theory in the Department of English and the School of Art & Design at the University of Michigan, and maintains four Limited Fork Theory resource web sites: 4orkology.com, The Mid-Hudson Taffy Company, 4orked. com, and Tine Mapped. She is a very happy Proforker even as intellectual, political, and meteorological climates change.

GARY PAUL NABHAN is a Lebanese American writer who lives on the United States–Mexico border. He works as a Research Scientist at the Southwest Center of the University of Arizona where he co-founded the Flavors Without Borders Foodways Alliance. His book *Arab/American* won the 2009 Southwest Book Award, and his other twenty books are now available in six different languages.

NALINI NADKARNI is a member of the faculty in environmental studies at The Evergreen State College. Her research concerns the ecology of tropical and temperate forest canopies. In 1994, she cofounded the International Canopy Network, a nonprofit organization that fosters communication among researchers, educators, and conservationists concerned with forest canopies. In 2001, she received a Guggenheim Fellowship to pursue her interests in communication of canopy research to nonscientists. In 2003, she created the "Research Ambassador Program," which offers training to scientists to disseminate their own research to nontraditional public audiences such as religious leaders, prisoners, legislators, and rap singers.

MELISSA NELSON was born in the San Francisco Bay Area and grew up in rural Mendocino County in northern California. Her PhD is in cultural ecology from the University of California–Davis, and she is an associate professor of American Indian studies at San Francisco State University. Nelson serves as the executive director of the Cultural Conservancy, a native nonprofit group committed to preserving traditional cultures and their lands. In 2005 Melissa coproduced the award-winning documentary, *The*

Salt Song Trail: Bringing Creation Back Together. Her first book is *Original Instructions: Indigenous Teachings for a Sustainable Future,* an edited anthology of over twenty indigenous leaders.

JENNIFER OLADIPO is a writer and award-winning journalist living in Louisville, Kentucky. She writes on environment, arts, international and social issues, and the many places where those subjects intersect. She recently became Kentucky's first African American state-certified environmental educator. Jennifer also heads a working group in the Sustainable Clifton initiative, a model for urban ecovillage design based on the United Nations-endorsed Gaia Education Curriculum.

LOUIS OWENS was a professor of English and Native American studies at the University of California–Davis, where he taught literature and creative writing until his death in 2002. Among his publications are the novels *Wolfsong, The Sharpest Sight, Bone Game, Nightland,* and *Dark River,* as well as several nonfiction volumes including *Other Destinies, Mixedblood Messages,* and *I Hear the Train.* Owens received several awards, including fellowships from the National Endowment for the Arts and the National Endowment for the Humanities, the American Book Award, the PEN Josephine Miles Award, and Writer of the Year from the Wordcraft Circle of Native Writers and Storytellers.

ENRIQUE SALMON learned from his Rarámuri mother and grandparents how to harness the medicinal and spiritual value of plants. He was founder of the Baca Institute of Ethnobotany, and a program officer at the Christensen Fund in support of indigenous communities in Mexico and the American Southwest. His consulting firm supports indigenous community cultural expression, landscape and ecological restoration, and language preservation.

AILEEN SUZARA is an educator, a food justice advocate, and a leader with the Filipino/American Coalition for Environmental Solidarity (FACES). She lives in Oakland, California.

A. J. VERDELLE, novelist and essayist, is mother to a daughter who was born in pre-Katrina New Orleans. Verdelle recently completed her second novel, about America's unheralded black cowboys, which will be published in

2011. Verdelle's novel *The Good Negress* won five national prizes, including a Bunting Fellowship at Harvard University and a distinguished prose fiction award from the American Academy of Arts & Letters. Verdelle teaches in the MFA program at Lesley University in Cambridge, MA.

San Francisco Bay Area–based poet-novelist-essayist **AL YOUNG** is the author of more than twenty books. He is also a world traveler and sometimes writing and literature teacher (at Stanford, University of California–Santa Cruz, University of Michigan, and St. Mary's College, among others) who often performs his own work to live music. Among Young's honors are Guggenheim, Fulbright, and NEA fellowships, Stanford's Wallace Stegner Writing Fellowship, the Joseph Henry Jackson Award, two American Book Awards, and two Pushcart Prizes. In May 2005 he was appointed California's Poet Laureate. Young's titles include *Heaven: Collected Poems 1956–1990*; *Conjugal Visits*; *Mingus Mingus: Two Memoirs* with Janet Coleman; *African American Literature: A Brief Introduction and Anthology*; and the novels *Who Is Angelina?*, *Seduction by Light*, and *Sitting Pretty*.

A Tohono O'odham linguist and poet, **OFELIA ZEPEDA** has helped native communities preserve their languages. She is a professor in the departments of linguistics and American Indian studies at the University of Arizona, cofounder of American Indian Language Development Institute (AILDI), and the author of the only pedagogical textbook on the Tohono O'odham language, *A Papago Grammar*. Writing in her native language, Zepeda is also the author of poetry collections including *Ocean Power: Poems from the Desert* and *jewed 'i-hoi/Earth Movements*. Zepeda has edited *mat hekid o ju:/When It Rains*, and coedited *Home Places: Contemporary Native American Writings from Sun Tracks* and a collection of Arizona tribal literature, *The South Corner of Time*. She has served as the series editor of SUN TRACKS from University of Arizona Press. Among her awards is a MacArthur fellowship.

Editors' Biographies

ALISON H. DEMING is the author of seven books including most recently a book of poetry, *Rope*, and is the editor of *Poetry in the American West*. Former Director of the University of Arizona Poetry Center, she is professor of creative writing at the University of Arizona. A tenth generation New Englander, she lives in Tucson.

Of mixed African American, Native American, and Euro-American heritage, **LAURET E. SAVOY** writes about the threads of cultural and ecological identity. She is a professor of environmental studies and geology at Mount Holyoke College, Massachusetts. Her books include *Bedrock: Writers on the Wonders of Geology* and *Living with the Changing California Coast.*

ACKNOWLEDGMENTS

The process of making a book that involves the work of many writers is a wild and unruly one, made possible thanks to the generosity of others. We are especially grateful to the writers who took the time and energy to generate new work for this book, sharing our vision of its importance. We are grateful as well to the many colleagues and dear friends who gave support and advice, shared ideas, and suggested potential contributors for this anthology, in particular Kris Bergbom, as well as Danyelle O'Hara, Karen Remmler, John Lemly, Carol Driscoll, Gerald Vizenor, and for the first edition, Louis Owens. Our editor at Milkweed Editions, Patrick Thomas, was an inspired collaborator. He shared our vision in the conception of this work, then nourished and strengthened it with his political conviction and editorial judgment, for which we give great thanks.

We are also deeply thankful that the process of collaboration led us into a friendship that has nourished us in personal and professional ways.

MORE NONFICTION FROM MILKWEED EDITIONS

To order books or for more information,
contact Milkweed at (800) 520-6455
or visit our Web site (www.milkweed.org).

The Nature of College:
How a New Understanding of Campus Life Can Change the World
By James J. Farrell

The Future of Nature
Writing on a Human Ecology from Orion Magazine
Edited and introduced by Barry Lopez

Hope, Human and Wild:
True Stories of Living Lightly on the Earth
By Bill McKibben

Toward the Livable City
Edited by Emilie Buchwald

MILKWEED EDITIONS

Founded as a nonprofit organization in 1979, Milkweed Editions is an independent publisher. Our mission is to identify, nurture and publish transformative literature, and build an engaged community around it.

JOIN US

In addition to revenue generated by the sales of books we publish, Milkweed Editions depends on the generosity of institutions and individuals like you. In an increasingly consolidated and bottom-line-driven publishing world, your support allows us to select and publish books on the basis of their literary quality and transformative potential. Please visit our Web site (www.milkweed.org) or contact us at (800) 520-6455 to learn more.

Milkweed Editions, a nonprofit publisher, gratefully acknowledges sustaining support from Amazon.com; Emilie and Henry Buchwald; the Bush Foundation; the Patrick and Aimee Butler Foundation; Timothy and Tara Clark; the Dougherty Family Foundation; Friesens; the General Mills Foundation; John and Joanne Gordon; Ellen Grace; William and Jeanne Grandy; the Jerome Foundation; the Lerner Foundation; Sanders and Tasha Marvin; the McKnight Foundation; Mid-Continent Engineering; the Minnesota State Arts Board, through an appropriation by the Minnesota State Legislature and a grant from the National Endowment for the Arts; Kelly Morrison and John Willoughby; the National Endowment for the Arts; the Navarre Corporation; Ann and Doug Ness; Jörg and Angie Pierach; the Carl and Eloise Pohlad Family Foundation; the RBC Foundation USA; the Target Foundation; the Travelers Foundation; Moira and John Turner; and Edward and Jenny Wahl.

Interior design by Rachel Holscher
Typeset in Adobe Garamond Pro
by BookMobile Design and Publishing Services
Printed on acid-free 30% post-consumer waste paper
by Versa Press